"Ahmad Fuad Rahmat's *Decolonization and Psychoanalysis: The Underside of Signification* is a groundbreaking work that brings an innovative lens to the study of psychoanalysis through the prism of decolonial thought. This book is essential reading for anyone interested in the intersections of psychoanalytic theory and postcolonial critique, as it masterfully unpacks how Jacques Lacan's ideas on the materiality of speech can be employed to critique colonial legacies within the field of psychoanalysis."
Robert K. Beshara, *author of* Decolonial Psychoanalysis *and* Freud and Said

"The most ambitious project yet to formulate a nuanced and robust vocabulary for decolonial psychoanalysis. Fuad's analysis does not simply underline the problem of how to break the colonial matrix that has formed the historical grounding of psychoanalysis, he advances, with critical skill and radical theoretical originality, a series of concepts that fundamentally shift the axis of what a decolonial psychoanalysis can be. Whether via his exploration of the materiality of speech as a basis for decolonial subjectivity, the notion of symbolic dispossession (as thought through Malcolm X), the idea of the 'unlanguaged subject', or the impetus to disrupt the primacy of European temporality, Fuad's powerful analysis of the decolonial unconscious profoundly unwrites what would have been the colonial future of psychoanalysis and produces a compelling vision for a global decoloniality."
Derek Hook, *author of* Six Moments in Lacan

"Fuad takes the reader on a journey from Bosnia and Herzegovina before the First World War to Malcolm X, via Joyce and Asia, betting that psychoanalysis can't realize its globalization, neither its decolonial potentiality, without a work of 'defamiliarization' on its own conceptual habits and political imagination."
Livio Boni, *Collège International de Philosophie, Paris*

Decolonization and Psychoanalysis

Decolonization and Psychoanalysis challenges conventional psychoanalytic assumptions by revisiting Lacan's conceptualization of the materiality of speech through a decolonial lens.

Ahmad Fuad Rahmat explores how Lacan's ideas about the symbolic order and its historical development are intertwined with decolonial assumptions, and proposes that critically considering these assumptions can pave the way for a decolonial psychoanalysis. The book begins with how Lacan uses Freud's Jewishness as a marginalized perspective that reveals the excluded dimensions of signification within the symbolic order, and examines James Joyce's anti-colonial politics and its significance for Lacan's conception of the sinthome. The book includes a critique of Slavoj Žižek's Eurocentric reading of Malcolm X as a foil with which colonized speech could be conceived as "symbolic dispossession". Finally, it reframes the notion of "the gap" by understanding global capitalism as a mode of exchange to advocate for a decolonial psychoanalysis that focuses on the non-spaces of transmission as opposed to a like-for-like export of the clinic from the center to the periphery.

Decolonization and Psychoanalysis will be of great interest to psychoanalysts and to scholars of psychoanalytic studies, critical theory, and cultural studies.

Ahmad Fuad Rahmat is Assistant Professor of Media and Digital Cultures at the University of Nottingham Malaysia.

The Lines of the Symbolic in Psychoanalysis Series

Series Editor: Ian Parker, Manchester Psychoanalytic Matrix

Psychoanalytic clinical and theoretical work is always embedded in specific linguistic and cultural contexts and carries their traces, traces which this series attends to in its focus on multiple contradictory and antagonistic 'lines of the Symbolic'. This series takes its cue from Lacan's psychoanalytic work on three registers of human experience, the Symbolic, the Imaginary and the Real, and employs this distinctive understanding of cultural, communication and embodiment to link with other traditions of cultural, clinical and theoretical practice beyond the Lacanian symbolic universe. The Lines of the Symbolic in Psychoanalysis Series provides a reflexive reworking of theoretical and practical issues, translating psychoanalytic writing from different contexts, grounding that work in the specific histories and politics that provide the conditions of possibility for its descriptions and interventions to function. The series makes connections between different cultural and disciplinary sites in which psychoanalysis operates, questioning the idea that there could be one single correct reading and application of Lacan. Its authors trace their own path, their own line through the Symbolic, situating psychoanalysis in relation to debates which intersect with Lacanian work, explicating it, extending it and challenging it.

A Social Ontology of Psychosis
Genea-logical Treatise on Lacan's Conception of Psychosis
Diego Enrique Londoño-Paredes

Ornette Coleman, Psychoanalysis, Discourse
Movements in Harmolodic Space
A.L. James

The Origin of the Subject in Psychoanalysis
Rethinking the Foundations of Lacanian Theory and Clinic
Alfredo Eidelsztein

Decolonization and Psychoanalysis
The Underside of Signification
Ahmad Fuad Rahmat

For more information about the series, please visit: https://www.routledge.com/The-Lines-of-the-Symbolic-in-Psychoanalysis-Series/book-series/KARNLOS

Decolonization and Psychoanalysis

The Underside of Signification

Ahmad Fuad Rahmat

Routledge
Taylor & Francis Group

LONDON AND NEW YORK

Designed cover image: Getty Images © markusspenger

First published 2025
by Routledge
4 Park Square, Milton Park, Abingdon, Oxon OX14 4RN

and by Routledge
605 Third Avenue, New York, NY 10158

Routledge is an imprint of the Taylor & Francis Group, an informa business

© 2025 Ahmad Fuad Rahmat

The right of Ahmad Fuad Rahmat to be identified as author of this work has been asserted in accordance with sections 77 and 78 of the Copyright, Designs and Patents Act 1988.

Trademark notice: Product or corporate names may be trademarks or registered trademarks, and are used only for identification and explanation without intent to infringe.

British Library Cataloguing in Publication Data
A catalogue record for this book is available from the British Library

Library of Congress Cataloging-in-Publication Data
A catalog record has been requested for this book

ISBN: 9781032482224 (hbk)
ISBN: 9781032482194 (pbk)
ISBN: 9781003387978 (ebk)

DOI: 10.4324/9781003387978

Typeset in Times New Roman
by Taylor & Francis Books

For Dian and Melur.

Contents

Series editor preface

The argument of this timely book is signalled, appropriately enough, in the subtitle, as if it were the obscured truth, the answer to the implicit question posed by the main title. How are we to decolonise psychoanalysis? This is not merely an academic question of juxtaposition, putting psychoanalysis as a predominantly Western or Global North practice alongside arguments for a decolonial or post-colonial sensitivity to language. To speak of and from debates in the East or the Global South is to pose a deeper challenge to how we conceptualise dominant theories and practices, and how we might resist them. That requires a linking of colonial oppression and repression, particularly an account of repression that makes use of a Lacanian psychoanalytic understanding and the unravelling of it.

A Lacanian psychoanalytic account of repression attends to the way each one of us is located in a symbolic order which, at one and the same moment, structures and conceals what it shuts out, what it refuses to speak about and then pathologizes those who dare to. That effective repression is reiterated in the play of signifiers that compose the symbolic, with imagery that is replicated ideologically in the imaginary lures that make it seem as if we understand what is said of us in direct unmediated form, as if it were not ideological, culturally historically structured. What is shut out from dominant discourse, the stuff of the symbolic, and experiential engagement, the line of the imaginary, is the real, which, in the case of colonisation, includes dispossession and material brute power.

The "underside of signification" is, in Lacanian terms, that which is both produced by repression and is able, if we listen and act on it, the repression, to contest it. Remember that, for Lacan, it is the process of repression itself that is crucial, and that it is hopeless to imagine that what is actually "repressed" can be excavated and made to simply shine forth; to speak the truth of repression is precisely to speak of how an "underside" of signification is manufactured rather than falling into the trap of celebrating a mirror-image of colonisation, a mirror-image that retains and repeats everything it seems to refuse. Repression is, Lacan argues at one point in his work, metaphor, but metaphor which makes us speak, speak within the contours of power.

Ahmad Fuad Rahmat shows us in a finely crafted psychoanalytic mode of argument in this book that where there is power, there is resistance. Colonisation calls upon metaphor to enact an ideological view of the world, one that repetitively recomposes the symbolic order in line with particular cultural-historical forms of power, and an understanding of repression as metaphor is crucial to the way we listen to the speech of those who resist that power. This then opens the way to grasping how decolonisation as a process of resistance must attend to the institutions that relay that power into the lives of each subject, and how we move from an individual to a collective level of resistance in which decolonisation as such is not viewed as metaphor so we might encounter the real.

Psychoanalytic clinical and theoretical work circulates through multiple intersecting antagonistic symbolic universes. This series opens connections between different cultural sites in which Lacanian work has developed in distinctive ways, in forms of work that question the idea that there could be a single correct reading and application. The Lines of the Symbolic in Psychoanalysis series provides a reflexive reworking of psychoanalysis that transmits Lacanian writing from around the world, steering a course between the temptations of a metalanguage and imaginary reduction, between the claim to provide a god's eye view of psychoanalysis and the idea that psychoanalysis must everywhere be the same. And the elaboration of psychoanalysis in the symbolic here grounds its theory and practice in the history and politics of the work in a variety of interventions that touch the real.

Ian Parker
Manchester Psychoanalytic Matrix

Acknowledgments

I was quite happy to never write a book, never mind an entire book on Lacan and decoloniality, until Ian Parker's encouragement led me to it. His writings were immeasurably significant for my introduction and eventual commitment to psychoanalysis. To be able to work with him is in many ways a major milestone in my intellectual evolution.

Jessica Wong and Azizah Rahmad also deserve an early mention for their love and unwavering conviction in what I have to offer. Their support and patience for the grind of countless re-reading, re-drafting and re-editing that the manuscript required was indispensable to getting me across the finishing line. I cannot thank you enough. Dian Zainab and Melur Aminah provided much-needed inspiration and lightness at every step and turn.

I also thank my colleagues at the University of Nottingham Malaysia's School of Media, Languages and Cultures. Khoo Gaik Cheng, Lee Seungyeon, Zaharom Nain, Joanne Lim, Dag Yngvesson, Gayatri Vekiteswaran, and Sandeep Ray made for the best combination of characters to work with every day, in a healthy dialectic of guile, earnestness and humour I'm sadly quite certain I'll never find again anywhere else. There was no other school in the world that offered what we did, and I was always happy to serve because of the wonderful people powering it. I proudly laboured on this book in large part because I took it to represent us.

My understanding of what psychoanalysis actually does owes a great deal to Eliana Silberfich and Gonzalo Prado. I must also thank the Centre for Lacanian Analysis in Aotearoa for letting me participate in their rich discussions and reading groups. I experienced my most productive phase of writing in-between the meetings with Andréa Guerra, Ursula Lau, Ilana Katz and Omar David Moreno to design a global-decolonial analytic training programme. Andréa deserves special mention as a most profound guide in my journey into psychoanalysis. My sabbatical at PSILACS (Psicanálise e Laço Social no Contemporâneo) at the Federal University of Minas Gerais, which was crucial for much of the book's most breakthrough insights, would not have been possible without Andréa's tireless support. This was also where I befriended Guilherme Spinelli Estevam, Lucas Fernandes

Silva, Edvaldo Ribeiro Brandão, Luca Anaruma Ribeiro, and Renally Xavier de Melo whose insights as young aspiring decolonial analysts were inspirational for my thinking.

I was encouraged by the gatherings that effectively became Malaysia's first-ever equivalent of the Wednesday Psychological Society. Jeannette Goon was an all-important catalyst. Victoria Cheng, true to her experimental spirit, was an important mainstay from day one. Regina Hoo is taking her questions in interesting directions to become another fellow traveller in decolonial analysis. I am happy to have our discussions feature in Hannah Kuah's very promising start as an educator and researcher. Clarissa Say will stand out for bravely taking the spirit of our critical inquiry into public advocacy.

Thank you Atik and Siti for always being there to hold the fort. Thank you too to the wonderful staff at Pustaka Raja Tun Uda for running the facilities that helped with my writing and editing. The decades of conversations with Syed Muhammad Muhyiddin al-Attas have also been spiritually rich.

Introduction

The materiality of language and decolonial psychoanalysis

This book turns to Jacques Lacan to explore the materiality of speech as the site for decolonial psychoanalytic thinking. If conscious speech is sustained through the crystallization of meaning, by which idea and utterance are thought to be seamless, unconscious speech surfaces out of the materiality of language by showing how the purported seamlessness was premised upon the exclusion of incompatible signifiers. The parapractic short-circuits, so crucial to the psychoanalytic operation, are triggered by the unintended and unwelcomed slippages and cracks in the tracks of speech wherein representation, as opposed to an ideal interface between person and world, is realized to be corporeally embedded. The decolonial opening is not difficult to see from here. Insofar as coloniality dominates as a mechanism of representation, speech as where representation is embodied is also where the unconscious dimension of coloniality functions and/or falters. This takes the colonial politics of language beyond the refusal or retrieval of a given idiom for its nativity or coloniality, to language as the formal basis of ordering an object world, of rendering the terms with which objects become visible or invisible to be worthy or unworthy of consideration and address. A decolonial use of this premise would identify the slippages in language as the site for analysis' decolonial potential.

If the materiality of language is what we call the formal possibility for the decolonial use of Lacanian precepts, I present "the underside of signification" in turn to refer to the textual and conceptual precedents that indicate the active germination of an anti-colonial outlook in Lacanian theory. Lacan does not often single out this notion for scrutiny but the few times when it is mentioned indicates his recognition of a crucial feature to the symbolic order. If the materiality of language speaks to the critical potential in the breakdown of speech, the underside of signification points to Lacan's attentiveness to how the materiality reveals the ways symbolization happens across historical differences, in which the question of European colonialism eventually cannot be avoided. Indeed, with "the underside" we are able to flesh out a key Lacanian premise: The symbolic order is not a static matrix always already structuring speech but is historically in movement to engulf entirely new worlds of different referential logics. The question of psychoanalytic decoloniality is thereby directed from how psychoanalysis

DOI: 10.4324/9781003387978-1

could be used for decolonial purposes toward how psychoanalysis itself could be decolonized from the site of another speech where different symbolic and theoretical possibilities could be had. Thus, rather than providing another conception of decolonial psychoanalysis, this project seeks to consider the materiality of language as the basis for a decolonial psychoanalytic standpoint, to indicate a point of departure with which psychoanalysis could be continuously reconsidered for a decolonial project.

The materiality of the underside is presented in recognition of the contradiction Mrinalini Greedharry (2024) finds in the decolonial psychoanalytic impulse. On one hand, psychoanalysis is being rightly deployed for decolonial aims. On the other hand, it remains reliant on a broad set of concepts whose coloniality remains unchecked. Greedharry presents Paul Preciado's (2021) infamous 2019 speech at the École de la Cause Freudienne as a case in point. Preciado's stirring reproach against the psychoanalytic establishment is widely noted for the strong reactions it generated. But Greedharry points out a curious moment when Preciado laments how psychoanalysis remains complacent within its Eurocentric heterosexual frame while he casually calls himself "Africa" to describe how psychoanalysis had colonized him as a queer subject. This use of Africa by a white European male is telling of how decolonial psychoanalysis, no matter how trenchantly pursued, remains locked in a colonial matrix owing to the absence of an alternative language with which psychoanalysis could pursue its decolonial aims:

> This flicker of the colonial imaginary at the heart of psychoanalysis, even in the hands of an avowedly decolonising psychoanalyst, should give us pause precisely because colonialism returns, in the psychoanalytic language, as an always available metaphor or analogy but seldom as the bare, lived experience of the colonised.
>
> (Greedharry, 2024, p. 61)

The challenge for psychoanalytic decoloniality is deeper than the mere transformation of psychoanalysis' uses and audience. It is about a blind spot in the very reproduction of the psychoanalytic outlook. Thus the importance of language, and psychoanalysis' use of it, as the site of decoloniality:

> The question that persists, then, is how we can grasp the psychoanalytic language in such a way that it could be used against its own institutional practice, a practice that certainly does continue to construct and reproduce the "autonomous and self-identified subject of self-realization." What I mean by language here is not simply the specialist, technical language that psychoanalysts use to speak to one another about analysands, but also language of analysis that analysands must adopt in order to carry out the task of analysis.
>
> (Greedharry, 2024, p. 62)

The exact practice of language as the resource to posit new decolonized concepts for psychoanalysis is beyond the scope of the book. There is enough in Greedharry's challenge, however, to trigger a realization – which to my knowledge is yet to be recognized or treated in any length – of a similar contradiction in how Lacan's conception of the symbolic order is understood, particularly where Lacanian psychoanalysis is being read for anti-colonial critique. On one hand, such a critique cannot but draw from the symbolic order given how the symbolic anchors a wide array of adjacent concepts that lends Lacanian psychoanalysis its critical import. At the same time Lacan is always clear that the symbolic order he speaks of is the Western-European symbolic order. Lacan does not theorize language in the abstract. He has in mind an experience of speech as it emerged out of the evental ruptures of symbolization supposedly distinct to Western history. He thus sees psychoanalysis as responding to the crisis of knowledge in the historical experience that amounted to the Cartesian cogito as a template of subjectivity. To theorize with the symbolic order as a paradigm molded out of this circumstance is to confine all possible modes of decoloniality within the European bandwidth of sameness and difference. This is even the case every time the real is placed whether logically or figuratively "outside" the symbolic, for such a relationality only acquires its salience because Europe was deemed the inside or the center that must be transformed in the first place. "The underside of signification" will be developed as a way out of this impasse via a key characteristic to Lacan's historicization of the symbolic, namely that it always implicates difference and incommensurabilities. It will be shown that Lacan theorized the symbolic order to show how it expands as a homogenizing trajectory through which the difference between what is symbolically within and outside could become a problem in the first place. Overcoming psychoanalysis' colonialty requires an attentiveness to how psychoanalytic theorizing should better position itself as to critically respond to the symbolic order grasped as a historical expansion of this particular objectal outlook. A key effect to this intervention is the reorientation of our conception of the psychoanalytic subject toward different historical sensibilities, evoking spatiotemporal imaginaries beyond whatever afforded by the story of European history.

The chapters that make up this book proceeds by way of firstly demonstrating the historicity of the symbolic order and its colonial challenges before considering how this could inform contemporary psychoanalytic politics. Chapters 1 and 2 can be read together to detail the spatiotemporality of symbolization where they are clearly central for *Formations of the Unconscious: The Seminar of Jacques Lacan, Book V* and *The Sinthome: The Seminar of Jacques Lacan, Book XXIII* respectively. The chapters see Lacan attentive to Freud's relationship to German and James Joyce's relationship to English as "unlanguaged", a term I bring loosely from post-colonial theory to refer to the estrangement unique to colonized subjects who are unable to identify with the languages they are expected to embrace. What the chapters come together to confirm in effect is that the alienation of speech so crucial in Lacan could not have been thought without the standpoint of the colonized as unlanguaged. That both seminars bookend the early and later phases of Lacan's thinking speaks to how the underside stands as a key preoccupation throughout his theorizing.

Chapter 1 will account for the underside of signification more particularly via Lacan's conception of "the trace" in *Seminar V.* This refers to the residual fragments of signification that trail the symbolic order's reproduction of signifiers, one that Lacan discerned in Freud's status as a European Jew. This is evident in Lacan's use of Freud's reading of Heinrich Heine (another outsider European Jew) as well as Freud's contentious instance of self-analysis in the Signorelli parapraxis, where the problem of difference and translation, anchored in preoccupations around what sufficiently signifies Europeanness, are integral to understanding how the symbolic order interpolates. The spatiotemporality is evident where Lacan references Heine and Freud's travels to speak of how the process of symbolic ordering also expands, particularly where it meets impasses at the margins of its trajectory. To take this seriously is to take Lacan's return to Freud as a return to Freud's historicity. Freud is the subject of the trace as the standpoint which could neither be expelled nor interiorized by the symbolic. He could only be both the irrevocable Jew and the urbane scientist because he was a contradiction that could not be reconciled. This consequently situates the discovery of the unconscious at the interstices of incommensurabilities, the liminal gap antagonizing an expansively devouring field of meaning.

My reading of *Seminar XXIII* in Chapter 2 will present what I call "the coloniality of the analyzable" to show how Lacan was eventually concerned with the domination inherent to the psychoanalytic paradigm. Lacan did not formulate this problem in a single document or treatise, but it is evidently presumed where he described Joyce's savoir-faire as "heretical", as a form of subjective defiance that resists the trappings of symbolic ordering. This "heretical" resistance furthermore was a provocation to rethink psychoanalysis' most basic precepts. But a consideration of how Lacan frequently referenced British colonialism throughout *Seminar XXIII* indicates that Joyce's savoir-faire was not simply a matter of individualistic non-conformity. Joyce's singular refashioning of the English language was also presented as a response to the longer history of power relations that produced psychoanalysis in which European colonialism was essential. The political profundity of Joyce's heresy shall be contextualized further by way of *The Seminar of Jacques Lacan: The Other Side of Psychoanalysis (Book XVII)* as another instance where savoir-faire was described in relation to colonial history. Here savoir-faire is positioned as knowledge on the side of the slave in the history of the master's theft of the slave's knowledge, amounting to an exploitative hierarchy Lacan also saw to be at work in the clinic. With this as the bigger historical picture Lacan was working with, we can think of Joyce's heresy as a call to defamiliarize psychoanalysis through the unlanguaged. This should compel us to radically reimagine how psychoanalysis should also travel as a result, beyond the north to south model of transmission we have all become familiar with.

Chapters 1 and 2 should come together to show that the gap between Freud's and Joyce's marginalized historical situation, on one hand, and the languages imposed on them to operate as 'European' subjects, on the other, enables Lacan to reflect on the historical conditions through which we can critically discern how the symbolic order functions, namely, by expanding into different historical standpoints, a difference that the underside of signification as a notion helps identify. To simplify for an introduction: where the standard subject of psychoanalysis meets the gap belatedly after the fact, unlanguaged speech unfolds through the very structuring of the gap. The unlanguaged speaks the quilting process. The unlanguaged is realizing at some level that the symbolic is gaping and that the terms of (non)sense-making consequently could be remade. Once the centrality of the symbolic underside is established, we discuss how it is operative in a more recent example of unlanguagedness in Malcolm X. Chapter 3 explores how Malcolm's pursuit of decolonial politics was fueled by his constant alienation through the different linguistic forms he encountered in his travels in Africa and the Islamic world. From the white American English he internalized, Malcolm was then estranged by the new Arabic terminologies he had to embrace to become Muslim. Rather than rendering this as a straightforward story of Islamic conversion, our attentiveness to how Malcolm was often lost across translations speaks to the ways his subjective experimentation was sustained through the gaps in speech as they manifest as gaps across historical differences. His political and spiritual conversions were not forged out of the tensions within the dominant Western symbolic order, but the antagonisms produced where the Western symbolic order's reach and effect were clearly limited by other dominant historical forces. The subjective experimentation at the threshold between the dominant European symbolic and its limits before different histories of symbolic possibilities, so unique to colonized subjects, will be termed "symbolic dispossession" to differentiate it from symbolic ordering as usually construed.

The three chapters assert the importance of thinking about the materiality of language in historical terms for a uniquely psychoanalytic contribution to decoloniality. The exact politics this produces, and their clinical applications are altogether different matters requiring a more elaborate venue. This book should suffice however to recast speech in a different light, that rather than merely symptomatic, speech is actively weaving together signifiers out of different historical dynamics. A decolonial psychoanalysis therefore should not think that all speech is empty by default. For the unlanguaged, situated as they are the margins of the symbolic order, speech is symbolization in the thick of historical (non)sense-making. The gaps in unlanguaged speech consequently reveal crossroads of different subjective possibilities and are thus productive resources for new concepts. But while this book does not explore the practical possibilities, its three chapters compel sufficient occasion to question how the notion of "the gap" should now be reconsidered for a globalizing decolonial clinic. For a decolonial psychoanalysis also bears the burden of trailing psychoanalysis' global spread as it travels along the growing demand for mental health awareness worldwide. If the underside reveals a different relationship to the gap, then we will do well to ensure that the psychoanalysis as a clinical service does not globalize only to further replicate the hegemony therein. The fourth and final chapter will therefore address this matter by way of introducing two interrelated terms by way of Kojin Karatani (2005), namely "the intermundia" and "non-space". They refer to the two interfaces structuring the world produced through the proliferation of capitalist monetary exchange. "The inter-mundia" refers to the essential "gap" underlying the international world that trade brings together, with "non-space" the implication I draw to emphasize the tenuousness of the spatial imaginaries therein. The notions are key for what Karatani takes monetary exchange to do wherein the regeneration of surplus serves to momentarily equalize the incommensurability between two differing value systems. Capitalism's growth and its unsustainability are therefore rooted to how the universality of surplus value occurs upon the intensification of difference. The critical task consequently is to be attentive to both registers of globalization in a gesture Karatani describes as "transcritical". This means traversing the world capitalism produces while discerning the incommesurabilities the exchange occludes. "Non-space" consequently is the difference underlying the seamlessness of apparent space. The transcritical transposition across sameness and difference could similarly apply to the psychoanalytic setting. The form of the clinic as we know it will be the way that psychoanalysis is sold to new markets beyond the Western-European fold it came from. But the purchase of the psychoanalytic outlook, as in the actual monetary purchase given that psychoanalysis is a service after all, must also be noted for the other values and affects occluded as a result.

"Coloniality", "colonialism", "empire", and "imperialism" will be used as interchangeable terms throughout the chapters given that they are understood and discussed differently across the texts being considered. They share, however, a common referent in the hierarchized spaces that are structured by the globalized world produced by the expansion of scientific capitalist modernity and its ideology of developmental progress. What is more important than strict definitions of coloniality and empire, however, is the reader's familiarity with certain key things. The first is the entrenched coloniality of Freud's texts and outlook.[1] This has been extensively recounted and detailed in various venues and will not be revisited unless necessary. To this we can add the problems of coloniality in Lacanian psychoanalysis which continues to be dissected especially where he is being read as a resource for anti-racist critique.[2] While colonial racism is relatively less of a burden in Lacan, he is not totally off the hook. Nonetheless I hope for the subsequent chapters to show that there are in Lacan rich and productive avenues for decolonial thinking in spite of it all. How to square the contradictions, should they even need to be, is an important question that deserves a more extensive discussion given that such an inquiry would require a command of Lacan's oeuvre. The third contextual point my book takes for granted is the unfamiliar forms psychoanalysis will take where it is finding new markets and significant growth in countries outside the West and the Global North. Much remains to be done to synthesize these developments into an overarching picture but a brief consideration of the clinical and theoretical psychoanalytic debates and experiments taking place in China, Japan, India, Indonesia and Brazil, to name just five examples, will be enough to indicate that the future of psychoanalysis will not be in Europe.[3] The International Psychoanalytic Association's apathy and silence throughout the Gaza genocide and the Israeli invasion of Lebanon will no doubt be viewed one day as a key turning point in the slow and certain multipolar decentring of psychoanalytic thinking that is in motion. With this in mind, the "deprovincialization" of the European psychoanalytic outlook will be pursued with a wide-ranging understanding of "the global" that underpins all the chapters. Rather than taking the global to mean the globalization of Pax Americana or Westernization, the global shall be understood as an uneven world consisting of many histories and temporal flows beyond the story of European history. If to provincialize is to decenter Europe's claims to universality, to deprovincialize is to resituate universal thinking - indeed, universal voicing - in the periphery, or non-European historical flows in this case.

Something should be said about the prominence of Žižekian themes throughout the book. In many ways Žižekian theory is a useful foil for any discussion on decolonial psychoanalysis given how Slavoj Žižek has done the most to both globalize and Europeanize psychoanalysis over the three decades of his worldwide popularity. Psychoanalysis is globalized as Žižek's books travel along the mass exportation of Western popular culture more broadly. Psychoanalysis is Europeanized, in varying degrees of directness, through the European orientation of Žižek's politics in which the cultural and political supremacy of the European way of life is taken as given. I should state from the onset that my book is not interested in pointing out Žižek's ethnocentrism and alleged racism, which have been treated in depth in any case on various occasions (the belief that the authors we enjoy should mirror our values is narcissistic).[4] The primary issue taken, which constitutes the general theoretical concern underlining all the chapters, is the globality of the negative. Rather than a discovery unique to the European historical experience which is to be then projected chronologically to the rest of the world, negativity, the gap in being as the gap in speech, is to be understood considering global flows and formations, flows and formations that are not confined to the dictates of European time. This will be the basis with which we can think of lack in decolonial terms.

Ultimately, the arguments presented by my book should amount to the radical refining of the rather dominant tendency in Lacanian psychoanalysis to think of the real as beyond relations and thus untranslatable. My conclusion will therefore discuss Naoki Sakai's (1997) notion of "heterolingual address." This sees the task of translation as affirming the lack of understanding, owing to how the very desire to translate already marks a recognition of the gap between addresser and addressee. Sakai's historical setting is a modernizing Japan in a globalizing Asia wherein the process of situating Japan's unique place in the emerging world market saw the pressing need for translation amidst mounting international trade. Translation, and the contradictions therein, became a basis with which the global was conceived from "the periphery" as it were. One can think of this as a way of democratizing the non-rapport or the failure in language that Lacanians privilege. Sakai, thinking of translation in ways that defy symmetric exchange, describes how heterolingual address "does not abide by the normality of reciprocal and transparent communication, but instead assumes that every utterance can fail to communicate because heterogeneity is inherent in any medium, linguistic or otherwise" (Sakai, 1997, p. 8). The globalized world is not a world of greater intersubjective failure. It is a world that binds us all in a perpetual state of mutual incomprehension. The more we need to translate, the more realize we are bound by misunderstanding. "Failure" can now be the basis to reconfigure rather than renounce rapports.

Notes

1 Brickman (2017), Gaztambide (2023) and Swarz (2022) are notable recent works to address this.
2 See Burnham (2022) for a theoretical overview of the issues in decolonizing Lacan. Khan (2018) and several entries in Hook and Sheldon (2021) also address coloniality in Lacan via his critiques of racism.
3 For the latest overview of psychoanalysis in India see Manasi, Dhar, & Mishra (2018). Psicanálise na Rua (2023) pursues valuable experimentations of the spatiality of the psychoanalytic clinic, and thus speech, among marginalized communities in Brazil. Other notable psychoanalytic developments in the non-European world are as follows: Koichi Togashi (2020) finds decolonial promise in what he coins, drawing significantly from the Eastern Asian philosophy, the "Psychoanalytic Zero", wherein the Taoist and Buddhist philosophy of emptiness is posited as the ground for the therapeutic encounter. Against Cartesian dualism and formalism, the Psychoanalytic Zero stresses "the liberatory dimension of emptiness as context-free exchange and reflection: A therapeutic dialogue, therefore, can be seen as a succession of context-free moments, inclusive of every possibility and continually creating context, moment by moment" (Togashi, 2020, p. xi). Ismahan Soukeyna Diop (2023) draws from the myths, narratives, and lived experiences of African femininity

among the women of Wolof culture in Senegal to rethink the Lacanian notions of adornment and masquerade with which a more inclusive clinic more critical of the male-colonial gaze could be envisioned. This grounds the clinical dyad within the broader realm of symbolic possibilities drawn out of African women's choices of how to express themselves bodily, through which "adornment can be the space of the expression for this ambivalence and mark the body as a desiring subject" (Diop, 2023, p. 3). Stefania Pandolfo (2018) addresses the legacy of colonial psychiatry and psychology in Morocco from the standpoint and speech of patients suffering from Jinn possessions. She challenges and extends the Lacanian notions of subjectivity and the ethical by way of troubling received notions of "madness" from the experience of subjects being wrongly diagnosed, and thus silenced, through a modern-Western clinical paradigm. Conducting the clinic under colonial duress is the subject of Lara Sheehi and Stephen Sheehi's (2021) rich and detailed documentation of therapy in occupied Palestine, drawing from queer, liberatory, and Fanonian approaches. Most crucial is how this is informed by the clinical experience and speech of therapists and subjects enduring the horrors and brutalities of Israeli occupation. The clinic's duality as a concurrent space of containment and potential liberation is thus theorized out of the mires of everyday anti-colonial resistance, wherein psychoanalysis itself is rewritten and rethought out of the "coherent material reality" of Palestine's pursuit of liberation (Sheehi & Sheehi, 2021, p. 7). Ankhi Mukherjee (2021) takes the question of coloniality to the field of analytic practice through her in-depth and moving ethnography of free clinics among the urban poor in India to demonstrate psychoanalysis' decolonial possibilities by detailing what it can do for the marginalized underclass in Bombay as a microcosm of a rapidly polarising Global South.

4 Criticisms of Žižek's politics from non-European perspectives, and the defences they have elicited from his non-European readers, are so voluminous they should be compiled into a reader of its own. Noteworthy criticisms include Dirlik (1999), Hart (2002, 2003), Dabashi (2015), Bjelić (2011b), Kolozova (2011) and Almond (2012). Noteworthy defences include Khader (2017, 2020) and Kapoor and Zalloua (2021), the latter of which will be addressed in detail in Chapter 3. Other relevant accounts are Thakur (2013).

Chapter 1

The unconscious is structured like the unlanguaged
The colonized and the traces of signification

Introduction: What to make of Freud's Jewishness

The question of psychoanalysis' relationship to colonialism will eventually have to contend with the contradictions in Freud's coloniality. Freud's developmental outlook, which was reinforced by a linear historical attitude toward non-Europeans, is widely documented because he so openly professed them as some of psychoanalysis' most central meta-theoretical assumptions. But Freud's Eurocentrism was often dampened by the fact that he was also writing as a victim of European racism. Jewish marginalization is also as a result a central feature of his theorization. Indeed as widely documented, the development of psychoanalysis, with psychoanalysis premised on the discovery of the unconscious as the margins of the psyche, paralleled his anti-Semitic exclusion from academic circles and the impediments he faced throughout his endeavors across continental Europe. That Freud had no choice but to flee to London to escape Nazi persecution ensured that psychoanalysis' eventual success in the United Kingdom, where it briefly secured unprecedented national-institutional recognition and legitimacy, remained rooted to his story of exile.[1]

This unique position sees a contradiction in the extent to which Freud's criticality could be deployed for decolonial purposes. On one hand, Freud could be engaged for an immanent critique of Europe, with his relationship to Jewishness taken as symptomatic of the ambivalences common to colonized subjects. On the other hand, this can only ever be a European critique of Europe. Symptomatic of this contradiction is Stephen Frosh's (2023) redeeming use of "barbarism" to show how the Jewish standpoint could be deployed for decolonial purposes. Frosh builds on Santiago Slabodsky's theorization of "Jewish barbarism" to reposition the European Jew alongside other colonized subjects as common victims of European imperialism. Barbarism in this regard retains the European Jew in the margins of the European ideal of progress, thereby sustaining their standpoint for the critique of Europe as a critique of coloniality:

> this means taking the elements written off by the colonial empire as barbaric and empowering them, disrupting the colonial project. Jews are

DOI: 10.4324/9781003387978-2

potentially as much part of this as any other colonized group because colonialism has made them the same.

(Frosh, 2023, p. 64)

Frosh (2023) situates psychoanalysis in this tradition. He takes psycho-analysis' political history of marginalization to mean that it is both Jewish and beyond Jewishness: "Psychoanalysis needs and can never escape its Jewish provocations; and in these can be found some of the energy with which it is possible for psychoanalysis to contribute to the ongoing struggle for a decolonised world" (Frosh, 2023, p. 74). This informs the parallel Frosh charts – drawing from similar themes in Judith Butler, Otto Fenichel, Emmanuel Levinas and Talmudic ethics – between psychoanalysis and the "ethical relationality" he takes to be central to Jewish theology and historical experience (Frosh, 2023, p. 27). Ethical relationality is the affirmation of an inherent otherness against the liberal view of the transparent and self-sufficient individual. Frosh presents it as the basis of a practical ethics for a broader anti-racist agenda:

> In opposition to what is essentially a narcissistic, antisemitic and racist vision of a uniform society founded on ethnically "pure" identities (as well as in opposition to other types of homogeneity, for instance around sexuality), Judaic ethics recognizes that we are always "unsettled" by our relations with others.
>
> (Frosh, 2023, p. 29)

But in formulating the political link between Jewishness and psychoanalysis, Frosh also retains Europe in psychoanalysis' decolonial potential. To link psychoanalysis to the perspective of marginalized "barbaric" Jewishness is to also sustain Europe's position as the cause of the marginalization:

> This is because of the insistent and it seems never to be entirely over-come marginality of the Jews, through which they are at times absorbed into the body of the social, and at times expelled from it.
>
> (Forsh, 2023, p. 74)

Frosh's critical use of barbarism therefore stands out for how Eurocentrism does not feature as a central problem. Frosh's decolonial psychoanalysis ultimately reads as a decoloniality of European political power without a critique of Eur-opean culture or the idea of Europe. This is because Europe is sustained through the very anti-Semitism that shapes Freud's outlook. The outcome of this unfortunately is an appeal to the exceptionalism of Jewish marginalization:

> although there are many genuine "origins" to psychoanalysis which have effects and are of importance, its Jewish origins are uniquely significant

because of the political, historical, social and emotional baggage that they brought with them, and which psychoanalysis has never been able to escape.

(Frosh, 2023, p. 17)

Thus, to affirm the unique standpoint psychoanalysis offers is to affirm this inherent link to an oppression that is essentially European. This implies that the engagement with Jewishness that decolonial psychoanalysis requires is an engagement with Jewishness as it was produced by European resentment. We are back therefore to the same problem in which psychoanalysis, on account of its origins in the modernity responsible for Jewish oppression, remains an essentially European phenomenon. Frosh's decolonial psychoanalysis will only be able to respond to the universal question of colonialism through a European lens. The range of critical possibilities therein would be contained within the parameters of whether European Jewishness is non-European enough.

The unlanguaged Freud

This chapter aims to overcome Freud's European impasse by framing his political position as neither Jewish nor European but as "unlanguaged". "Unlanguaged" to be clear from the onset is not a Lacanian term. It is a term with varying definitions that populates post-colonial theory, with few occasional mentions in psychoanalysis. In general, however, the unlanguaged refers to subjects who are marginalized on account of the prejudice and/or disregard they experience because of the language they are associated with. This is pertinent for our understanding of Freud's decolonial potential because he himself suffered the anxieties of being unable to identify with languages that were marginalized due to their association with Jewishness. Austro-Hungarian Jews were recognized as a "people" (*Volksstamm*) but not as a "nation" (*Nationalität*). This distinction meant that Jews did not have the same territorial or linguistic rights as other nationalities within the empire. They were not granted the right to teach their children Hebrew or Yiddish, where other recognized national groups such as the Poles, Hungarians, and Croats were. The Jews' unlanguaged state was not simply a matter of historical exile but the political pressures at the time. This takes us to the second more specific way Freud was unlanguaged: He spoke neither Hebrew nor Yiddish but was nonetheless marginalized on account of his linguistic association with them. Freud was unlanguaged therefore for being linguistically European but racially non-European. This status links Freud's standpoint with a predicament common to post-colonial subjects who suffer the impossibility of feeling at home in both their native language and the language of the colonizer.

If Freud's anxieties of language and their post-colonial resonances should be of interest to a decolonial psychoanalysis, it is because they inform Lacan's theorization of the symbolic order and the unconscious in *Seminar V.* While Lacan does not put it exactly in these terms (indeed *Seminar V* should not be regarded as a primarily political text) he draws from history in enough detail and consistency to demonstrate an indispensable reliance on Freud's Jewish standpoint as a disenfranchised European qua the unlanguaged. Thus while coloniality, postcoloniality or the unlanguaged do not feature in Lacan's vocabulary, a close consideration of what he does with Freud in the seminar clearly shows his detailed attentiveness to Freud's political predicament in ways that speak to struggles characteristic of colonized subjects.

Lacan as one would expect takes this to purely formal directions charting elaborate mathemes to describe how the unconscious works via desire. There is no discussion of Judaism, never mind colonialism. "Jew" is mentioned only three times, despite the obvious themes of Jewish self-consciousness in the examples Lacan constantly returns to. "Empire" is mentioned only as a historical point of clarification without any serious consideration of its political implications. What is clear, however, is that Lacan cites Freud's displacement to provide a psychoanalytic account of the symbolic order as historical. More particularly, it becomes the basis of theorizing a scientific capitalist modernity by way of how the symbolic order regenerates "the beyond" that orients the reproduction of meaning. Consequently this regeneration of meaning in the beyond that Lacan evokes frequently throughout the seminar is the frame with which Europe and history - and by implication, the ideology of "progress" - would feature in his theorization, as we shall soon see. Specifically, Lacan provides a picture of a scientific capitalism whose salience is acquired through what he calls the process of "purifying" signifiers. "Purification" is the process of abstraction by which signifiers are emptied of their corporeal and historical specificity for the production of clarity, "that is, of reducing it to the necessary minimum for it to be able to grasp onto things" (Lacan, 2017, p. 333). Lacan does not single out purification as a notion to develop in detail. But it makes significant enough appearances in key moments in the seminar to be worthy of featuring.

For it is through the abstracting that purification ensures for the symbolic order that Lacan will situate the marginalized European Jewish standpoint at the margins of symbolization, as the subject whose speech is undergoing and at the same time resisting the symbolic. This reveals an antagonism that cannot be accounted for without considering how Eastern European Jews had the burden of inheriting an unmodern mother tongue deemed unsuitable for the beyond-oriented temporality of Western European modernity. In many ways we see the "excess" so crucial to Lacanian thought conceived through this example, with the Jewish standpoint being that which Europe can neither incorporate nor be rid of. This in general strokes resonates with broader post-colonial concerns about the loss of native symbolic sensibilities to European languages as colonial institutions. But Lacan takes this further to show it happens at the materiality of speech, at the sounds and affects that speak to the historicity unique to the lack in the word, more than the crystallized idea therein. In other words, it was only through Jews as the unlanguaged that Lacan could re-theorize the unconscious.

As we shall see, this informs Lacan's eventual formulation of the symbolic order as a process of regulating the failed expulsion of signifiers through which the excesses within "the body" and "identity" could be tentatively sustained. The symbolic could be understood only upon paying attention to the fissures that underscore the fundamental exclusions that constitute how symbols are made and ordered. These fissures, moreover, are only known indirectly through those subjects at the margins of the symbolic who Lacan situates at the threshold where "Europe" and "non-Europe" are being differentiated.

But this is only one side of the purification process. Lacan also demonstrates that purification is inherently unsuccessful. Purification is not just about making new self-sufficient concepts, the concepts are also shown for their inherent lack. This reproduction of lack indeed is how the desire for "more" is regenerated. This similarly is how we should understand the excessive nature of "the beyond" which in turn accounts for how modernity is fundamentally volatile. Purification consequently is never an absolute process for it produces a real that persists where the clarified signifier is outlined. Thus, Lacan deploys Freud's unlanguagedness as similarly unsettled. Being European and non-European was not a playful mask of mimicry Freud could put on and off as he wished. It was an antagonism that underlined his corporeality and this divide across time and civilization was how Freud could theorize the unconscious. It is to detail this process that Lacan in *Seminar V* turns to Freud's theorization of witz and humor by way of Heinrich Heine in *Jokes and their Relation to the Unconscious*, and forgetting via the Signorelli parapraxis from the *Psychopathology of Everyday Life*. They are presented as examples that attest to the granularity of the purification process wherein fragments of significations, in their most fundamental pieces of sound and the varying meanings they might carry, are torn apart and reconstructed to be purified into lacking signifiers. Our introduction of the underside will be aided by considering how Lacan uses the notion of "the trace" in Seminar V to describe purificiation in more detail.

The underside of purification

The Lacanian notion of "the trace" provides two critical uses: The first is to show how the unconscious works in the concrete disruptions of smooth speech wherein changes in the tones, sounds and emphases of words have the effect of disrupting their initial intentions. The trace disrupts to reveal the emptiness in signification insofar as there is underlying the otherwise stable exchange of symbols, a chaos that initially compelled the symbolic ordering process. The second more important feature of the trace is how this disruption reveals another meaning that had to be excluded, that there is in the momentary chaos underlying symbolization another possibility of ordering the symbol. Thus, the trace is crucial for how it disrupts the production of meaning by exposing the raw, acoustic, material of signification that had to be purified. The power to work against the purification process is signaled by how Lacan also describes the trace is in *Seminar V* varyingly as the "waste," "scraps," "debris," "fragments," and conseqently "underside" of signification.

We shall have more to say about the significance of the trace in the coming parts of the chapter, but our introduction of the politics of the underside should note that the purification of signifiers would not have been required if the "impurity" of language was not a problem to begin with. It is in this curious presumption that we find how symbolic ordering works in spatiotemporal terms. Lacan's rereading of the Jewish examples in Freud's theorizing shows that the purification of language implicates the fundamentally diasporic nature of the unlanguaged Jew. Lacan to be sure does not use the term "diaspora" in the seminar but he sufficiently referenced Jewish dispersal across Europe especially where the question of nationality, belonging and translation across differences were often evoked. In many ways they speak to how Lacan took the unavoidable historical details in Freud's reading of Heine for granted. Recall how Eastern and Central European Jews often spoke more than one "Jewish" language in Yiddish and Hebrew (as non-European languages with etymological and grammatical roots in Slavic and West Asian languages) along with the distinct accents of their German or French. This was an unsettling enigma at a time when national uniformity was a pressing demand. Recall also that Freud was writing during the fall of the "old" European imperial world and the rise of nationalism. This in temporal terms meant that the Jew did not have a natural relationship to the language of a European modernity that saw its historical destiny in national terms. All this goes to show that Lacan had presented psychoanalysis' critical purchase as one that is intrinsically afforded by the Jew as "neither here nor there". Consequently, psychoanalysis is Jewish if we accept that it is a Jewishness that is impossible, and this is a real impossibility located at the margins of the symbolic. The marginalization of Jewishness in this regard is neither psychoanalysis' conscience nor critical lens. It is the historical condition for the possibility of symbolic disruption that psychoanalysis works with. This outlook disentangles Jewishness from psychoanalysis by showing that this impossibility is not in any person or identity but in the repeated encounter with the traces of signification, which was fueled by the otherness that persists in bodies and languages deemed insufficiently European (or Europeanly modern) for symbolic ordering.

With this a line between clinical theorization and historical event can be drawn. For Lacan what parapraxes reveal in the signifier is this "primordial" and "disorganized" aspect of pre-purified meaning. But this is noteworthy to begin with because there was a historical problem of "difference" that required symbolic organization. Thus, the symbolic order may be European in the sense that it is the producer of linear time measured as productive and "meaningful" time. But to say that symbolic ordering leaves a trace also means that its workings could only be known from the obstinate residues that form its underside. The unlanguaged is neither a perspective that is absolutely marginalized by Europe that it does not see what is happening. Nor is it purely colonized that it is uprooted. It is best understood rather as uneven: Oscillating across different spatiotemporal sensibilities between solidified symbolic ordering and the other time of the traces, the time that is "known" only where the symbolic is fissured.

The evocation of language and national belonging in *Seminar V* takes us to the unstated although essential theme of "bordering" in Lacan's evocation of the trace. If the discovery of value in meaning – indeed that "discovery" is to be regarded as a default virtue is already telling of our temporally modern situation – demarcates past and present and consequently insider and outside, the trace positions the Jew, however momentarily, as the subject whose speech cannot be dichotomized or placed properly in any stabilizing opposition. Consequently reclaiming the defiance of Jewishness that birthed psychoanalysis, should not be a gesture of exile, of being at home without a home. Exile works with the presumption of a territorial "inside", of a sealed interior in an ideal perpetuated by the converse discourse of "return", that risks further differentiation. The traces rather speak to the threshold where the past and present or inside and outside could never be properly placed. It trails progress to see what cannot be squeezed into the lacking "beyond" that necessarily haunts all demands for belonging. Thus, with the Lacanian trace as a historical lens into how the symbolic order works, Jewishness should not be construed as a positive cultural feature of psychoanalysis. It should be upheld as the basis with which psychoanalysis found its conditions of theorizing in the problem of marginalizing other speeches and bodies. Psychoanalysis by this is not essentially European, but the threshold that critiques the lack demanding the world to be organized, for the question of past, present, and future to be constantly posed.

This, however, should not mean that Lacan is off the hook. If this chapter is needed, it is because he neglected to push the insights he presents to their logical conclusions. Lacan builds significantly on Freud's reading of Heine while staying shy of their political implications. Thus, he points out the politics of naming that Heine and Freud grappled with (Freud's original name was Sigismund and Heine's birth name was registered as Chaim) without highlighting how it was a problem borne out of European racism. Racism was why they could not feel at home and thus the reason why they could confront symbolic ordering as a problem. But this was a racism they could unpack from the trace confronted from their unlanguaged standpoint. Lacan's take on

Freud's reading of the wordplay in Heine's joke about "the Golden Calf" and "famillionaire," will be crucial as we shall soon see. But nowhere is the question of belonging more evident than Lacan's rereading of the forgetting during Freud's train ride across the Balkans. Those familiar with this vignette can understand the allegations of its coloniality. During a casual conversation with another passenger, Freud struggles to remember the painter of the Orvieto frescoes. He eventually arrives at the right answer in Botticelli but along the way realizes that he had been struggling to come to terms with the death of a friend. The trigger was the fact that the conversation happened as the train went through Muslim Bosnia. Freud suddenly was taken to his memory of a friend who recalled the Turks he encountered in Bosnia and their contradictory attitude in which sex is pursued openly while death is feared. It was through meeting with this contradiction in an Oriental other, while he was thinking about something European, that Freud could recall the death of his friend. The theoretical lesson, that a forgetting revealed a repression, rests on an Oriental trope and this is taken to indict Freud's embedded coloniality. Lacan's structural approach offers a more productive reading of this moment to detail how purification happens across translation. Lacan accepts the location – the border between Europe and the Islamic world – but sees forgetting as the parapraxis that reveals how the symbolic order purifies difference across time and space. The forgetting is symptomatic of Freud's (failed) intention to symbolically (read: civilizationally) order his speech. We must, however, build our case from the beginning, namely, the details of Lacan's structural and linguistic use of Freud and how the trace works primarily through disrupting the temporality demanded by the symbolic order. That the trace barely features in Lacanian literature requires that we piece together its elements from the many times Lacan describes it throughout the seminar, particularly to grasp its relevance as a crucial notion at the heart of Lacan's historical outlook.

Part 1: Discourse and the trace

We can begin to think of the trace by comparing it with how Lacan launches *Seminar V* with a discussion on discourse. Discourse refers to "the reality we all share" and is thus the circuit where "the person who speaks" also "makes himself understood" (Lacan, 2017, p. 10). But Lacan's descriptions, while appealing to the quotidian, are geared to explain what is unique to speech in the ego as it relates to the symbolic order. Lacan describes discourse to show how the perceived variety experienced in normal everyday exchanges is actually contained within a circumscribed set of possibilities. Thus Lacan declares that ultimately "discourse says absolutely nothing" (Lacan, 2017, p. 11). Discourse is actually "empty discourse" because it functions "at the level at which the fewest meanings are created," since the meaning exchanged in everyday speech is just there and already given in advance (Lacan,

2017, p. 10). Discourse is ultimately empty because it is about ensuring rapport where there is none. Insofar as speech and language are centered on a broader dynamic of identification, the emptiness of discourse is a good way into the emptiness that structures the wider process of symbolic ordering and subjectivity. The deceiving regularity of discourse is a key setup for the more elaborate argument Lacan is to present in *Seminar V* in which discourse is so defined to account for how the unconscious disrupts the apparent regularity of speech and language and thus the seemingly reliable constancy of the world as we know it. But before we get to the nature of this disruption, we need to first understand the tenuousness. For this Lacan presents metonymy and metaphor in *Seminar V.*

Metonymy ensures regularity in the signifier's content. This requires that there is a constant pattern of possible relationships between varying signifiers. In linking different signifiers together into certain recognizable patterns, Lacan describes metonymy as functioning through the "combination" or incorporation, of different pieces of signifiers to produce an established framework of meaning: "Every relationship of derivation and every use of a suffix or an ending in inflected languages uses the contiguity of the chain for signifying purposes" (Lacan, 2017, p. 67). It goes without saying that difference constitutes the essence of the metonymic process given the endless possible combinations of words there could be, and that as a result metonymy functions to equalize and stabilize signifiers. With this we should begin, following Lacan in this seminar, to take it for granted that there are many metonymies being applied at a given time. This will in fact be key in our discussion later, as Lacan situates Freud's self-analysis of the Jewish predicament at a juncture where varying metonymies clash. For now, just note that metonymy's handling of difference ensures that there can be context, that is to say differently demarcated parameters of meaning within a given time:

> A word may be linked in different ways in different contexts, and this will give it two completely different meanings. By using it in a certain context with the meaning it has in another, we are in the metonymic dimension.
> (Lacan, 2017, p. 53)

Meanwhile, metaphors expand the chain of signification with new meanings. By this, Lacan is not referring to particular metaphors. Rather, he has in mind a structure - "a completely general function" - that accounts for "the world of meaning to be conceived" (Lacan, 2017, p. 24). Metaphor is discourse's creative and productive capacity and thus the basis of new "signifieds" that orient or expand the range of discourse. Where combination marks the metonymic operation, metaphor is defined by "substitution" in that it forges more links in the chain of signification, thereby producing more new meaning to uphold for discourse. New meanings felt in discourse are nothing more than "the pure and simple purring of repetition, idle chatter, short circuiting" that happen within the confines of the signifying chain that ensures their stability (Lacan, 2017, p. 11). Note that metaphor does not recycle signifiers as if to paste them onto new things and spaces. What is new in metaphor is a link between signifiers. The new is not an actual new entity but merely another link within the given chain. As Lacan says, "New meaning emerges through the action of a metaphor when, taking original circuits, it enters the everyday, banal and accepted circuit of metonymy" (Lacan, 2017, p. 83) Thus Lacan describes that what actually happens is just "a sort of shifting or equivocation." (Lacan, 2017, p. 67).

Thus Lacan stresses the two sides of metaphor. On one hand, it accounts for the innovation language affords. Metaphor is language's "creative mainspring" (Lacan, 2017, p. 24). It provides insight into "the evolution of meaning" (Lacan, 2017, p. 26). But the regulation and extension of meaning in signification and their perpetual recycling do not just happen. The process works to produce things by lining "emptiness" thereby including them in the broader network of already-ordered symbols. Thus, metaphor is also referred to interchangeably as the metonymic object given that it shapes a new objectal focal point around which metonymy revolves. With this we have an idea of how the object is lined by the materiality of signification, in the sounds and affects that make the basic components of the symbol. The networked nature of symbolization is important to note because it does not just explain how "nothingness" is signified, it is also the loop that makes the metonymic object the object of the Other's desire. We cannot account for there being an Other to communication if there is not to begin with an exchange between signifying fragments that indicate an exchange of meaning is taking place. But rather than there being a speaker here and a receiver there, there is only the combination and substitution of signification fragments in the network through which speakers speak. This is why Lacan says that "the only object is a metonymic object" and that the metonymic object is "the object of the Other's desire" (Lacan, 2017, p. 7). Consequently, metonymy and metaphor are the fundamental parts of the symbolizing process that ensures that desire is oriented to the Other's speech, given a direction and purpose that, however generalized and abstract, nonetheless ensures the circulation of predictable meaning.

Now why this void has to be perpetually "Othered", and that the circuit cannot remain in a self-same process of recycling without any need for new concepts, is an interesting question that this seminar will account for in ways that show the indispensability of Freud's Jewish position in Lacan's thinking. For now, it is important to note that the stability of speech – the ordering of symbols that sustain predictable meaning – is particularly important at a time when language has been rendered purely instrumental, a tool to purify and formalize phenomena "reducing it to the necessary minimum for it to be able to grasp onto things" (Lacan, 2017, p. 334). This takes us how Lacan uses "purification" to describe the experience of language unique to secular modernity. Speech has been made fundamentally interrogative and exploratory where things are broken down to produce clearly conceived concepts. Lacan takes this pursuit of comprehension for its destructiveness: "do we not observe strange upheavals in things which are certainly not unconnected to the way in which we question them?" (Lacan, 2017, pp. 333–334). This historical location is important for us to understand the world Lacan takes for granted in *Seminar V*. The ordering of symbols the Other's desire enables occurs at a time when

> people have contrived to disconnect language as much as possible – not totally, of course – from the things with which it was deeply connected up until a certain period that corresponds more or less to the beginning of modern science, in order to reduce it to its interrogative function.
>
> (Lacan, 2017, p. 333)

When Lacan speaks of the perpetual sliding of signifiers, he is referring to signifiers as they are experienced in this historical circumstance. The evental nature of this change is presumed in how Lacan, in a moment that sees him evoking a common Marxist and post-colonial expression, describes the sliding of signifiers in one instance as a "decentering" (Lacan, 2017, p. 71).

The underlying chaos to signification then is not a default feature of language that the symbolic order naturally finds its purpose to regulate. It is a distinct time which requires a specific outlook, and this should also signal how Lacan cannot, despite his formalism, ignore the importance of history to account for Freud's standpoint and thus the politics of his Jewishness. Before detailing this further we shall have to consider a crucial implication to the historicity Lacan has in mind. What is implied in the destructive way that language functions in the era of secular modernity is that the symbolic order is essentially fragile. This fragility is what Lacan will account for by way of "the trace". Lacan did not develop the trace into a standalone concept, but it will be clear that he evokes it frequently enough in *Seminar V* to stress a fundamental point. The trace represents the gap in the flow of metonymic circulation and metaphorical production of the new from the old. The idea is that signification always produces a remainder, that what is asserted through a new signifier is stained by the enduring presence, however partial, of the meaning contained in the previous signifier. But the insight Lacan wants to convey from the trace is not that there is something "left behind" in the production of metaphor. We know of the "past" fragments of signification because the trace reveals the signifier's fundamental emptiness. As such speech is constituted not by the smooth exchange of words but by the breaking down and linking of different pieces of signification in time. This is how the trace reveals the truth of symbolic ordering. The idea that the emptiness of language is revealed in breaking down the signifier is conveyed more clearly in the ways Lacan describes the trace as the "waste," "ruins" and "scraps of signifiers" (Lacan, 2017, p. 8). In one instance we get a more precise description of the trace as "the residue of metaphorical creation" (Lacan, 2017, p. 45). In another, the trace is "the debris of the metonymic object" (Lacan, 2017 p. 44). There is always a leftover emptiness in the anticipated unity of meaning that a signifier is meant to provide.

The trace's intervention is most obvious in metaphor. Another fragment of meaning is re-introduced into the sliding chains of metonymy, to form what Lacan describes as the "repressed signifying scrap" (Lacan, 2017, p. 48). It is here that the trace, as the "underside of the signifier," trails the metaphor (Lacan, 2017, p. 44). The key implication of the trace is how discursive purification simultaneously produces another chain of sense among the scraps of excluded signifiers. Again, it is worth stressing that we should not position the trace "in the past" as it were. The trace is not relegated to a prior moment. It has rather "fallen out in the interval [of signification and speech], which has been eluded in the articulation of meaning" (Lacan, 2017, p. 24). In other words, if the trace is significant in metaphor, it is because it evades the containment of meaning in metonymy. Metaphorical production and the trace then are inseparable: "the material of signifiers always partakes in something of the evanescent character of a trace" (Lacan, 2017, p. 322). If metonymy is a chain, the trace is lined along the gaps therein. Consequently, if time as we experience it occurs along the reproduction of metaphors, the trace is the suppressed element whose weight is acquired through this process of exclusion.

The effect, which is key to this seminar, is the gradual disembodiment of signification where the circulation of signifiers is about the production of concepts, wherein meaning is registered as the mental process of comprehension, against the meaning imbued in the signifier's sonic and phonetic corporeality. The mentalization of the signifier constitutes a key aspect of purification. The dislayering of the signifier, in which an idea is extracted out of its affects, accounts for how the unconscious could find an opening in the regulated rhythm of banal everyday speech. For it reveals the tenuousness and fragility of the new in everyday discourse as it comes at the cost of intensifying the trace. But this only speaks to the insight Lacan finds in the trace, namely, how it "punctuates" a moment in the broader chaos underlying discourse formation (Lacan, 2017, p. 324). This is the linguistic underpinning, the structural condition for the possibility, of parapraxes and thus the formation of the unconscious that makes the seminar's concern and title. Repressed meaning does not just "show up," it acquires its force from the *movements* in the signifying network, particularly, in the reorientation and re-combination of the signifier through the scraps of metonymy. The reality of this dimension is what makes the trace "indestructible", felt through the endurance of the new in the old and vice versa (Lacan, 2017, p. 83). This location in between conscious speech and the unconscious chains of signification accounts for what Lacan highlights as the trace's crucial feature, namely its opacity. For if metaphoric creation expels a remainder, the ensuing trace cannot be regarded as a crystalized signifier. The trace, rather, is "the effect, mark, imprint or wound of signifiers" (Lacan, 2017, p. 427). Thus, the trace cannot be encountered as one would encounter a regular signifier as is normally presented in discourse. The trace, as residue, cannot be known directly as if it is another object of knowledge or experience. As the excluded, it can only be felt indirectly as if a "clue" in signification (Lacan, 2017, p. 32). This indirectness will be the opening to a new, unconscious, association of signifiers: "in what is a signifier, in fully developed signifiers in speech, there is always a passage, that is, something following each of the elements that are articulated together and that are by nature fleeting and evanescent" (Lacan, 2017, p. 322).

Lacan likens the metaphorical creation of new objects for metonymy and the produced trace with the regeneration of exchange and value, one which Lacan takes to also explain how capitalism works. Lacan contrasts metaphor's dimension of meaning with metonymy's dimension of value for two reasons. Metonymy as we know functions as a chain of signification because it is a network of general sameness by which one signifier could link with another. Indeed, Lacan is clear that metonymy at heart is about "levelling out and equivalences" (Lacan, 2017, p. 87). This is why signifiers are said to slide as they can only be described – and thus be rendered exchangeable with – other signifiers in a process ensured by the broader rules of meaning the Other sustains. Signifiers are deemed valuable and in demand only insofar as they can be incorporated into this chain. Whatever new meaning metaphor produces therefore is not singular. It is always to be situated in the realm of equivalence by which contact with the Other could be maintained. If metaphor is the product of discourse, ensuring that something new could be the focal point of speech, metonymy is language's "mode of production" (Lacan, 2017, p. 72). But the trace is important in this scheme because it accounts for the excess in the exchange. To describe this Lacan refers to *Das Kapital*, to the well-known discussion on how cloth and clothes only have value in relation to one another in that they could be exchanged for money with capital as the third term. Similarly, it is upon emptying or purifying the meaning of words for the Other that the exchanges in discourse could happen. Just as in capitalism "no quantitative relations of value can be established without the prior establishment of a general equivalence" so too does "the equivalence necessary from the start of the analysis, and on which what is called value is based, presupposes, on the part of both terms in play, abandoning a very important part of their meaning" (Lacan, 2017, p. 73). Lacan stresses this further by distinguishing a sign's meaning from its value. If meaning merely refers to a definition, value is about the excess in the definition which signals that the subject has a lacking relationship with the signifier, a lack that must be rendered exchangeable with the lack in the Other.

This conception of value in speech as the mystery of value in capitalism could be the basis of tracking the globalization of psychoanalysis as a service that responds to those very subjects who feel the need to pay to treat their excesses. This in turn could be a window into the subjective dimension of capital's crisis (or reveal that the crisis of capitalism is a crisis of subjectivity). While the subsequent chapters will deal with this convergence between the gap in language and the crisis gap in capital, we should first elucidate how this crisis happens where the signifier is circulated in a loop of perceived commensurability with the Other in a dimension that equalizes, that is to say stabilizes, meaning. This equalizing dimension to the symbolic order is important to note because this is why metaphor's function culminates in its production of the metonymic object. It is through the metonymic object that the "message" to the Other's lack is sent and that the object in turn finds its value as something desired by the Other. This ensures the dimension of the truth stated by the subject, which the Other will ostensibly reciprocate in the form of a "code". Message and code are very important aspects of discourse as it indicates the moment of rapport anticipated between subject and Other that the metonymic object shapes. The unconscious is ordered where meaning – which in effect is the exchange, indeed substitution, between message and code – is consistently projected, thereby giving form to the lack through which subject and Other ostensibly relate. So metaphorical substitution ensures the exchangeability of signifiers with the Other, and metonymic incorporation ensures that the signifier can be processed, that is to say, combined and exchanged with other signifiers in the signifying chain. "Meaning" would not function otherwise.

The excess as the beyond

It goes without saying that the "trace" in all this attests to that which cannot be absorbed and thus must be reintroduced into the circuit of exchange. To put in broadly Marxian terms, the trace stands for the excess waste of production that must be recirculated but cannot be sold. This indeed takes us to the trace's critical purchase. The persistence of the trace within the signifying network, the fact that it must be recirculated into the flow of metonymic substitution ensures that there is always excess to whatever order the symbolic attains. The excess in the trace indeed is how we can think of the "beyond" as that which cannot be symbolized. The excess in the purified symbol accounts for what Lacan describes as "the metabolism of the signifier" and the "crux and mainspring of formations of the unconscious" (Lacan, 2017, p. 29). It is here, with the trace as a fragment of signification that accounts for the beyond of speech that Lacan also produces a rather clear statement of the unconscious:

> this beyond I have posited, inasmuch as I am attempting to determine the requisite stages for the integration of speech to enable desire to take

its place for the subject, remains unconscious for the subject. Henceforth, this is where the dialectic unfolds for him, without him knowing that this dialectic is only possible insofar as his desire, his true desire, finds its place in a relationship, which therefore remains unconscious for him, with the Other's desire.

(Lacan, 2017, p. 346)

By this point we should note the temporal assumptions in Lacan's theory. It first explains the shape of the present. If science and capitalism, viewed together as a historical horizon, are about the purification of the signifier as the condition for new knowledge, metonymy and metaphor account for how language serves as the domain where the new is extended to be circulated and exchanged around the lack that appears as "the beyond". But with the trace as the building blocks of the entire process, Lacan has also accounted for what he believes is the primordial form of language, namely language at its most basic level of signifying chaos, of signifiers sliding across and running into one another. This is why for Lacan there can be no metalanguage because ultimately there is only the sliding – the combination and substitutions of elements – which are only granted tenuous meaning:

There is no such thing as a metalanguage in the sense in which it would mean, for example, a complete mathematization of the phenomenon of language, and this is so precisely because there's no way of formalising any further than what's given as the primitive structure of language.

(Lacan, 2017, p. 66)

Lacan's rather frequent reliance on the word "primitive" throughout the seminar is an unfortunate derivative of his reliance on Freud's concepts and their colonial and developmentalist baggage. He evokes the primitive, however, for the purpose of indicating a transition to a formal structuralist account where the pleasures of speech are to be found less in the libidinal acquisition of words *per se*, than their incorporation and stabilization through the understanding guaranteed via the signifying network. This process of incorporation is relevant and will be detailed shortly where we discuss unconscious desire. What we should note at this point is the issue at heart. There is no need to produce equivalence if difference was not a problem to begin with. Consequently, the trace would not acquire its disruptive force if the trajectory of equalization did not need to be maintained. If the trace is produced where the distinct corporeal meaning of signifiers had to be purified for the efficient circulation of ideas, it is because something of the body bore an impossible difference that had to be equalized. In what will become more obvious in our discussion, especially when we soon unpack Heine's identity crisis and Lacan's reading of Freud's forgetting, the "primitive" element of language, understood structurally, takes the form of

encounters across a world conscious of linguistic and civilizational differences. Lacan's description of metaphor will draw exhaustively from the
interplay of words and their similar phonetic and conceptual counterparts
across a wide array of European languages where the sliding of signifiers
acquires a more palpable presence. It is noteworthy indeed that Lacan presents a homology between metonymy's equalizing function with Polish and
French nationalism: "One cannot fail to recognize the metonymic dimension
in these examples" (Lacan, 2017, p. 68). Lacan's claim that "the phenomenon of witz" and "the forgetting of a name" both "share a topography"
appears more telling in this light (Lacan, 2017, p. 42).

But noting the problem of difference will only take us halfway. Recall that
the metaphor and metonymy of discourse work through the Other's desire
and that the trace appears as a problem because of the impossibility of discourse to evade the underlying chaos of signification. It is in this need to
continuously pacify the impossible difference that the Other acquires its place
in "the beyond" of speech. This is the impossible point of signification that is
pursued in the proliferating purification of signifiers which must be sustained
lest the scientific capitalist world reproduced by the symbolic order collapses.
The trace intervenes to show that the beyond, rather than a truth or solution
to be found "elsewhere," is immanent in the workings of language. The pursuit of this mythical something in the beyond is important as a segue into
our discussion of witz and forgetting, for they happen to question the lack in
the Other's desire qua the lack that shapes the beyond of speech. Witz and
forgetting find their symbolic purchase in revealing the signifier's core emptiness. Witz and forgetting inserts the gap in the signifying trajectory of
sameness by perching the Other as the "beyond" of the symbolic. The political implication is obvious from here too: this occurs through Heine and
Freud's distinct situations as unlanguaged.

Part 2: Lacan, Heine, and witz

The Golden Calf and the millionaire

We can simplify the distinction between discourse, and its metonymic and
metaphoric dimensions, on one hand, with the trace on the other, as trajec-
tories of equalization and differentiation, respectively. While Lacan does not
use the language of sameness and difference, its politics is evident when
Lacan situates his theory of language with reference to capitalism and
nationalism, as the modern scientific conduits of producing abstractions, and
thus key aspects of the world that psychoanalysis responds to. This is the
world that gives the trace its impact and conceptual significance for the
seminar. The formal linguistic mechanisms Lacan describes refer heavily not
just to Freud's texts but to concepts that speak to Freud's historical location.
The implication here is key. If the chaos underlying the metaphoric

reproduction of discourse is where the formation of the unconscious is to be identified, then Lacan found it in Freud's neither here nor thereness. The dislocation is more evident when we consider Lacan's sensitivity to the Jewish relation to European history and geography. We shall begin with the former, through reading Freud's theorization of witz through an anecdote recounted by Heinrich Heine.

Witz is what happens when an unexpected meaning is introduced through wordplay. To say that witz is unexpected is to say that it has a temporal effect because the words are expressed phonetically with an element of surprise that suggests other possible meanings that could be conveyed at the same time. Lacan indeed takes witz's temporal effect as its primary distinction. Normal jokes have "the capacity" to "leave the question in suspense" (Lacan, 2017, p. 92). Witz, on the contrary, finds its impact immediately through the meaning of words or lack thereof: "A witz doesn't need to be massaged at length for it to work, whereas for the comic a simple, brief encounter is not enough" (Lacan, 2017, p. 120). There is then a revealing simplicity witz affords to the nature of the unconscious: "it just pops out like that, and that's how you recognize that someone is witty" (Lacan, 2017, p. 54). Two examples from Heinrich Heine from *Jokes and their Relation to the Unconscious* will be central to *Seminar V*: the joke about the "Golden Calf" and "famillionaire". The first is presented on technical grounds as an account of how metonymy works to enact a temporal effect. The second situates the same temporal effect within a broader historical transition. We shall proceed from the former to the latter.

Heine's joke about the Golden Calf is as follows:

> Heinrich Heine is with the poet Frederic Soulie at a salon, and the latter says to him, talking about a person who was rolling in money, a character who occupied an important position at the time, as you can see, and who was very popular, 'You see, my friend, the cult of the Golden Calf isn't yet over.' 'Oh!' Heinrich Heine replies after looking the person over, 'For a calf he strikes me as being a bit past it.'
>
> (Lacan, 2017, p. 53).

Freud, according to Lacan, highlighted this joke as an example of diversion: Heine "made use of the double meaning of which the phrase 'Golden Calf' is capable to branch off along a side-track" (Lacan, 2017, p. 51). Lacan takes this to emphasize how the branching off occurred along the metonymic signifying chain, as a mark of the concurrent negotiation of difference and sameness that a signifier undergoes as it crosses the jumbled networks of signification. Lacan's breakdown of the joke is as follows: Heine begins by taking Soulie's claim that the millionaire is a calf. This plays on the link between the millionaire's popularity with gold's "fetishistic function" (Lacan, 2017, p. 62). The flatness of Soulie's remark is contrasted with the intelligence in the play with meaning in Heine's memorable reply. Rather than a marker of wealth, Heine appeals to its meaninglessness as an object of exchange. The millionaire is old and is therefore no longer a calf, and he is desirable only because he has money: "Suddenly, this calf is taken for what it is, a living being that the market, itself effectively instituted through the reign of gold, reduces to being only sold as stock, a head of cattle" (Lacan, 2017, p. 63).[2]

Lacan highlights that the witz does not happen in the transition between referents. Anyone can use two different meanings for the same word. Heine's cleverness rests on the ability to find the emptiness of signification in the flow of words. "Calf" is decomposed and recomposed into different senses because it is revealed to be an empty signifier beholden to the fragments of meaning transported across the chain of signification. Witz shows the inner mutation a signifier undergoes as it moves across the signifying chain:

> there is a referral from the message back to the code, that is, along the line of the signifying chain and, in a way metonymically, the term is picked up again on a plane which is no longer the one along which it had been sent, and this makes it possible to see the collapse, reduction or devaluation of meaning brought about in metonymy quite clearly.
>
> (Lacan, 2017, p. 72)

The calf is clearly a reference to the famous moment in the Old Testament where the Israelites worshipped their gold (after Aaron, Moses' brother, had molded them into a calf upon fearing that Moses would not return from his meeting with God at the top of Mount Sinai). The Golden Calf was made in the absence of God thereby linking money and wealth to the void. But Heine subverts this by showing how it is not about the meaninglessness of worshipping the wealthy but how the millionaire, upon being worshipped, also turns himself into another empty object of circulation. Soulie's rendition of the Golden Calf then is incomplete because it assumes the biblical critique. Heine does one better to take the biblical critique to its logical conclusion by pointing to nothing rather than God. By this point, the tensions surrounding the failure to limit the meaning of "calf" is evident. Consequently, the millionaire is "the Golden Calf" in the joke not because of what they both "have," but upon the absence of meaning in which wealth circulates.

Heine, Freud, and famillionaire

If the Golden Calf offers a glimpse of what happens in the metonymic chain of signification, famillionaire plays the more crucial role of describing metaphor and the trace. If metonymy is how meaning is contained within a signifier, the trace in metaphoric creation speaks to the divergences therein. The many layers of meaning that this one piece of witz reveals across three different authors in Heine, Freud and Lacan requires that we unpack it step by step. The famillionaire example occurs during Heinrich's Heine's recollection of his conversation with Jewish lottery ticket agent Hirsch-Hyacinth. While trimming corn with Nathan the Wise of the Rothschild family, Hirsch-Hyacinth recounts his kitchen encounter with another member of the family, Solomon Rothschild, who also happens to be a lottery agent. Solomon, upon knowing of Hirsch-Hyacinth's occupation, told the latter to leave the kitchen. Hirsch-Hyacinth concluded this story by accidentally saying "he treated me in quite a famillionaire manner" (Lacan, 2017, p. 16).

The joke is that Hirsh-Hyacinth's uncle treated him like a millionaire would and not like family should. Freud focuses on the wordplay to show how its novelty stands on its transition from bewilderment to resolution. The utterance of an unfamiliar word ("famillionaire") is instantaneously resolved by noting the different words that form it. The laughter happens where the combination of the two words makes sense in the moment. Lacan takes Freud's point to be as follows: the "'joke' must no doubt be ascribed to the formation of that word and to the characteristics of the word thus formed" (Lacan, 2017, p. 13). For Freud the joke compresses "familiar" into "millionaire" in a way that stresses the estrangement in the moment: it "is precisely on this verbal structure that the joke's character as a joke and its power to cause a laugh depend" (Lacan, 2017, p. 18). This would become the structural basis for Freud to theorize the unconscious link between the timing in the cadence of speech and its indirect unexpected mutations, which Lacan will build on as a formal account of language and the unconscious.

Freud's interest in the structure of the joke, however, moves toward its social sources and implications. He recognises that jokes are necessarily intersubjective in that they are meant to be shared with someone else. From here he ponders about how jokes, despite significantly relying on tacit and contextual assumptions, can circulate and regenerate without a known source. Freud is careful to draw presumptuous links between the content of a joke and the psychology of its teller. Nonetheless he concludes – ultimately returning to famillionaire after considering many other examples – that if the source could be found it will be in the instinctual conflicts of neurosis: "its significance seems to lie in the fact that the person concerned finds criticism or aggressiveness difficult so long as they are indirect, and possible only along circuitous paths" (Lacan, 2017, p. 142). What this means is that the joke, as unconscious, acquires its weight and impact from uttering the unspeakable, unspeakable that is in light of social conventions. This takes us of course to the heart of Freud's theoretical claim, that jokes relieve tension through the aggressiveness conveyed by indirectly saying things that would otherwise be unacceptable. The indirectness of the aggression becomes more apparent when we consider how the subject of the joke is twice removed from its object. Freud finds the most relevant link in the names that would have to be evoked to explain the joke: The combination of two Hs forming Hirsh-Hyacinth resonates with the two Hs that make up Heinrich Heine's name. But even this is not a direct mirroring but a "self-parody" rooted in real-life family drama (Freud, 1960/1905, p. 14). Heine has a real-life uncle named Solomon who also delivered a bitter blow of rejection. The following is Freud's explanation:

> What seemed in Hirsch-Hyacinth's mouth no more than a jest soon reveals a background of serious bitterness if we ascribe it to the nephew, Harry-Heinrich. After all, he was one of the family, and we know that he had a burning wish to marry a daughter of this uncle's; but his cousin rejected him, and his uncle always treated him a little famillionairely, as a poor relation. His rich cousins in Hamburg never took him seriously.
>
> (Freud, 1960/1905, p. 141)

The self-parody behind the name change speaks to a broader predicament. Freud highlights that Heine, after his baptism, had changed his first name from the more Jewish-sounding Harry to the more Christian-sounding Heinrich, and that this resonates with how Hirsh-Hyacinth had opted to drop the first half of his name "so that I don't need to have a new one cut" (Freud, 1960/1905, p. 141). The background is of course Freud's more fundamental assertion about how Jewish jokes are the best exemplifications of the instinctual conflicts that move humor and its reception, owing to how they're made as coping mechanisms for a marginalized people. The detail Freud is more concerned with is how the neurosis in the joke is linked to Heine's personal conflict with his family and how it speaks to his alienation as a European Jew.[3] Freud's own identification with Heine's double-bind between Europeanness and Jewry is clearly at work here. Eliott Oring (2007) reads the joke to note that Freud too had to change his name from the obviously Jewish birth name Sigismund to the more Germanic Sigmund.

However, understanding how the joke achieves its effect through a disruptive signifier requires a consideration of how this was in turn produced out of an unlanguaged standpoint. To appreciate this, we should look not simply into Heine's critique of Jewish culture (he once said that "this race will do anything for gold"), but also the relationship he had with Hebrew as a result (Heine, 1879, p. 396). He registered his ambivalence toward learning languages clearly enough (he had disparaging things to say about Latin and Greek). But Hebrew was singled out for its extimacy, as something he was both close to and unfamiliar with:

> It went better with Hebrew, for I always had a great predilection for the Jews, although they to this very hour have crucified my good

name. In fact, I never could get so far in Hebrew as my watch did, which had a much more intimate intercourse with pawnbrokers than I, and in consequence acquired many Jewish habits for instance, it would not go on Saturday and it learned the holy language, and was subsequently occupied with its grammar, for often when sleepless in the night I have to my amazement heard it industriously repeating: *katal, katalta, katulki kit'el, kitfalta, kittalti pokat, pokadet! pikat pik pik* [italics in original].

(Heine, 1879, p. 184).

The wit, in disassociating himself with other Jews by way of an object and a stereotype (the pawned watch), is consonant with the overall critical posture Heine, as a committed secular progressive, assumed toward the demands of Jewish culture. For our purposes it is important to note not simply his estrangement from his heritage but the distinct way this resonated phonetically in which cultural foreignness is accentuated further by way of a sonic foreignness, a revulsion felt in bodily ways as to amount to long sleepless nights. Ian Miller finds in famillionaire the important insight in how "Freud recognizes that this joke discloses a significant fact, Heine's poetic observation of the bitterness of Jewish suffering, emitted through the vehicle of Hirsch-Hyacinth's mouth" (Miller, 2019, p. 6). But the mouth in this case is uttering and responding to Jewishness as an extimate presence that he embodies in the real but cannot manifest in the symbolic. This is an important threshold of corporeality we should keep in mind as we consider Lacan's reading of famillionaire. It is the antagonism between flesh and symbol that he will take as the basis to uncover the fundamental gap in symbolization that witz addresses and plays with.

Lacan and famillionaire

Lacan's reading of famillionaire is brief but complex so it will help to break it down schematically into two main points. Instead of viewing famillionaire only as a reflection of Heine's Jewish predicament, Lacan highlights its broader historical significance, namely as a discovery of what happens in the gap in signification. Heine's profound innovation in famillionaire speaks to how metaphor works with the materiality of the signifier, that is to say, the sounds and fragments from other signifiers that are required to form another signifier. The material nature of the process more importantly reveals a crucial fact about metaphor, namely its residual production:

Heinrich Heine has, then, managed to create a character out of which, with the signifier "famillionaire," he generates two dimensions – one of metaphorical creation, plus a sort of new metonymic object, the famillionaire ... As I showed you last time, even though our attention isn't drawn to this aspect of the thing, we can find in it all the debris or scraps typical of reflecting on an object used in any metaphorical creation.

(Lacan, 2017, p. 44)

Let's clarify by way of comparison: while the example of the Golden Calf shows the tensions between differing meanings a signifier internalizes, famillionaire is an example of how those tensions cannot be contained. This also allows us to track the different moments of the trace. Metonymic witz does not strictly speaking produce a trace, seeing that the signifier manages to limit the multiple senses it evokes within certain presumed boundaries, however much it may come at the cost of the signifier's integrity. Metonymic witz shows how unwanted associations are cut short through the metonymic process of combination. The famillionaire is presented, on the other hand, as an example of the latent trace in metaphoric witz, that in metaphor there is a leakage of unwanted sounds and senses where the boundaries of the signifier are lined to retain coherence. This opens greater possibilities to map the tensions within the symbolic order. This indeed is what Lacan will ultimately do with Heine's famillionaire. We cannot account for how famillionaire pieces signifiers together, without also noting how they are each to be differentiated at the same time.

We begin with what makes famillionaire a memorable wordplay. We first register the interconnections between familiar, family and millionaire. With this, we are allowed insight into the gap in metaphoric creation, between the audible and obvious "famillionaire," and the trace where family and familiar trails the utterance of the word. "Famillionaire," in other words, is the metaphor producing the new by having "millionaire," push "family" to the remainder. There is a clear historical presumption here: the auditory slide from "familiar" and "millionaire" is noteworthy because it attests to how the family was no longer an autonomous institution but must contend with capitalism as the new sphere of value in which desire now circulates. This is how we can render the thinking presumed in the famillionaire story.

However, the millionaire's symbolic significance, while important to note, is not Lacan's point. If that were only the case, then Lacan need not resort to a theory of language at all. Here Lacan points to how the temporal prominence of the millionaire is at the same time undermined by the phonological trace ushered in family and famillionaire. Famillionaire works as a piece of witz not only in the moment of convergence between different signifiers but also in their concurrent dissolution. In this, the imprint in the debris is not in any word but the tracks of signifying formation and composition. It is along these tracks that the unexpected could occur. This does not stem from the word play but the phonological twists required to form the witz. Here Lacan diverges from Freud. For Lacan, the most significant moment in the pun is neither millionaire, familiar nor family but the sliding between them. Consequently, we cannot think of metaphorical production in static terms, as if "famillionaire" readily emerged beside "millionaire" as a fully formed concept. Unlike the "standard" production of symbols, witz is fundamentally about the momentary shifts that occur along the production of meaning. As causal, these shifts give the witz's unique phonological trajectory. Consequently, if the form of "famillionaire" places millionaire in a primary position, its content reveals a certain critical standpoint afforded by the disintegrating "family". Thus the millionaire's dominance over the family is not presented as an example of straightforward negation that represses the latter. The witz is noteworthy because it marks the historical tug-of-war of symbolization that was happening at the time. Family and millionaire appear as enigmas to one another's standpoints, enigmas realized through Freud and Heine's lived experiences as unlanguaged.

Lacan and history

Thus rather than thinking of family and capital as conflicting territories, Lacan reads famillionaire to point to how they were symbols emerging at a distinct historical juncture in which they were, to put in a term accounted for earlier, "purified" to become signifiers. Famillionaire acquired its significance at a time when the millionaire as figure and symbol became "excessive". He has "become transcendent, as it were having become something that exists in being and no longer as a sign pure and simple" (Lacan, 2017, p. 46). The same was also happening to the family. Lacan notes how "family" slides into "familiar" with reference to the curious word "familial" which he spotted in the 1881 edition of the *Littre Dictionary*, a word which can be regarded as a compromise formation between family and familiar. In this Lacan finds it instructive that the word is situated "when it was possible to treat the family as an object at the level of an interesting political reality ... insofar as the family no longer had the same structuring function for the subject it had had up till then" (Lacan, 2017, p. 47). With Heine and the famillionaire we can think of how this gap was addressed and dealt with through the symbolic order's historical dimension. Indeed, it is with Heine's examples that we can think of two axes of meaning. There is the part that already makes sense at the level of the metaphoric object. There is also the part that is actively trying to make sense qua the organization of signifiers in the gap within the symbolic order that occurs at the level of the trace. This is the axis of meaning manifested by metaphoric creation which occurs within the parameters of understanding. But Heine's wordplay attests to another, more fundamental axis. As unconscious this axis "may not be immediately perceived" because it stands for the structural possibility for meaning "by virtue of the combinations that we could extend indefinitely, the word is crawling with all the needs that proliferate around an object" (Lacan, 2017, pp. 36–37).

Thus, where family and millionaire were already established words, famillionaire disrupted their stability by revealing the traces of their fragmentation as live sites of symbolization. This is where Heine for Lacan was most momentous, for Heine conjures the presence of "all those signifying fragments into which the term 'famillionaire' shatters – 'fames,' 'fama,' 'famulus,' 'infamy' and, ultimately, whatever you want whatever Hirsch-Hyacinth actually is for this caricature of a master" (Lacan, 2017, p. 44). The same applies to how "millionaire" could be fragmented for other "possible decompositions" in "affamillionaire," "famine-llionaire" and "fat-millionaire" (Lacan, 2017, p. 36). Thus, Lacan concludes that "'Famillionaire' has thus played, it seems to me, many roles, not simply in the imagination of poets, but in history as well" (Lacan, 2017, p. 35). This is what Lacan understands Heine's standpoint to have provided: "Without us in any way ending up with a being of poetry, it's an extraordinarily rich, swarming and proliferating term, much like what we find at the level of metonymic decomposition" (Lacan, 2017, p. 36). The affective impact famillionaire forms cannot happen, in other words, without echoing the essential fragmentation of meaning that is taking place. At the level of metaphor famillionaire organizes a meaningful message. But as an enunciated moment of an accidental and bungled wordplay, famillionaire happens through the coming together of fragmented signifiers. The latter can only be accounted for through unpacking its component parts, further stressing how it is formed upon a prior decomposition. By the time the subject is put back into the circulation of discourse he would have registered how the fragments of "family" emerge not only as the cause of the joke but how it also troubles the millionaire's emergence. This only happens, more importantly, indirectly when famillionaire unfolds "in the after-effects of the phenomenon" (Lacan, 2017, p. 22)

Unconscious desire

If "famillionaire" stands for a telling moment in metonymic decomposition, the Golden Calf attests to the fundamental processes of limiting tensions in the different senses within a word that metonymy manages. If famillionaire shows how the imprints of residual meaning survive puns, the Golden Calf shows the leveling out that occurs to ensure that signifiers are stabilized to retain a certain range of possible meaning at the cost of doing away with other aspects of their meaning. Metonymy ensures "the equivalence necessary for both terms in play, abandoning a very important part of their meaning. The meaning effect of the metonymic line is located along this dimension" (Lacan, 2017, p. 73). Put simply, if metaphoric witz offers a view of the sliding chain from an external vantage point in the imprints of meanings that trail what was said, metonymic witz shows the same tensions from "within" the signifier, from what is contained in the unsaid. The Golden Calf and famillionaire come to reinforce Lacan's fundamental claim, that "everything you can find in plays on words, and very specifically those called conceptual plays on words, consists in playing upon how bad words are at maintaining a full sense" (Lacan, 2017, p. 87). This, situated in Lacan's view of language in the era of scientific scrutiny, allows us to enlarge this joke and its components to understand them as moments in the process of purification discourse is built on, the mess of signification it leaves in its wake, and how this mess in turn serves as the building blocks for metaphorical creation.

But note what has happened by now. By formalizing Freud's use of Heine as an account of symbolization rather than identity, Lacan has universalized Heine's politics by making it a source for insights into the primordial workings of language. With the trace we have a way of accounting for the "unconscious combination of signifiers" as the origin of language, particularly metaphoric creation and its tensions (Lacan, 2017, p. 46). We find further resonances between Lacan's theory and Freud and Heine's preoccupations with the Jewish question in how it is attentive to the dynamics of inclusion and exclusion that ensures consistency in language. Just as the value of metaphor is acquired through metonymic exchange, so too does witz reveal how the signifier does not enter the chain of signification without first losing its past significance. Thus, if value is produced in the crystallization of meaning metonymic production provides, the trace attests to the process' underlying materiality via the expulsion of signifying fragments. Lacan in fact summarizes this straightforwardly as if a formula: "the material of signifiers always partakes in something of the evanescent character of a trace" (Lacan, 2017, p. 343).

Lacan's formalization of Heine's standpoint should not be seen as precluding the significance of Freud and Heine's socio-political situation. Rather the politics is framed in terms of the signifier. Consequently, we can recast Freud's observation about the pressures for Jews to change their names in a similar light in which their plight, beyond the historical details of Eastern European Jewry, is ultimately about the loss of meaning which psychoanalysis deals with in the breakdown of signifiers that happens in clinical speech. In this regard, as yielding insight into the core workings of language, Lacan effectively reads Freud and Heine as theorists of the trace. The convergence of Lacan's formal theory of language and Freud's historical situation as unlanguaged should now afford us an appreciation of the temporal dimension of metaphoric creation, namely how this dimension originates from non-discursive time. This is the time that occurs before the smooth flow of metonymic speech, which accounts for the similarly temporal nature of the unconscious' disruption. Lacan of course does not describe what this "other" time amounts to and in many ways it would be beside the point. It would suffice for us to note the location where it happens, namely in the flow of signifiers in their dissolution and reconfiguration. There is a crossroads of signification wherein diachronic time, construed as moving forward or backward, dissolves into untimeliness, where the signifier is shown for its material constituents and this could be viewed only from another place than the metonymic flow, as it were, a view that the trace affords however momentarily. Put simply, if Lacan's account of language presumes a temporality that fragments along with the trace, it is because of Freud and Heine's insight into what is included and excluded from progressive time.

This is the point at which we could appreciate how the trace shapes the temporality of desire as to provide it with critical potency. This is the dimension of desire that emerges in the demand for meaning against the familiar "beyond" discourse affords. This is desire at the threshold of the signifier's breakdown and recomposition, in the "certain level of circulation of signifiers" that is "between the message and the Other" (Lacan, 2017, p. 83). Remarkably Lacan situates the unconscious desire moving the trace as the culminating lesson of the unlanguage qua Freud's reading of Heine's witz:

> The point of a witz is in effect to re-evoke for us the dimension by which desire, if it does not recapture, at least indicates everything that has been lost along the way, namely, on the one hand, what scraps it has left behind at the level of the metonymic chain and, on the other, what it has not fully actualized at the level of metaphor.
>
> (Lacan, 2017, p. 87)

It is being able to grasp the "past" that had to be relinquished for the signifier's exchangeability that desire emerges where the unconscious is formed. The past of signification is therefore intrinsic to unconscious desire: "The only desires that enter the unconscious are those that, having been symbolized, can, on entering the unconscious, be preserved in their symbolic form – that is, in the form of this indestructible trace" (Lacan, 2017, p. 83). As Lacan puts it more summarily later, "An entire aspect of desire continues to circulate in the form of scraps of signifiers in the unconscious" (Lacan, 2017, p. 86).

In other words, if metonymy and metaphor sustain the value in signification by keeping the subject in an ebb and flow of exchange with the Other, desire's place in the trace qua the past of signification allows us to question the process. Just as the trace yields affects from the past of signification, so too is unconscious desire in touch with the meanings excluded in the purification signifiers undergo to be incorporated into the chain. Desire therefore is where two temporal standpoints converge. There is time in the desire for the Other's lack at the level of metaphor. But then there is also the desire that "leaves, somewhere, not only traces but also a circuit that insists" (Lacan, 2017, p. 80). This is the desire which, for a moment at least, is homeless insofar as it was articulated before the crystallization of the Other's lack. It is here in desire's place between two registers of the symbolic – the before and after of purification – that we can account for what Lacan mentions as true value. This is the value that is revealed by the joke's evocation of the lack in the Other, which has yet to be fully stabilized into the object of the Other's desire. There is the value confined within the ebb and flow of metonymic exchange. There is, on the other hand, the "true value" revealed by the joke (Lacan, 2017, p. 88). This is similarly how we can understand the critique witz inserts, as it is able to formulate a standpoint from within the formation of meaning, and thus the formation of the unconscious.

Bit-of-sense and step-of-sense

To think of time in the trace therefore is to think of time not as abstracted from speech and the symbolic order but as fundamentally rooted to the flow of speech wherein the symbolic is at work as such. It is in the disruptions found along the way, the very disruptions that make parapraxes memorable, that the traces forming metaphoric creation are brought to light, and the materiality of time could be felt and the value of discourse could then be scrutinized. But if we aren't with an exact formulation of an alternative temporality, we are nonetheless given an account of the point at which its perspective emerges. To deduce that witz undoes linear time synchronically is to note how it undercuts the flow of discursive time by introducing a new object. It will do this by identifying a lack in the Other from a different temporal flow and standpoint from discourse. Thus, Lacan is keen to stress the suddenness of the witz's intervention, that it "breaks free from the constraints of the format," from the supposedly smooth exchange that fuels discourse (Lacan, 2017, p. 99). The sense in the trace's imprint is evident not in the sounds that are made or the meaning of words. Rather it is through how the witz takes our attention to the fragmentation of meaning that shapes it. The trace does not merely dismantle meaning. It has the effect of revealing the beyond by way of critiquing the lack that even the Other had not yet registered. It reveals the lack within the process of symbolic formation itself: "A joke is indissociable from the Other, who is charged with authenticating it" (Lacan, 2017, p. 88). This view the trace affords into the signifier takes us to the radicality of Lacan's conception of comedy. While Lacan certainly recognises comedy's critical element, he goes on to stress that this is not what the structure of comedy ultimately does. Rather, jokes disrupts the range of possible meanings that are available. Because of this, and unlike many interpreters of his theory of comedy, Lacan disassociates comedy from nonsense insofar as it is still essentially a symbolic operation.

This is how we should begin to understand two key trace-related concepts in *Seminar V,* namely the "sense" in bit-of-sense and the step-of-sense, especially where they are presented as alternatives to straightforward associations of comedy with "nonsense". They both clearly reference the inevitably of humor to entail some degree of the nonsensical. But the bit-of-sense and step-of-sense go further to stress how the supposed nonsense is a prelude for two key moments that we can break down schematically as follows. It first signals a particular lack in the Other, in the form of a lack that the Other itself affirms. In doing so it produces a new object. Jokes are neither nonsense nor Real because they detect a lack to actively respond to the demand for meaning at the same time. In this regard, jokes can be understood as signifiers that anticipate a lack in the Other to ultimately add something new to it. This "new" object however does not represent the closure of the symbolic process but rather the lack that yields the space for critique. Key then is the causal dimension to the bit-of-sense and the step-of-sense. They are not simply about short-circuiting the symbolic order so much as they are about leaving the big Other perplexed. It is about identifying how and why the linguistic operation peculiar to witz could unsettle the Other qua the symbolic order. This is why they are beyond nonsense. It is not about merely exposing the lack of the big Other but playing with and teasing it for other symbolic possibilities.

The bit-of-sense is a dimension situated in the "reduction of meaning" in "the signifying chain" (Lacan, 2017, p. 87). It emerges where "something occurs" that "reduces the message to its scope" in the formulation of a demand (Lacan, 2017, p. 87). Recall that "reduction" is one of Lacan's ways of accounting for how signifiers are formed, while the "message" refers to the truth that is delivered to the Other for a reciprocating code. With reduction and message we are still in standard discourse territory. A joke, however, occurs when "the message questions the Other over this bit-of-sense" namely the trace produced by the process of reduction (Lacan, 2017, pp. 87–88). Lacan finds the bit-of-sense's distinct effect in questioning the meaning of the signifier as it is being produced: "this is where the nature of the message specific to a joke lies" (Lacan, 2017, p. 88). It is in this capacity to question that the bit-of-sense marks "the interrupted path of metonymy" to indicate a lack in the production of discourse (Lacan, 2017, p. 88). If the bit-of-sense is the lack in metonymy, the step-of-sense in turn marks the actualization of the metaphoric object. This is the lack that emerges in something "new," whose novelty takes the subject beyond anything that could be explained from the signifying chain, that is "beyond metonymic use and beyond anything commensurable, beyond any received values to be satisfied" (Lacan, 2017, p. 89). Thus where the step-of-sense produces a new signifier, the bit-of-sense sustains the question of its meaning to the Other. It isn't difficult to see how both moments occur at once in the utterance of "famillionaire." The piece of witz that is "famillionaire" is the metaphorical creation, the step-of-sense, that reveals the combination of signifiers, in a way that unpacks the lack, the bit-of-sense, in both "family" and "millionaire." Noting the lacks therein takes us immediately to the lack in the Other that shapes the rapport where "famillionaire" was uttered and registered. The same process is operative in the Golden Calf where the Golden Calf's manifest association with the millionaire occurs through the latent implication, delivered so instantly as without utterance, that the millionaire was in effect just another object of exchange.

The highly theoretical direction Lacan has taken us should not obscure the more significant point that not only could the lack from the other be disrupted, but that the view into the disruption is afforded particularly to those who are with the standpoint to discern the lack from another perspective. The witz does not simply mark the expression of a "new lack". It is an intervention that arrives sideways as it were from the margins. To affirm this conclusion is to also recognize how we arrived to it: The historical fragmentation of language that is the key premise for Lacanian psychoanalysis finds its most telling account in the seminar's reference to Jewish history. The former provides the universal theater of speech psychoanalysis addresses as the latter is where its intricacies could be demonstrated in detail. This is how the double takes in famillionaire and the Golden Calf allows us to simultaneously experience the symbolic order and the lack that at once structures its ordering. With this we can understand why Lacan says that the bit-of-sense is a "happy shadow" in the trail of metonymic creation (Lacan, 2017, p. 87). And nowhere is this more evident than how the impact of witz occurs from what the symbolic order cannot immediately register: "For a joke requires that the Other has perceived what is there as a demand for sense – that is, as an evocation of a sense that lies beyond" (Lacan, 2017, p. 88). If the Other is to play a role as authenticator for jokes, it is in its authentication of the lack of meaning in the signifier itself. Jokes, by this, anticipate a lack that the Other can in turn verify through surprise. This ability to "awaken the Other" as it were is where the pleasure of the joke comes from (Lacan, 2017, p. 104). Awaken, that is, "inasmuch as he has succeeded in surprising the Other with his joke" (Lacan, 2017, p. 89). The joke seeks verification from the Other while doing something to it: when "I prepare a joke I evoke something in the Other that tends to set him in a certain direction," that is to say to to a new lacking signifier (Lacan, 2017, p. 107).

Part 3: Lacan, Freud, and Bosnia

Freud and Heine's geopolitical movements

We now discuss how the great deal that Lacan does with the material provided by Heine's witz could be taken as an unconscious decolonial moment. Heine critiqued Jewish orthodoxy as a secular and progressive leftist. As a contemporary of Marx, Heine presented his work as a response to the global political changes taking place at the time. This displacement should also be acknowledged for its own unique anti-colonial value for Heine was a vocal supporter of revolution and global decolonization. Heine once defined "the question of the age" as the question of emancipation:

Not simply the emancipation of the Irish, Greeks, Frankfort Jews, West Indian negroes, and other oppressed races, but the emancipation of the whole world, and especially that of Europe, which has attained its majority and now tears itself loose from the iron leading-strings of a privileged aristocracy.

(Heine, 1879, p. 290)

This to be sure was a Eurocentric view of "decolonization", which in any case was not a term Heine used. Nonetheless, Heine identified with other struggles of emancipation from a self-conscious position at the margins of Europe. Under-lying his comparisons of the different characters and societies he encountered in his travels was a question of history and progress (where France, to Heine, stands out most as the standard bearer). But if Lacan missed this opportunity to pursue Heine's politics, he nonetheless is attentive enough to how Heine's witz happened across differences. Lacan acknowledges that the "famillionaire" exchange happened in Luca, Italy as if to further stress the displacement that informed Heine's perceptiveness. To this we can add another detail: the incident happened along the passage of Heine's journeys across the North Sea, Britain, Italy and Germany. Thus, it is noteworthy, although admittedly we should not make too much of it, that Lacan too would speak on many occasions of how signifiers "travel" along the circuit of metonymy.

We do, however, find movement across geographies in another case study that will be crucial to *Seminar V*, namely the famous Signorelli parapraxis in Freud's 1898 train trip across Southern Europe, from Italy to present-day Bosnia-Herzegovina. If witz anticipates the Other's lack through the untimely formation of a new object, forgetting will stress the underside of discourse by showing how discursive speech emerges upon the reassembling of signifying traces across different languages. There are many significant details to this scenario. Dusan Bjelić (2017) reminds us that the Balkans, as the site of a historical scramble between Christian Europe and the Islamic Ottoman Empire, was Freud's only trip outside Europe proper and to "the Orient". Bjelić is also certain that Freud must have palpably felt this difference given that the conversation took place in Trebinje, which at the time was a colony of the Austria-Hungarian empire. We should not discount the likelihood of a certain superiority complex here given that Freud eventually supported Austro-Hungary's occupation of Serbia in 1914.[4] The significance, however, was not simply historical. It was also spatial. The Balkans was the bloody site of conflicts between Austro-Hungary, Russia, Ottoman Turkey, Britain and France. In this, Austro-Hungary suffered the most pressing predicament of being the Balkans' immediate neighbors. In many ways, the Balkans' location as the ever-contested threshold between Christian Europe and the Islamic world saw to it that Austro-Hungary remained stuck to the continent as rival European empires modernized to acquire overseas territories. Ottoman Turkey at that point was the Habsburgs' fiercest imperial rival, as it was the military deadlocks at the long borders they shared across central, Eastern, Southern, and Mediterranean Europe that led the Habsburgs to their eventual downfall. Thus even non-post-colonial readers of this scenario from Peter Swales (1982, 2003) and Diane O'Donoghue (2018) acknowledge the role difference plays in triggering Freud's attempt to grapple with the forgetting. Gil Anidjar (2002), interpreting the parapraxis from a religious standpoint, sees Freud's reference to the Ottoman Islamic Turk after being humbled upon a Christian work of art in the Orvieto frescoes, as symptomatic of the monotheistic unconscious in Freud's early attempt to secure psychoanalysis status as a universally secular science. A general comparison in any case could be drawn by this point. If Freud's conversation with Heine attests to symbolic dissolution from a standpoint within Europe, Freud's trip to Bosnia shows how symbolic formation is felt at the margins of Europe. Psychoanalysis' most basic possibility was produced at a time of geographical fragmentation between familiar and foreign places. If Heine speaks to how traces disrupt the temporality in the signifying chain, Freud's Signorelli forgetting situates this disruption within a "European" spatial imaginary.

This again reiterates the point made in the former section, that the gap in discourse is to be found from the margins of the symbolic order that the European Jewish experience instantiates. But what Freud's forgetting in Bosnia shows more prominently than witz is the element of different sounds and affects by which the chain of signification flows. Freud's conclusion is that ultimately the parapraxis is neither about Bosnia nor forgetting. It concluded to become about Italy and repression. The twists, however, are precisely the point for it showed just how the unconscious emerges as if by surprise, out of the names and words that appear unexpectedly while on the train (and in this case it included an actual train) of speech and thought. Lacan here builds on the insight Freud himself stressed. The point is not that Freud was disturbed by a forgotten name. It is that Freud had forgotten a name in such a way that he was compelled to think psychoanalytically, of an unconscious motive force moving his recollection of the different sounding fragments of foreign names. Recall that Freud had presented this forgetting as a form of self-analysis which in concretely historical terms means that it was an attempt to symbolize a real as an unlanguaged subject. Lacan built on this premise to take it to its linguistic implications by showing that Freud's forgetting has much to do with how he had to traverse many languages to produce the metaphoric object. The Golden Calf and famillionaire were examples that take us to the chaotic emptiness of the object. The example of Freud's trip across Bosnia speaks to the foreignness entailed in the chaos, that the chaos is fueled by the meeting of incommensurate meanings.

Now let's look at the forgetting closely: Freud's story about forgetting in Bosnia-Herzegovina is full of geographic twists and turns.

The conversation took place during a trip in the summer of 1898 from Ragusa (then a part of the Austria-Hungarian Empire and today Dubrovnik, Croatia) to Herzegovina (at the time a part of the Ottoman Empire). The forgetting happened as Freud asked a stranger on the train if he had seen the frescoes of the Last Judgment in the Dome of Orvieto in Italy when Freud was struck by his inability to remember the frescoes' artist Luca Signorelli's name. Instead of Signorelli, two other Italian names came to him: Botticelli and Boltraffio. Freud immediately ruled out the oddity of the names as the cause of forgetting: "The forgotten name was just as familiar to me as one of the substitutive names" (Freud, 1938/1901, p. 4). He also did not think much of the forgetting until, a few days later, the right name was relayed by someone. Freud instantly remembered it and wondered why there was a chain of association that took him from Signorelli to Botticelli and Bol-traffio. His recollection led him to a flashback of an exchange that preceded the discussion about the frescoes. This concerned a comment made by a friend of Freud who practiced medicine among Turks in Bosnia and the peculiar irony in how the Turks' "full confidence in doctors" is belied by a "complete submission to fate" (Freud, 1938/1901, p. 5). This was the premise that led to Freud's conclusion, summarized essentially via the following two sentences in which the signifying elements that explain the forgetting are brought together. When the Turks were told that there is no help for the patient, they answered: "Sir [*Herr*], what can I say? I know that if he could be saved you would save him" (Freud, 1938/1901, p. 5). Freud notes "In these sentences alone we can find the words and names: Bosnia, Herzegovina, and Herr [sir], which may be inserted in an association series between Signorelli, Botticelli, and Boltraffio" (Freud, 1938/1901, p. 5).

Unpacking each of the terms and their interconnections, however, requires another detour for the point eventually was not even the Turks' attitude to doctors but a different, more difficult, thought associated with them, one which Freud lastly opted not to utter. It concerned the claim, which he took as true at the cost of much post-colonial ire, about how Turks value sexual pleasure "above all else," and how this stood in stark contrast to their fatalistic attitude to death. Here Freud recalled what his doctor friend in Bosnia was told by a Turk: "For you know, sir [*Herr*], if that ceases, life no longer has any charm" (Freud, 1938/1901, p. 5). Freud acknowledged that he was hesitant to bring up this comment because he did not want to broach an awkward topic with a stranger. But Freud thought further to wonder if there was something more to his reluctance. Now Freud felt an after-effect of a memory regarding a patient in Trafoi [Italy] who had committed suicide due to "an incurable sexual disturbance" (Freud, 1938/1901, p. 6). This meant that there were two forgettings in which one forgetting (Signorelli) was in effect, unconsciously, moving thought away from the actual forgetting that mattered more: "The disinclination to recall directed itself against the one content; the inability to remember appeared in another" with each happening toward different objects, Signorelli being one and the death of the patient being the other (Freud, 1938/1901, p. 8). Consequently, the different moments in each track of forgetting overlapped with one another to form a deflective chain of associations. *"Herr"* came in place of the *"Signor"* in "Signorelli," the *"bo"* in Bosnia was deflected into Botticelli, while *"Trafio"* hid in Boltraffio. This leads to one of Freud's widely cited conclusion: "besides the simple forgetting of proper names there is another forgetting which is motivated by repression" (Freud, 1938/1901, p. 13).

Freud's self-analysis has invited allegations of Orientalism. For Gil Anidjar (2002) Freud's recollection ultimately saw the Ottomans "othered" as to refuse his own non-Europeanness and assert his European worldview. Dusan Bjelić (2011a) shows how Freud's self-analysis took his recollection of the patient who had died due to a sexual disease to further assert the sexual nature of repression, placing the Orientalist stereotype of the sex-crazed Turk at the heart of psychoanalytic theorizing: "Freud's unconscious had attached a sexual content, which concealed itself through forgetting the name 'Signorelli'" (Bjelić, 2011a, p. 36). As Bjelić summarizes it, "In hysterical amnesia, [Freud] postulates, the unconscious has blocked a disturbing sexual memory, and concludes his short paper by stating that psychoanalysis is able to cure amnesia by bringing this sort of blocked memory into the ego-consciousness" (Bjelić, 2011a, p. 37). The unconscious in this case serves as a merely rhetorical handmaiden to assert a Eurocentric worldview.

Before engaging with these criticisms, let's consider Lacan's reading. The zigzagging across signifiers entailed in the recalling and forgetting is about the formation of the object out of the chaotic traces underlying the symbolic order. He asserts that the point of this anecdote is not the suicide resulting from sexual dysfunction. Lacan takes it rather to be a demonstration of a structuring process: "the object is *behind* the various specific elements that are at play there in the immediate past" [italics in original] (Lacan, 2017, p. 31). In other words, behind the death in Freud's recollection of *"Herr"* there is the "death" of the signifier through which the significance of *"Herr"* "moves on, fades away, withdraws, and is repelled" (Lacan, 2017, p. 32). Thus it is not *"Herr"* as a static moment that Lacan is interested in, but how *"Herr"* dissolves to make way for the trace. It is the point at which the signifying chain disintegrates to make way for *"bo"* as trace - "an ersatz, the debris or ruins" - of *"Herr"* by which it can then combine with "other ruins of the name which are repressed at that moment" (Lacan, 2017, p. 32). Lacan takes this as accounting for the structure of speech itself, which shows where "what we call free association is located insofar as it enables us to track what happens in the unconscious" (Lacan, 2017, p. 32).

But to Lacan's reading we can draw out a decolonial opening in how the zigzagging problematizes identity. If the object is "behind" the signifiers, it is also the gap that recognises the differences that are being brought together for combination. The simple distinction to be made is that *"Herr"* is European for being a German word and non-European where Freud contended with it literally in Herzegovina. But this is not about differentiating solid established identities so much as recognizing the problem of difference at their most basic linguistic constituents. The case of *"bo"* reveals how Freud grappled with the problem of foreign sounds. *"Bo"* is doubly foreign to Freud because it is Italian and Bosnian. Indeed, Lacan directly describes this as a problem fundamental to the need for translation.

We may pursue the decolonial potential further by noting how this example was the occasion, and the only one at that, where Lacan speaks of "heteronymous substitution", further stressing the centrality of the difference entailed in metonymy (Lacan, 2017, p. 33). So central are the heteronyms to this moment that Lacan proclaims: "This is what happens in every translation – the translation of one term into a foreign language on the substitutive axis, in the comparison required by the existence of different linguistic systems" (Lacan, 2017, p. 33). The question of difference is more apparent in the *"Signor"* in *"Signorelli"*. The issue here is crucial in that *"Herr"* and *"Signor"* are supposed to mean the same thing, but it wasn't *"Signor"* that led Freud to his realization but the crucial *"bo"*. This is the *"bo"* that hid Signor*elli* in Bottic*elli* and the *"bo"* that eventually blended with *"traffio"* to make way for *"Trafoi"* to surface in Freud's speech. Lacan, however, does not regard *"Signor"* to be secondary to the process. It rather marked a crucial moment in the production of the trace, in the signifying disintegration, that exemplified the "phenomenon of metonymic decomposition" (Lacan, 2017, p. 33). In the first place, if *"Herr"* and *"Signor"* could not be linked in the moment, it is because they have been situated at differing sections of the chain: *"Herr"* was going to the substitutive level at the metaphoric object and *"Signor"* "repressed … in the message code-circuit" (Lacan, 2017, p. 35). *"Signor"* "went off and followed its own little circular circuit somewhere in unconscious memory" (Lacan, 2017, p. 45). In other words, the entire point of the story is that the word *"Signor"* in that moment did not mean *"Herr"* where the emptiness of the object was in the un-symbolizable death of the friend. This is why one signifier (*"Signor"*) could be uttered alongside another signifier (*"Herr"*) of the supposedly same referent without their equivalence being posited. *"Signor"* in this case floats in the chaos of the signifying chain to register where the fracture from the metonymic object goes before its meaning emerges to be registered again: "we can think of 'Signor' as in constant rotation between code and message, until it's refound" (Lacan, 2017, p. 34).

But if this split is thinkable at all it should not be taken to mean that *"Herr"* had totally ejected *"Signor"* from thought. *"Signor"* is a trace insofar as it was the meaning excluded to make way for the realization Freud experienced when *"Herr"* was uttered. If their gap could still be posited it is because of an enduring connection expected between them. But this was the connection that could be made owing to the disruption marked by the gap qua death. Here Lacan points to why the gap could not be immediately recalled and it is because Signorelli connoted another "death" for Freud, that is to say, the death represented in the frescoes and thus the "death" that triggered the initial haunting Freud was trying to grapple with in the loss of his friend: "the Orvieto frescoes and the evocation of the last things, represents the most beautiful elaborations there are of this impossible-to-confront reality that is death" (Lacan, 2017, p. 34). "*Signor*" then was pushed out before it could fully form into "Signorelli," to become a metaphor on its own. The death in "*Herr*," precisely because it is the death Freud was most implicated in, won out in the end as it became the death that Freud could not come to terms with. The foreignness indeed is less about the meaning of the words but the lack felt in their utterances at the time. The death qua the gap could not be symbolized as it was taken across three realms of differences which we can simplify as follows. We have, on one hand, the death qua excess as symbolized in the frescoes as a cultural historical statement and monument. There is the "death" qua excess in the racist imaginary Freud internalized in the Turks' attitude to health. There is then the death in the real in the loss of his friend which evoked Freud's status as a doctor, and consequently as the innovator of psychoanalysis, an outsider. Freud evoked signifiers across recollections in a way that reflected the broader gaps in languages and land-scapes he traversed at the time. The forgetting took Freud to gaps as they were instantiated in different linguistic dynamics.

Freud in-between borders

But this formalism is less important than why Lacan felt that the fragmen-tation of signifiers was ultimately resonant for Freud. Lacan is not insensitive to the fact that the recollection of names across the threshold of Europe speaks to Freud's own fraught relationship with naming. Note that what was ultimately disturbing but significant about the forgotten names was their relative proximity in sound and meaning. They are unfamiliar in their familiarity. It is here in the excess within the familiar that we find Lacan acknowledging Freud's cultural predicament. The foreignness in this example is merely incidental. What is undeniable is that Lacan is making a universal point about language: "It can occur with the words of your own language, but the reason Freud started with the forgetting of a foreign name is that the example was readily available and conclusive" (Lacan, 2017, p. 49). This takes us to Lacan's clearest statement on the centrality of difference in sym-bolic ordering. The ordering of symbols succeeds when the incompatibility in different words is equalized through definitions that merely capture their most general qualities. This is what makes for discourse's efficiency. But Lacan also finds in this example of forgetting, the foreignness more characteristic of Freud's unlanguaged subjectivity:

> The proper name in question is a foreign name, in the sense that its ele-ments are foreign to Freud's own language. "Signor" is not a German word, and Freud stresses that this is not unimportant. He doesn't tell us

why, but the fact that he singles it out in the initial chapter proves that he thinks it's a particularly striking facet of the reality he is addressing. If Freud states this, it's because this introduces another dimension than that of proper names as such, which is always more or less attached to cabbalistic signs. If a name were absolutely proper and particular, it would have no homeland.

(Lacan, 2017, p. 30)

This rich passage is telling of Lacan's sensitivity to Freud's political predicament: the fragmentation is "striking" for a reality whose geographical and political stakes were directly relevant to Freud's status as a Jewish subject where the foreignness of the names he was trying to recall eventually evoked the foreignness of his own name and consequently his desire for a home (Lacan, 2017, p. 49). The same point about the failure of exile – and in this case Freud was in exile from his Jewishness and his Europeanness - was made in another section in *Seminar V* where the ego-ideal, rather than resolving foreignness is shown to merely exacerbate it. Lacan here is speaking of the psychoanalytic subject in general but will eventually evoke the question of nationality and identification: "what he acquires as ego-ideal is like the country of an exile which he carries stuck to the soles of his shoes" (Lacan, 2017, p. 272).

Actually, we know little of what exactly happened in Herzegovina. It has been a bone of contention in psychoanalytic literature because it was varyingly documented across three different texts: twice in an 1898 correspondence to Fleiss for a technical and theoretical exchange, and once most notably in 1901 in the *Psychopathology of Everyday Life* which has become the standard reference for the Signorelli parapraxis given that it was presented for a lay public. But beyond this there are also reasons to question the basic details of the scenario. Nicholas Weber (2017) thinks it was likely that the exchange happened in a horse carriage more than a train. He also finds it difficult that the conversation that triggered the forgetting – which quickly veered off into an exchange about death, doctors and Turkey – happened with a stranger. There are also the limitations of the present lens. None of the countries in discussion today were independent entities at the time. Bosnia and Turkey are also known to be different Islamic contexts, with the former largely recognised to be among the most secular countries in the Islamic world after decades of Communist rule. Turkey meanwhile has seen its secular experiment severely hindered due to the rise of Erdogan and the AKP. The Balkans, to be sure, continues to be a religiously fragmented region but it is for different reasons than those of Freud's time. There is also something archaic about how Freud had contemplated the parapraxis on a train. The passage across rapid sceneries was a crucial symbol for Freud's description of what free association is like. But if there is a coloniality to conceiving the pursuit of the unconscious by train, it certainly speaks to a coloniality of old imperialism, a condition Austro-Hungary was all too self-conscious of, rather than rivaling ones rapidly advancing by air and sea at the same time.

But this is only a problem if we take the state of the world today as "final," when we have more of a reason to anticipate greater fragmentation in the oncoming of a more unfamiliar world. Difference will not be something we go elsewhere to find. "Other countries" will be felt in the speech of our everyday encounters with neighbors, colleagues and friends. The ebb and flow of symbolic dissolution and symbolic ordering, felt as it is in the materiality of speech as the materiality of representation, will shape the tensions out of which much of the capitalist world is shaped. With this, Freud's Jewry finds a universal purpose for speaking to the displacement that happens in the very ebb and flow of symbolic ordering and the traces therein. Consequently, a return to Freud in this light is a return to the necessity of thinking of symbolic fractures. In Freud we do not see a Jew but an ever-tenuous colonial modernity that cannot repress the traces of its discourse. This experience is sure to reverberate if nowhere else when trying to come to terms with the Signorelli parapraxis: the impossibility of grasping what is really at the bottom of Freud's Southern European forgetting is symptomatic of the gap that moves psychoanalytic thinking itself, as the gap which will ultimately take us into the underside of signification, in the senses and affects whose historicity is such that they will be impossible to contain through theory alone.

But to begin and end with the gap in Freud's Herzegovina is to also recognise the unique positionality it affords. As Diane O'Donoghue reminds us, the polarities were presented after the fact: "What Freud encountered as chaos we encounter as polarity: As he recounted the story, he needed to create polarities – acceptable/repressed, manifest/latent, and Italy/Balkans – in order to make the mechanism of psychical 'forgetfulness' plausible to his readers" (O'Donoghue, 2018, p. 178). The goal is to listen to the anxieties in the need for polarities as they stem from being unlanguaged in a world of increasing enclosures. The decolonial opening consequently emerges in the gap afforded in Freud's belatedness. The gap then is in the certain temporal drag from the past which we linguistically experience in the debris of productive speech. This appears to be the realistic standpoint as psychoanalysis globalizes. It can be attentive to the underside of its own significance as it confronts the incommensurabilities it will be sure to meet along the way.

On a more speculative note, this attentiveness to the materiality of language as the repressed differences in purportedly smooth speech, could even account for why Lacanian psychoanalysis has thrived more in the untimely margins of modernity (Slovenia, Argentina, and Brazil, and currently it seems China) than in late capitalism as the regeneration of value as the clarification of speech is more palpably felt in the clinics of uneven development and their multiple temporalities. We shall describe this in a subsequent chapter. What is crucial to note in the meantime is that the idea that psychoanalysis could be re-found in the post-colonial world was not considered as a one-off event. What follows is a reconstruction of how the linguistic premises in *Seminar V* inform Lacan's later reading of James Joyce wherein knowledge in the breakdown of symbolic ordering is accounted for by way of two concepts. *Pere-version* signals the turning away from the father as the quilting point of symbolic ordering. *Savoir-faire* is the unique experience of knowing that occurs within this torsion. Both will come to suggest how psychoanalytic decoloniality could be thought of as a form of what I call "defamiliarization". For this we need to begin with another psychoanalytic controversy.

Notes

1 This coincided and in many ways responded to England's War and post-War traumas and the collapse of the British Empire. For more see Overy (2009).
2 Lacan's rendition of the Golden Calf is brief. It leaves out more telling wordplay. Soulie and Heine were in a salon when the millionaire entered as "one of those financial kings in Paris whom people compare with Midas" (Freud, 1960/1905, p. 47). Freud also renders the punchline as follows: "'Oh, he's not a calf any longer; he's an ox already!' And in this reduced version it is still a joke. But no other reduction of Heine's mot is possible" (Freud, 1960/1905, p. 48).
3 There are personal stakes to this story. The famillionaire is a character based on the real-life person in Baron James Rothschild, a friend turned benefactor. The Baron invested money on Heine's behalf in the stock market (which no doubt inspired the lottery agent as a character trope in the joke) while feeding him insider information on French politics Heine would then comment on in his columns. It is also well known that Heine struggled financially throughout his career and had to constantly vie for his stakes in the family inheritance. For more, see Kossoff (1983).
4 See Clarke (1980) for how Freud's resentment for The United States was apparent when he blamed Woodrow Wilson for the fall of Austro-Hungary. For a more extended account of Freud's relationship with Wilson and its significance for the emergence of the liberal world order in the wake of the fall of Europe's "older" empires, see Weil (2023). Weil's book details Freud's eventual and unlikely collaboration with analysand William C. Bullitt, which culminated in a highly criticised unauthorised biography of the President that was only released decades later.

Chapter 2

Transmission or defamiliarization?

Savoir-faire and the two impossibilities in
Lacan's decolonial unconscious

Introduction: Of Japan and heresy

Lacan's many claims to the effect that "the Japanese are unanalysable," in the
rare times when they are recalled, have been met with a mix of perplexity and
awkwardness. Lacan's characteristic panache means that he was not short of
deliberately troubling proclamations. But this claim, especially when read in
today's globalized circumstance, is immediately concerning. It is a reminder
that Lacan actually did not regard psychoanalysis as a universal practice for
all times and places. "Subject," "desire," and "lack" are not conceptual
templates to be applied anywhere but are specific to the world Lacan envisioned when he formulated the clinic. The very need to contextualize or jus-
tify the analysability of the Japanese already signals an unresolved question
regarding the extent of psychoanalysis' global relevance, not to mention the
transferences triggered by the anxieties in the answers. The peculiarity of the
statement transcends Lacan's relationship to Japan to provoke further doubts
regarding psychoanalysis' universality.

The complexity is further compounded today some four decades after the
statement was made as psychoanalysis has globalized far and wide enough to
have a certain history in Japan. Luke Osagarawa, Director of the Tokyo Lacan
School, stresses how the relationship to the master signifier in Japan differs
from the context that Lacan took for granted in his theorization of the master
signifier.[1] This is further rooted in deep linguistic differences that dislodge any
simple equation between Japanese and European modernity. The Japanese
language features a duality of *on-yomi* (Chinese-derived readings) and *kun-
yomi* (native Japanese readings) for Chinese characters. This duality compli-
cates the process of assigning meanings to words, as the pronunciation in
speech may not directly correspond to the meaning in the Japanese language.
This means the master signifier is not "produced" to stabilize speech. Meaning
rather is given *a priori*. Applying the Lacanian way of looking at things would
show a contradiction. The location of the signified so differently positioned
means that there is less of a need to hystericize the master and thus less of a
demand for analysis in Japan. Regardless, some adjustment of the analytic

DOI: 10.4324/9781003387978-3

paradigm cannot be avoided should the two – psychoanalysis and Japan – be thought together. Osagarawa to be sure does not present this as a colonial problem but the challenge from an altogether different historical dynamic where the Japanese language marks Japan's civilizational roots in China in a relationship that since the Second World War been damaged due to Japan's imperial crimes throughout the region. The implication in any case is clear, psychoanalysis cannot have a future if it does not contend with the challenges of working in a world of deep epistemic differences.

The fundamental question about the extent to which psychoanalysis has the resources to think through a globalizing world will be handled in more detail in the subsequent chapters. We ought to begin, however, by recognizing that this was a question that Lacan himself anticipated. For the challenge of difference presented by Japan was also mentioned a few times in *The Sinthome: The Seminar of Jacques Lacan, Book XXIII* (2016). But the seminar, curiously, is not about Japan. Lacan explores the writings of James Joyce to present Joyce's sinthome as a way of conceiving a subjectivity that is not bound to the Other's desire. Lacan upholds Joyce as an occasion for psychoanalysis to radically reconsider its most fundamental theoretical and practical assumptions, going so far as to call into question the "standard" relation between the real, the symbolic and the imaginary. But a point that appears neglected is how this was premised less upon Joyce's solitary genius than a recognition of the coloniality of Joyce's situation. Shaped thoroughly by a Jesuit education in an Ireland torn by anti-colonial struggle, Joyce's sinthome was accounted for as a fundamentally historical and political, rather than a strictly clinical, manifestation. Therefore, Lacan's remark on the Japanese, considering its location in a historically and politically sensitive seminar in this case, provides enough for us to suppose that Lacan was concerned with what can be called "the coloniality of the analysable". This is more than simply about who psychoanalysis is for. *Seminar XXIII* goes further to show that the very question of who is analysable and not already risks replicating a colonial dynamic. The coloniality of the analysable presumes, in other words, a coloniality in the very deployment of the analytic lens.

But that Joyce is also presented as an alternative indicates that something could similarly be done to overcome psychoanalysis coloniality. One could, in other words, deploy the analytic paradigm and its concepts to subvert it, as it were. To pursue this line of thinking, however, is to encounter another challenge in the fact that *Seminar XXIII* holds a marginal place in the Lacanian corpus. Its timing, having been conducted at the final phases of Lacan's career, and unreadable delivery, in which he flamboyantly dangled threads and used string theory to describe knotting, make it all the easier to overlook. It is also considerably shorter than Lacan's other seminars. As a result, we are more likely to assume that many of its new concepts are introduced as teasing provocations rather than sustained reflections. There is also little explanation as to how they relate. The most common conclusion therefore is to regard the event as a homage to Joyce's equally enigmatic style, a performative and literary-aesthetic event as opposed to a text with clinical-political relevance. This is no doubt compounded by Lacan's own emphasis on the private nature of Joyce's jouissance. Lacan lists Joyce among Meister Eckhart and Moses as fathers of "deologue", as those who against convention fashioned their own relationship to God. Joyce's art, consequently, is something "he alone enjoys" (Lacan, 2018, p. 103). Thus, the Lacanian Joyce is often recalled as an alternative, though impossible, model of subjectivity rather than a provocation to radically rethink psychoanalysis. Few have turned to the Lacanian Joyce to explore psychosis, and even fewer to explore perversion, despite Lacan himself upholding Joyce's aesthetics for a reconsideration of the clinical structures. To say that there is a problem as pressing as "the coloniality of the analysable" in Lacan would appear to be asking too much of a seminar whose current place in the Lacanian psychoanalytic canon is quirky at best or at worst negligible.

Rather than getting to the bottom of what Lacan meant to say, we may find the decolonial insight to *Seminar XXIII* in the very confusion of its delivery, where the point was to show that psychoanalysis should be defamiliarized. I am using the term "defamiliarize" in a general sense to refer to the need and possibility of looking at psychoanalysis anew in light of "the coloniality of the analysable" as a problem. But I base the occasion and need for this notion where Lacan reads Joyce to think about psychoanalysis' colonial issues. We may find a telling point of departure for defamiliarization in Lacan's brief but significant description of Joyce's "heresy". At the face of it, Lacan appears to just be saying that Joyce is heretical where his sinthome manifests a mutation of the symptom, by which Joyce could forge his singular relationship to the imaginary, the symbolic and the real. Indeed Lacan would even stress the heretical significance of this relationship by presenting it as a new reiteration of Freudian perversion. But by heresy Lacan is also stressing the novelty of the pursuit. Heresy evokes a departure from symbolic ordering to return to the materiality of language for newer possibilities of signification. And insofar as the symbolic order is the fundamental structure of identification and authority, the experience of symbolization Joyce ushers should be appreciated for its political potential. Luke Thurston summarized the point incisively when he describes Lacan's heretical reading of Joyce as "turning away from the consistent fictive domain of symbolic identification towards the dangerous, unpredictable singularity of a language-event" (Thurston, 2004, p. 166).

With this we can appreciate how Lacan saw in the heresy of Joyce's sinthome a distinct type of politics, "Contrary to how things might appear at first glance, namely somewhat detached from politics" (Lacan, 2018, p. 6). For an actual political reading would show that Lacan accounts for this divergence by clearly situating Joyce's subjectivity in an anti-colonial zeitgeist. The implication is that the sinthome is not simply about individualistic singularity. The possibilities of what singularity should entail, and thus where the symbolic order is limited, must also be thought anew in light of anti-colonial politics. With this we also have a point of departure to answer our question. The coloniality of the analysable could be overcome when psycho-analytic concepts are subject to radical reconsideration via the symbolic antagonisms unique to anti-colonial subjectivities. Far from simply cutting and pasting the psychoanalytic gaze onto a new context, it is about ensuring that the paradigm itself is brought to bear upon a decolonial circumstance. In this sense, Lacan's use of Joyce could be considered as a kind of decolo-nial unconscious, in that Lacan was unrealisingly thinking about how the unconscious cannot be grasped without taking decolonization seriously.

This is particularly evident in Lacan's interest in Joyce's remixing of colo-nial English. For Lacan what is at stake here is not simply the British erasure of the Irish language but how Joyce as an anti-colonial subject could render English unfamiliar. Joyce could defy the symbolic order where it was regis-tered for its contingency as foreign. Indeed with Joyce we find Lacan's con-tinuous interest in the margins of the symbolic qua the unlanguaged that we had just considered by way of Freud and Heine. It is in the clear acknowl-edgment of how Joyce wrote and spoke in a different tongue that Lacan could in turn pursue the defamiliarization of psychoanalytic concepts throughout the seminar. The allusions to jouissance in "joui sens", of "lalangue" from langue and "pere-version" from perversion – not to mention the sliding of symptom into "sinthome", "saint-homme" and "sinthomadaquin" - are less about the introduction of new terms than they are about the disruptions that are to be felt when the familiar becomes unfamiliar in the materiality of the utterance. The new is to be known not through the literal production of new concepts but through the cracks of language embodied where concepts must be understood within anti-colonial antagonisms. Psychoanalysis by this is not something to be offered to colonized subjects. It becomes a stranger unto itself where colonialism is a question that cannot be avoided. With this Lacan affords us a sense of what psychoanalytic decoloniality could be about. It is less an exportation of psychoanalysis than the dissolution it experiences where its concepts are estranged, where it becomes, in Joycean terms, heretical.

Savoir-faire and the real slave

I will develop the centrality of the defamiliarizing ethos underlying Lacan's concern with psychoanalytic coloniality by enlarging his description of Joycean heresy as a "savoir-faire". This should be noteworthy because it resonates with another instance in which savoir-faire was contrasted against colonialism, namely in *The Seminar of Jacques Lacan: The Other Side of Psychoanalysis (Book XVII)* as a know-how that was historically "stolen" by the master's discourse of which European imperialism was central. Indeed, I shall be read-ing *Seminar XXIII* to show how it in many ways responds to an impasse in *Seminar XVII*. Where savoir-faire in *Seminar XVII* was knowledge concealed in the master's discourse, by *Seminar XXIII* savoir-faire represents a knowing that cannot be "stolen", or "exploited", as it cannot be purified to be ordered into the symbolic. We can underscore a thematic continuity across the two texts when we consider how the father's historical significance in the master's discourse is presumed in *Seminar XXIII* only to be subverted. This indeed is where the heretical nature of Joyce's savoir-faire culminates into what Lacan calls "pere-version", where corporeality endures in a certain polymorphousness without recourse to a paternal metaphor. Consequently, Lacan's Joyce is not an idiosyncratic one off. It must be read as a response to a longer-standing problem about the relationship between psychoanalysis and coloniality, particularly the extent to which we can overcome the coloniality of the analysable.

Reading the two texts together speaks to a crucial implication for decolonial psychoanalysis for it shows that Lacan was theorizing in effect with two "slaves" in mind. Lacan saw that the slave of the signifier, or the hysteric, that we theorize for the clinic is just one side of psychoanalysis. There is also the question of the other slave in history who produces the more pressing problem of knowledge analytic theory is meant to address and develop. The place of the second slave in the history of psychoanalysis should trouble us enough to pursue the decolonial unconscious seriously as an agenda built into the foundation of analytic theorizing itself, rather than an incidental question. With the two notions of slave we have therefore two "impossibilities". There is the impossibility the hysteric suffers in the loss that structures surplus jouissance. There is also more importantly the impossibility of speaking of the colonized's savoir-faire. Joyce's savoir-faire as we shall see will resonate very much as Lacan's attempt to come to terms with the real against the master. Should we want to conclude that Joyce's savoir-faire points to the importance of colonized speech for psychoanalytic rethinking, then psychoanalysis' future should orient itself to speech not on the side of the master's symbolic order but that of the real slave qua the impossibility of colonial knowledge. Thus, to take this seriously as a decolonial unconscious is to take Lacan's conception of Joyce's savoir-faire to its most obvious implication by showing how defamiliarization, through an encounter with the impossibility of the slave's standpoint, is not an intellectual option. It is an inevitable development that is integral to a historical-materialist grasp of psychoanalytic politics. Until then, we shall only be working with the master's psychoanalysis. Psychoanalysis' future consequently should not be oriented toward the regeneration of the master's knowledge. It must be defamiliarized through the slave's real speech.

Part I: *Savoir-faire* against the master

The problem of colonized speech

Lacan's use of savoir-faire is rooted in the French distinction between two types of knowledge in *connaitre* and *savoir*. *Connaissance* refers to technical and/or organized knowledge. This is the knowledge that is clarified and systematized to be upheld for thought and speculation. *Savoir*, on the other hand, refers to practical knowledge, knowledge that is found in doing rather than contemplation. It is often translated to practical wisdom or know-how for this reason. This difference in where knowledge happens is the basis for Lacan to differentiate more generally between "episteme" as knowledge as it appears to the ego and savoir-faire as knowledge in the unconscious. In Seminar XVII, episteme emerges upon a process of "purification," in which knowledge is produced by way of "extracting" from the real (Lacan, 2007, 149). This occurs through abstracting from phenomena, or emptying the signifier, for information that would then be imposed onto a similarly projected world. In this regard, episteme is very much premised on mastery and thus the basic form the master's discourse takes. In contrast, savoir-faire, refers to the knowledge that is unique to the analytic encounter. Clinically, it is derived from the art of listening that unfolds through the concreteness of the transferrential breakdown. This takes the form of "making" or doing, a realization in the here and now, rather than the pursuit of more meaning where knowledge is to be sought in a master signifier: "It prescribes a proper way, adequate, but from which there is no separate knowledge. A savoir-faire, it is not knowledge in the sense of the symbolic ... It is a knowledge that is entirely invested in the making" (Miller, 2016, p. 109).

Note, however, that savoir-faire is not simply different from *connaissance*. Lacan in many ways presents it as an alternative to masterization. He does not put it literally in these terms but there are sufficient indications. For example, according to Jacques-Alain Miller savoir-faire enables Lacan to "establish his distance with regards to science" (Miller, 2016, p. 109). It

> goes as far as knowledge that would be to the benefit of art, of art as the supreme form of savoir-faire. So, the distance taken by relation to science, to the benefit of art, is at the same time to the debasement of philosophy and of thought.
>
> (Miller, 2016, p. 109)

The revelatory "non-scientific" truth savoir-faire is to usher, however, is belied by the little that can be known of it. Presumably, to ask if we have arrived at savoir-faire is to commit an epistemic error, as the former is fundamentally opposed to the scientific attitude to rational scrutiny. This is probably why savoir-faire stands among the least developed concepts in Lacanian secondary literature.

Lacan does nonetheless leave us with some significant indications. *Seminar XXIII* is crucial in this regard as we find Lacan positing two different truths, where savoir-faire's half-said truth is distinguished from the master signifier's home truths. "Home truths" are what we can say default truths (Lacan, 2016, p. 50). They constitute the "very first stirrings of what is called ponderings," of what makes sense in that it "entails a reference" (Lacan, 2016, p. 50). Lacan equates home truths with cognizance where thought proceeds through an active-passive subject–object dichotomy. They are first more particularly "insofar as the discourse of the master reigns" (Lacan, 2016, p. 14). The truth in savoir-faire, on the other hand, is formed in the real and in disregard for the need for a master signifier and whatever this might personify in the form of a guarantor. It is half-said because it is always lacking symbolic support. This half-saidness is what makes Joyce's relationship to language unique as "There is no Other of the Other to perform the Last Judgement" (Lacan, 2016, p. 47). This should move us to recall what Lacan describes to be happening in *Seminar V* where the traces of speech are encountered in the breakdown of symbolization. Like Joyce, Freud and Heine too worked with the fragments of signs. Lacan describes Freud's forgetting – and the recollection that occurred across foreign signifiers in the Signorelli parapraxis – as the traversal across half-names, for example. The Freud of *Seminar V* in this regard is positioned much like the slave in *Seminar XVII*, namely as speakers at the threshold of symbolization. But with Joyce we appear to be *within* the fragments of symbolization itself. If Freud met with the underside of signification through their short-circuits, Lacan seems to situate Joyce in the flow of linguistic chaos and this is key to understanding the symbolic value of Joyce's relationship to language and thus the evental uniqueness of his writings. Lacan therefore describes savoir-faire, similarly, as a "*savoir-faire* tethered by a practice of the signifier" as opposed to knowledge stabilized (or destabilized if we are to keep in mind what Lacan said about the underside of signification) in the representation of a master signifier [italics in original] (Lacan, 2018, p. 165).

With this different relationship to the signifier, Joyce also points us to a different relationship to lack. This is the basis of Lacan's conception of the sinthome. If the master signifier is what makes the subject's symptom, the subject of the sinthome, on the contrary, is formed where such recourse was not sought. It is here at this divergence from the Other that we are taken to Joyce's heresy. Lacan describes Joyce as a heretic not only because Joyce personifies a different mode of knowing from science. It is also to describe how the sinthome actively dismantles the master's discourse. The question at the heart of it all is "In what way is artifice expressly able to target what presents itself in the first instance as a symptom?" (Lacan, 2016, p. 14). Lacan's description of how the sinthome undoes the symptom and that savoir-faire captures the truth should be similarly understood in light of this heresy, as ushering a break from the established order of representation.

Lacan, having acrimoniously exited a few psychoanalytic organizations by this point, including some he founded himself, avows his identification with Joyce's heresy on this radical basis. The sinthome is not simply a structure without an Other. It is a structure whose difference is marked by a certain refusal or disobedience against the symbolic order.

Joyce's heretical manifestation of savoir-faire, however, is not simply about defiance. It is also about epistemic possibilities for the sinthome. The *haeresis* is most evident where it inverts the symptomatic treatment of God. Instead of the neurotic's Name of the Father qua the receiver of jouissance, the sinthome reveals God as artisan, artisan that is, as the primordial attitude to being that fuels the "art" or "creativity" that sustains our experience of the object world: "God is not the one who made this thing that we call the universe. People impute to God what is the artist's business, the first model of which is the potter, as everybody knows. It is said that he molded but with what, though? – this thing that is called, not by chance, the universe" (Lacan, 2018, p. 50). In other words, rather than a God that is "beyond" science, beyond insofar as it is to be understood within the confines of masterized knowledge, Joyce's savoir-faire points to God as the very constitution of our object world. Lack, or what in the symbolic would manifest as the mystery in the origin of things, is also reconfigured as a result. The many iterations of "God" in the neurotic timeline is consequently revealed as an unconscious recognition of real knowledge beyond the master signifier, a knowledge that does not conform to the master's drive for purification. This is why Lacan says that savoir-faire reveals the artisan's God not as substance but as real structure.

The formation of the sinthome then does not simply disregard the master, it is a know-how enabled by a certain insight into the master's limits. This is the know-how that enables Joyce's heretical diversion from the symbolic order. We can extend the heretical nature of this insight via Lacan's account of Joyce's "epiphany", in which the subject experiences a new object-sensibility as the world isn't purified and segmented for thought. In this, the unconscious and the real are knotted together as language is unbound from a fixed chain of meaning. Raul Moncayo's description of Joycean epiphany as meaning without comprehension is particularly useful here: "Epiphany is related to a sudden revelation or a manifestation of the real that at first may appear insignificant or ordinary but the ordinary soon becomes something of a different order (of the real) revealed in ordinary experience" (Moncayo, 2018, p. 61). This ordinary difference in the new that epiphany ushers makes way for a non-masterized difference that does not fold into science's ethos of discovery and the conceptual conquest that entails. This prevents Joyce from psychotic collapse, by which incomprehensibility does not amount to destabilization. Instead, it paves the way for Joyce's joui-sens, an enjoyment in meaning that emerges where the possibility of meaning isn't to be formally confined.

It is important to note that sinthome formation does not produce a different world. The idea of a differential break resonates too closely with the masterized outlook of hard categorization. This is where I suggest "defamiliarization" to describe what Joyce's savoir-faire ultimately does. The artisan's savoir-faire is heretical where it disorients our notion of origins and reveals the possibility not of another world but another mode of knowing. This is not occluded knowledge so much as a mode of being in the world irreducible to formalistic demands for linguistic clarity and consistency. Thus, savoir-faire is not about knowing literally different things. As a practice, it entails enduring in a non-masterized object world. This indeed is where Lacan stresses the impossibility in Joyce's savoir-faire. It is a mode of knowing that masterized knowledge cannot register, in a world whose absence of clarity does not translate to a demand to know. Lacan affirms that savoir-faire nonetheless retains a locus, a "real Other of the Other", in the sinthome the Joycean subject fashions (Lacan, 2018, p. 50). This Other is not the master's drive for purified knowledge. Rather, "it is the idea we form of the artifice, inasmuch as it is a form of making which eludes our grasp" (Lacan, 2016, p. 50). Consequently, in its impossibility, it does not offer, unlike the symptomatic semblant, a jouissance we can manipulate. It "far exceeds the jouissance we can derive from it" (Lacan, 2016, p. 50).

It is to describe the impossible artisanal form of knowing-through-making that the fragility of the Borromean link acquires its significance in *Seminar XXIII*. On one hand, Lacan presents it to think of how the real, symbolic and imaginary are equivalents, as they are logically related to each other. On the other hand, Lacan also stresses that they are equivalent only insofar as the central trefoil knot that sustains them is contingent. It is only salient insofar as it is a presupposition that enables us to think of the registers separately, which is needed to conceptualize the subject. Thus, while the link accounts for the existence of a subject, the established link between the imaginary, the symbolic and the real that purportedly constitute the subject's stability should be retained only insofar as it is conceptually helpful. The goal is to think without it. To stress the knot's provisional quality, Lacan explains that what makes the Borromean knot unique is that none of the rings could be removed without altering the connection between them: "by making a mistake at one point of the knot, the whole knot evaporates" (Lacan, 2016, p. 76). As Roberto Harari explains: "The decisive property of the triple knot" is "precisely what causes anyone eagerly trying to draw it, or tie it, to make boo-boos" (Harari, 2002, p. 9).

The fragility in the making – the subject's actual contingency – explains why Lacan describes the knot as a "pure and simple" ring whose sole use is to be eventually folded into a trefoil knot (Lacan, 2016, p. 72). This marks the "true hole" – the real before the knot– out of which Joyce would fashion his subjectivity. What defines this fashioning is where the real is sustained for its fragile, indeed disruptible, quality. The subject – in language and embodiment – therefore remains in a constant state of slips, faults, and gaps which Lacan takes to be emblematic of Joyce's literature. Joyce is constantly entangled with the real and is therefore able to continuously work with the interconnectivity between the three registers. Speech is consequently defamiliarized, where meaning appears and fades across newer possibilities found in the twists and turns of their sounds and spellings. Consequently, the savoir-faire in the sinthome too is to be conceived topologically. It is not based on propositional knowledge. It is know-how qua creativity in the real, "that which enables the trefoil knot, not to go on forming a trefoil knot, but rather to maintain itself in a position that looks like it is forming a trefoil knot" (Lacan, 2016, p. 77). It is less about the thing that is formed as it is about the subject's continuous deformation by which the impossible nature of its knowledge is sustained.

Savoir-faire against empire

We are through Lacan's Joyce taken to creative possibilities wherein speech disrupts not as evental breaks but a constant refashioning of symbolic possibilities. And we will understand why this should be of post-colonial interest when we consider the politics that Lacan presumed in his conception of Joyce's savoir-faire. Contrary to how Lacan's Joyce is presented as a figure of non-conformity, we should instead note two things.

The first is that savoir-faire does something against the master's discourse. It is an alternative that does not simply depart from the master. Something also happens to mastery as a result. The second thing to note is that Joyce's savoir-faire is causal. The dissolution of epistemic knowledge is meant to show the real at its most foundational qualities. This indeed is where Lacan's evocation of topology is politically significant. Joyce isn't presented merely as an exemplary form of singularity but one that is in tune with the real that underwrites the symbolic. The lining in Joyce's savoir-faire is subjectivity formed through a certain knowledge of the cause of things. This accounts for the symbolic undoing that Lacan believes Joyce represented. It allows Lacan to think of an alternative form of subjectivity where its most foundational components are realized:

> in most people, the symbolic, the imaginary and the real have become intertwined to the point that each forms the continuation of the other, for want of any operation that would set them apart as in the link of the Borromean knot ... Why not grasp that each of these loops continues in the next in a way that is strictly distinct?
>
> (Lacan, 2016, p. 71)

In fact, Lacan is clear that the subject that psychoanalytic theory presupposes is the exception, that the subject of lack "only makes 3 through imaginary forcing" (Lacan, 2016, p. 11).

Lacan is sure to set this radical rethinking Joyce ushers, however, in history. The topological un-knotting and re-knotting occurs amidst a broader symbolic breakdown. This is where we must recognize Lacan's equation of masterization with the historical master in imperialism. Lacan describes the symbolic order's law of substitution as "the arbitration between two signifiers" that is regulated by an "umpire on the basis of empire" (Lacan, 2016, p. 10). Joyce's subjectivity is immersed in other words within a chain of signification determined by British imperialism. But Joyce was particularly significant where he became subject to the symbolic order's imperial reach through the destruction of the Irish language. Without a connection to his native tongue, Joyce manifested his subjectivity via the defamiliarization of English as both his first and foreign language. Lacan does not see this as a matter of linguistic reappropriation. Joyce' was unique in how he found a way of dismantling the English language: "Joyce wrote in English in such a way that the English language no longer exists" (Lacan, 2016, p. 3). Similarly, Joyce's subjectivity could be re-found through rendering the symbolic order foreign from his post-colonial position. This is where Lacan regarded Joyce to have given a new meaning to lalangue. Joyce's situation in the cracks of language in Britain's erasure of the Irish reveals how "One creates a tongue inasmuch as, from one instant to the next, one endures it with meaning, one gives it a little nudge, without which it would not be a living tongue" (Lacan, 2016, p. 114). Lalangue by this is no longer reducible to singular speech. It is a singularity that reveals the underlying truth of discourse. Lalangue is similarly no longer individualized. It is instead, causal. To quote Colette Soler, lalangue in Joyce about "the letter outside meaning" altogether (Soler, 2018, p. 62).

Joyce's causal standpoint afforded a view into the real of language beyond a symbolic that is conceived in specifically anti-imperial terms. The other aspects of his singularity would not make sense otherwise.

Joyce's decolonial resonances are also evident in Lacan's play with the term "sinthome". Lacan describes it at one point as "*sint'home rule*" in recognition of Home Rule as the dominant strand of Irish nationalism in Joyce's time [italics in original] (Lacan, 2016, p. 6). Immediately in the same paragraph the sinthome is also described as "*sinthome roule*" to stress the open-ended, phonetically rolling nature of Joyce's heresy as it unfolds in the decolonial atmosphere [italics in original] (Lacan, 2016, p. 6). This defiance no doubt includes, what is ultimately at stake in decolonization, Joyce's sense of place. Lacan recognizes the significance of the "country" or as Lacan quotes Joyce directly, "the uncreated conscience of my race" (Lacan, 2016, p. 14). Lacan describes Joyce's sinthome as the "sinthome of Dublin which only takes on a soul from his own" (Lacan, 2016, p. 105). But we must be sure to note that if the master's discourse could be overcome it is not because of the knowledge savoir-faire produces. Savoir-faire may be presented as an alternative. But it is wrong at the same time to invest it with some inherent power. If Joyce's sinthome could do something to the master's discourse it is also in light of what it reveals about the master. In Joyce, Lacan finds a disorder in a symbolic order that could be grasped fully by way of history. When Lacan asks us to "consider that Joyce's case corresponds to a way of making for the knot's coming undone" it is because there is a broader undoing that is shaping Joyce's subjectivity, an undoing that Lacan describes in decolonial terms (Lacan, 2016, p. 71).

Lacan's evident appreciation of Joyce's anti-colonial context is belied by the little that has been said of it. Luke Thurston's (2004) influential work argues that Joyce provided Lacan with a way to overcome the confines of thinking about psychoanalysis in applied terms. With Joyce, Lacan could think of the shock in the encounter between the theoretical and the aesthetic. This shock, however, is to be regarded as a purely textual one, presumably a kind of feeling one gathers from Joyce's unparalleled style or genius wisdom. The decolonial factor that conditioned the linguistic antagonisms that made such a shock conceivable to begin with, the very encounter Lacan clearly shows is evident in Joyce's use of language, is not addressed. Colette Soler's reading of *Seminar XXIII* is also characteristic of this neglect. She explores Lacan's reading of Joyce with great care without stressing its most important political implication. The anti-colonial is relegated to a background detail rather than an essential structural fact. Thus, what we see first is word play rather than decoloniality. Consider, for example, her deconstruction of "sinthome rule". Soler recognizes its anti-colonial contours but ultimately makes it about "government" instead: "writing it as 'sint'home' with an apostrophe no longer isolates 'homme' (man) but rather 'home.' 'Home rule': this was the great rallying cry of the demand for Ireland's autonomy and local government" (Soler, 2018 p. 22). This same point is presumed when she emphasizes the French accent in the wordplay: "To the French ear, the English word 'rule' evokes something that rolls; Lacan plays with this translinguistic homophony by speaking a little later about the 'symptôme à roulette.' 'Rule' is basically what orients government" (Soler, 2018, p. 22). But the political connotations of "home" is rendered secondary. The decoloniality is relegated instead to a point about language in the abstract: "The 'sint'home rule.' the symptom on wheels, this alone commanded him, allowing him both to sustain himself as autonomous and to sustain himself in the world" (Soler, 2018, p. 22).

The neglect of the colonial fact of Joyce's subjectivity is likely due to Lacan's emphasis on Joyce's singularity. Joyce is ultimately, it bears repeating, to be grasped as a figure of symbolic defiance rather than an expression of the Irish anti-colonial struggle. Remember that Joyce is supposed to remind us about the impossibility of knowledge first and foremost. So even if the anti-colonial thrust of his savoir-faire is to be acknowledged, this should not reduce Joyce's psychoanalytic politics exclusively to an anti-colonial politics. Joyce is not to be read in the same vein as Franz Fanon. The latter theorized on behalf of the Third World with a dialectical outlook that anticipated the rise of former colonized peoples and the eventual downfall of imperial Europe. While the British Empire was a force Joyce had to confront and overcome, his singularity was ultimately in defiance of everything that constituted his symbolic circumstance. Thus, his heresy unfolded not simply against the British Empire but also the Catholic Church. Colette Soler describes Joyce's heresy as "a triple choice of heresy: Oedipal, religious and political" (Soler, 2018, p. 24). To reduce this to anti-colonial politics, from this perspective, would be to narrow the possibilities of Joyce's savoir-faire. But if we are to recognize that the sinthome marks a culmination of Lacan's longer-standing theorizing of the real beyond the master's discourse, then we must consider the seminar's post-colonial concerns within a broader light, that Lacan had also thought of the real in a historical frame in which the real of colonialism is integral. This requires that we recognize how Joyce resonates with Lacan's longer-standing thinking about the relationship between savoir-faire and the coloniality of the master's knowledge in *Seminar XVII*. Viewed from here, Joyce's savoir-faire does not simply point to a different mode of knowing but one that overcomes the master discourse's limitation of knowledge, one that cannot be understood without the history of colonialism. Joyce's savoir-faire is therefore anti-colonial insofar as the master's discourse against which it is framed is colonial.

Lacan of course does not use "the coloniality of the master's knowledge" as a notion but it is evident that colonialism is crucial where Lacan had to account for the world-historical nature of the master's discourse's expansion, that the master's discourse is not simply "knowledge" or "science," in the abstract but a certain experience of knowing that is formed through the historical exploitation of *episteme* at a global scale. Indeed Lacan's claim that in Joyce the name as "the proper noun does all it can to make itself more than the S1, the master's signifier" cannot be understood without the history which made the master signifier a problem to begin with, the history in which colonialism is indispensable (Lacan, 2016, p. 73). To see this is not to simply enlarge the tension between savoir-faire and the master signifier in light of the broader history that fueled it. It is to also link what we know of Joyce to the figure with which Lacan previously conceived of savoir-faire in historical terms, and that is "the slave" in Seminar XVII. Should Joyce's savoir-faire be an extension of Lacan's theorizing of knowledge and the master, then we can posit not simply the salience of a decolonial unconscious in Lacan but that this unconscious is premised upon the necessity in effect of there being two "slaves" in his theorization of the master's discourse. This refers first to the slave whose speech psychoanalysis is meant to address and the slave whose speech is lost to the psychoanalytic paradigm altogether. But this difference is underlined by the challenge that sees the latter slave positioned on the other side of what psychoanalysis' knowledge can register. The latter will be the basis of our call to explore psychoanalytic defamiliarization. To see the two slaves, we shall begin by reconstructing the history of the master and the slaves' place in it.

Part 2: Two slaves, two impossibilities

Slave 1: The slave to the signifier

The problem of speaking about the slave's savoir-faire in Lacan is that the very notion of the slave is often used interchangeably with, or to refer to, the analysand, or the more generical psychoanalytic subject. Thus one usually finds the slave mentioned in Lacanian theory to more or less refer to the slave under the Other's desiring gaze. For Ellie Ragland the slave in Lacan is the "slave in discourse" (Ragland, 2006, p. 69). The same goes for Justin Clements who characterizes the slave as the "slave to the signifier" (Clements, 2013, p. 83). In both cases, the slave is the subject whose speech is beholden to the lack in symbolization. This reduction of the slave into a metaphorical figure is in many ways due to Lacan's reworking of the Marxian use of the master–slave dialectic in which history is to be understood less as a struggle for recognition or a contradiction between labor and capitalism but the "theft, abduction, stealing slavery of its knowledge, through the maneuvers of the master" over time (Lacan, 2007, p. 21). This is where the slave's knowledge qua savoir-faire, as an artisanal know-how, is presented as the antagonistic contrast to the master's discourse. This forms "episteme" qua systemic theoretical reflection whose current political implication Lacan finds in "the capitalist's discourse, with its curious copulation with science" (Lacan, 2007, p. 110). This is the historical antagonism Lacan charts all the way from antiquity to the present. It goes without saying that psychoanalysis as *Seminar XVII* formulates it is placed on the side of the master's discourse.

Thus, savoir-faire properly speaking is not simply a different type of knowledge. Viewed historically through the master's discourse it should be more understood as the productive activity of the exploited that is transformed into knowledge for the master's discourse. The master signifier, similarly, is associated with science but it is also accounted for as the mastery in the distinct form of knowing that fuels scientific capitalist hegemony. Savoir-faire therefore is not simply another type of knowledge that was excluded. It was excluded from an extractive antagonism where one loses at the expense of another's gains. This element of exploitation is important to note because it clearly shows Lacan engaging with dominant Marxist and Hegelian accounts of history that were influential among his student-activist audience at the time. Thus, Lacan would refer to "the slave" in varying ways to speak to this political atmosphere: *Seminar XVII* refers to the ancient slave, the colonized, the proletariat and the psychoanalytic hysteric beholden to the subject-supposed-to-know as similarly "slaves". Indeed, Lacan clearly charts a historical continuity, where in one instance the subject of "consumer society" – "those who are themselves products, as we say, consumables" - are spoken of as contemporary versions of "the ancient slaves" (Lacan, 2007, p. 34). In building on Hegel and Marx, Lacan effectively presents his understanding of "master" and "slave" as standpoints grounded in concrete events of world-historical relevance. But more than that the history of colonialism is taken for granted as one of the factors why analysts should take the master's discourse's historicity seriously. The broad historical strokes with which the slave is described here easily links Joyce's savoir-faire to the slave's historical standpoint.

But if we are to pursue the assumption of there being two fundamental notions of "slave" in Lacan we must go beyond figurations and see how Lacan's use of "slave" is informed in the first place by a certain picture of history's trajectory, as it were. For if we have all become slaves, it is also because there are no, properly speaking, "masters" anymore either. For what reigns above any particular instantiation of the master today is the "fantasy of totality knowledge" (Lacan, 2007, p. 33). Thus we are all "slaves" only insofar as we are also "masters" in our conviction in the value of this fantasy. It goes without saying that psychoanalysis finds its epistemic location, and critical purchase, within this historical antagonism. Psychoanalysis occupies the place from which the discourse is ordered, "from which, if I can put it in these terms, the dominant is issued" (Lacan, 2007, p. 43). It is dominant as it teases mastery in the recourse it offers for subjective suffering. But the analyst discourse is also a "counterpoint" to masterization where it can subdue lack through dismantling the fantasy imbued in the need for such a recourse (Lacan, 2007, p. 99).

But this is based on another key premise regarding how the master's discourse has mutated to become all pervasive in the first place. The contemporary slave of discourse did not emerge as an object overnight but only at the point where the master fantasy of knowledge reigns. Something happened in the path that gave the exploitation of the slave's savoir-faire its history, from the time when the slave was the literal slave of antiquity to how the hysteric is to be regarded as the generic template for the subject of modernity. The question becomes how we are to chart the story of the master and slave in Lacan as a historical development, on one hand, with how master and slave has dissolved into the fantasy of totality knowledge that now predominates, on the other.

For this we must be attentive to a crucial detail in Lacan's picture of history whereby the fantasy of totality knowledge is produced through the exclusion of the slave's knowledge as its cause. This should considerably contextualize our understanding of "the slave" in Lacan. The historical nature of the slave's standpoint means that "the slave", as the source of the master's knowledge, has been expelled to become the real. This is because the master's theft of the slave's knowledge occurs through what Lacan describes, in line with what we saw in *Seminar V*, the "purification" of knowledge (Lacan, 2007, p. 149). This sees the slave's know-how converted into theories and formulas that ensure that knowledge is produced as clarity and consistency in thought. Thus the master's discourse is formed through "the very ideal of a formalization in which henceforth everything is merely to be counted" and continually quantified (Lacan, 2007, p. 80). This formalization of knowledge explains the nature of surplus jouissance as the jouissance that is crystalized to become "calculable, could be counted, totalized" (Lacan, 2007, p. 177). But Lacan is also clear that this occurs as a process of exclusion that produces the real. Formalization gives "primacy to everything at the beginning and at the end" to "neglect everything in between" (Lacan, 2007, p. 80). That which is rightfully "in the order of something arising in knowledge" is replaced along the way with "pure numerical truths" (Lacan, 2007, p. 80). Thus Lacan asks,

> Doesn't this make it the case that in the place of the master an articulation of completely new knowledge, completely reducible formally, is established, and that in the slave's place there emerges, not something that might be inserted in no particular way into this order of knowledge, but something which is its product [of said order] instead.
>
> (Lacan, 2007, p. 92)

Episteme is a fundamentally repressive process insofar as it entails the active *rejection* – or "purification," to use Lacan's term again – of a prior form of knowledge that Lacan will call savoir-faire.

This should take us to a clear statement of what I just earlier described as the "coloniality of the master's knowledge." Put simply, there could be no episteme if there was nothing to purify in the first place. But to take the dominance of the master's episteme seriously is to take a step further to recognize the more structural implication. Lacan has it that if "the master" has become a fantasy of total knowledge, it is not simply through the slave's erasure. It is that the exclusion of the slave as cause constitutes the loss that defines episteme. The expulsion of the slave's savoir-faire, in other words, is not simply central to Lacan's account of the exploitative nature of the master's discourse. It is also the basis for the unique experience of knowledge loss – unique that is in terms of what the master's discourse does – that psychoanalysis works through. For if purification is the basis for the surplus jouissance, which is in effect a jouissance in loss, then we must conclude that this loss is premised upon the exclusion of the slave's savoir-faire. In other words, it is in the master's epistemic exploitation of the slave that knowledge could be experienced as loss. The master's episteme is produced through the erasure of its origins in the slave's savoir-faire. The erasure in turn manifests as the lack of the knowledge that the hysteric will continue to demand, and thus suffer with the desire for more knowledge experienced as a kind of loss-recovery. The Other's jouissance is thus imagined as a "jouissance of being deprived", that is, of a desire moved by the urgency of recuperation of an impossible loss (Lacan, 2007, p. 99). This allows us to fine-tune a lot of the talk about the waste entailed in the enjoyment of surplus (for example, where Alenka Zupančič describes "Surplus value is nothing else but the waste or loss that counts") (Zupančič, 2006, p. 170). Waste is what is experienced in the sphere of master. But the cause of the production of the waste occurs in the exclusion of savoir-faire as the exclusion that produces the real. What is known as the loss of knowledge occurs through the slave's erasure.

The master's historical dynamic of expulsion culminates in Lacan's historicization of the objet petit a's impossibility. This, as we know, is the fantasmatic object around which the surplus jouissance in loss is sustained. Now we can grasp the salience of this object at the threshold of the hysteric's speech where the encounter with knowledge is also an encounter with knowledge qua loss. But we are also able to encounter this to begin with because the impossibility in the very desire to know has become palpable. Thus, the mystery of loss that is felt at every new consumption of knowledge is not to be regarded as some inherent feature of the objet. It is rather the objet as we have come to know it through the historical expulsion of the slave's knowledge. This is why Lacan in *Seminar XVII* could describe the objet petit a as the "opaque" thing "that has been misrecognized for a long time" (Lacan, 2007, pp. 42–43). For we are at the historical juncture when we are finally able to see that what manifests as "mastery" is structured by the objet petit a as the empty kernel that gives the signifier its loss-ness. This impossibility constitutes a key aspect of the intensification of loss that gives the objet petit a its enigma, namely, the purification entailed in the increasingly formalized nature of knowledge under scientific capitalism. For Lacan the point is not just that surplus jouissance entails the production of loss. It is that this loss must be continuously reproduced because it has reached a breaking point, where the "beyond" that is structured around the opacity of the objet a is no longer tenable. Surplus jouissance is registered where the slave's knowledge is expelled as the purification of knowledge attains a certain idealized, purely mental as opposed to real state.

Slave 2: The colonized

The banishment of the slave's knowledge in the real is presumed where the impossibility of the objet a is positioned across the quarter turn, as it anticipates the eventual repudiation of knowledge that the subject will eventually meet in his jouissance across the four discourses. The university discourse is that which "guarantees the discourse of science" in its institutional structuring of subjects for the organization and circulation of knowledge (Lacan, 2007, p. 104). The university is thus characterized as "the place of more or less tolerable exploitation" (Lacan, 2007, p. 178). The analyst's discourse is ascribed a critical function within and against this process, as occupying "the place from which the discourse is ordered" (Lacan, 2007, p. 43). The analyst is the subject-supposed-to-know – as the reason the analysand speaks – but only insofar as "he eliminates himself completely from his own discourse" (Lacan, 2007, p. 63). So situated, Lacan stresses that the work of the analyst, as the elusive objet a, should remain in "an uncertain zone where he is vaguely in quest of being put on the path, of being put on the scent, of knowledge, which he has, however, repudiated" (Lacan, 2007, p. 136). If the analysand is to eventually confront the impossibility of knowledge it is because historically speaking the cause of knowledge – the slave's savoir-faire as the origin of the master's discourse – has become impossible. The picture of "history" Lacan provides should now allow us to further refine how the problem in the coloniality of the master's knowledge entails two impossibilities. There is, on one hand, the impossibility of extracting which coalesces around the objet petit a. There is also on the other hand, the impossibility of knowledge where the slave as the source of the master has become fully excluded from discourse. But what is key to the entire formulation is how we have come to know about this exclusion. Lacan remarkably concludes that it is because we have come to face the colonized directly. This point becomes more obvious when Lacan mentions "the real of decolonization" in reference to the immediate politics of his time (Lacan, 2007, p. 34).

We should be careful of making too much of a brief aside in a seminar as rich as *Seminar XVII* but it is noteworthy that Lacan makes this statement not simply to mark the limits to what the master's discourse can process. It is also the real he presents as an answer to the historical reproduction of the cause in the master's desire:

> what remains a mystery is how the desire to do this could have arisen for him. Desire if you take my word on this, he can easily do without, since the slave satisfies him even before he himself knows what he might desire.
> (Lacan, 2007, p. 34)

Note what this question presumes is that mastery has nothing to do with the product of the slave's labor but the desire for knowledge itself, a knowledge situated moreover in the excess of satisfaction. But more importantly Lacan will imply that this is a question only the slave knows the answer to. Instead of answering what is effectively the question at the heart of his account of the master's history, Lacan references a chance meeting with an analysand, a soldier who had just returned from "the former Algeria" (Lacan, 2007, p. 34). What exactly we are to make of this encounter – in which the master standpoint of the psychoanalyst faces its opposite – Lacan also does not say. But he does pause to suggest that any desire to clarify this encounter by giving it meaning is itself a form of hysteria, another enjoyment of loss. His non-answer then is less a statement of agnosticism than a refusal to speak for the colonized subject. Lacan concludes this meeting by saying that "there is a domain here that must not be spoiled" (Lacan, 2007, p. 34). The broader implication of what the hysteric means in *Seminar XVII* should be noted. If the master's historical theft of the slave's knowledge is the basis of the modern hysteric, the analyst should not simply do whatever he wishes with the slave's speech. The analyst should not, to put it in terms of the current chapter, extend the coloniality of the analysable. But most importantly, this is realized only when the psychoanalyst must now face the choice of speaking to the colonized.

This demarcation between what is properly sayable and what is not effectively charts two domains of psychoanalytic inquiry. There is the domain of the hysteric's enjoyment of loss on one hand, which the master discourse's history accounts for, and this "domain that will not be spoiled" on the other, where the question should not be subject to the hysteric's search for satisfaction. This brings us closest to Lacan's two-slave presumption. If colonialism is integral to account for the master's discourse world-historical significance, then decolonization has revealed the colonized as the real in the master's history. Insofar as psychoanalysis works within the domain where the master's discourse is dominant in its expulsion of the slave's knowledge, then it can only speak to those within this hegemony. There are subjects on the other side of the master's discourse whose speech should not serve the hysteric's desire.

This concern with the difference between the colonized's standpoint and the history of masterization will be expressed later in the seminar where decolonial Africa is again evoked. This time Lacan critiques the coloniality of analytic training via how his Togolese analysands were forced to recognize a Western oedipal unconscious:

> This was the unconscious that had been sold to them along with the laws of colonisation, this exotic, regressive form of the master's discourse, in the face of the capitalism called imperialism. Their unconscious was not that of their childhood memories – you could sense it – but their childhood was retroactively lived out in our familial categories.
>
> (Lacan, 2007, p. 92)

The implications of this direct statement about psychoanalysis' coloniality are rarely stated. The history of colonialism affords a view into how psychoanalysis colonizes subjects by imposing concepts that were produced within the domain of the master. Thus Lacan here denies psychoanalysis' universality by denying it any anthropological legitimacy: "one cannot understand an ethnographical inquiry through psychoanalysis" (Lacan, 2007, p. 92). Lacan, however, is clear why the psychoanalyst cannot speak of the colonized and it is because psychoanalysis is unable to "relativize" scientific discourse, unable to think outside the master's discourse insofar as it is historically constitutive of modern European science (Lacan, 2007, p. 92).

Part 3

From pere-version to defamiliarization

Lacan's treatment of colonialism and its significance is torn between the refusal to reproduce the symptom, by reducing the colonized into another object of knowledge for the master's discourse, and a recognition of how psychoanalytic practice was produced in a history in which colonialism was indispensable. The consequence is that Lacan turns to colonialism to explain the colonizer more than the colonized, to broaden our understanding of capitalist discourse than to understand colonial subjectivization. He says as much by stressing psycho-analysis' failure to speak about the other side of the master's history. Lacan's insistence that psychoanalysis is a product of a unique juncture of an exploita-tive history, rather than a timeless universal lens, may allow us to revisit a curious comment that occurs in this section of the seminar. Lacan says that

> what psychoanalysis enables us to conceptualize is nothing other than this ... namely that discourse is bound up with the interests of the sub-ject. This is what, from time to time, Marx calls the economy, because these interests are, in capitalist society, entirely commercial.
> (Lacan, 2007, p. 92)

This could be read to mean that the subject that psychoanalysis is most interested in is the capitalist subject, the subject for whom surplus jouissance is both a product and a problem. Or one could be more consistent and follow Lacan's assumptions about history to its most logical conclusion: the subject is an incomplete theoretical construct for as long as the real of decoloniza-tion, and the slave we can only understand through an oedipal frame, remains unaddressable. And insofar as we encounter this problem from within the master's history of exploitation, we can say that the subject is not simply a flawed concept with which we can understand the world. The sub-ject occludes its cause in the slave. To take the master's discourse, of which European empires were essential – as the historical path with which psycho-analysis came to find its form and purpose – is to also expand our view of the bigger picture of the world the master's discourse was introduced as a concept to explain. If the lacking subject developed historically through expelling the source of its jouissance, then the production of the big Other too has its source elsewhere. The master's discourse is less as a tension within the master's epistemic exploitation of the slave's labor than it is about the master's knowledge and its tensions in the real of decolonization.

Joyce's decolonial significance for Lacan should be situated in this tension. Lacan needs the slave's perspective to theorize psychoanalysis historically, to situate psychoanalysis in the symbolic order as the development of a parti-cular experience of jouissance in the "beyond". But he is also unable to properly theorize the colonized perspective in *Seminar XVII*. Joyce's heretical use of language, understood as a manifestation of a unique relationship to language possible only to the Irish resistance to British colonialism, appears politically useful in this regard. It allows Lacan to speak of psychoanalysis as a historically situated endeavor without committing to the need to understand the colonized. Indeed, at the risk of simplifying matters for convenience, Joyce will be read by Lacan as the resistance possible within the sphere of non-comprehension. The historical outlook presumed here is evident where structure or "the problem" for Lacan is framed neither as just "the Other" as in *Seminar V,* nor the master's discourse in *Seminar XVII*. Structure in *Seminar XXIII* is understood by way of "the father". Lacan would frame this with reference to Joyce's distinct relationship with his father to explore just how differently identification with the symbolic center manifests in the anti-colonial circumstance. Here the notion of defamiliarization is useful not simply to describe what should be done but the certain inevitability that must be confronted where a different paternal structure of identification is at work.

This provides us with the basic coordinates for a psychoanalytic post-colonial politics. Lacan shows how resistance entails the more sustained work of refashioning symbolic relations, that something could be done through an experimentation with newer subjective possibilities. This most importantly is not about producing new meanings. It is about a speaking subjectivity that moves with the sonic and phonetic possibilities of corporeality rather than a slavish attitude to the fantasmatic object. More technically, this does not happen in some hard-hitting encounter with the lack in the symbolic but its playful or creative deployment. We can grasp this through the politics of defamiliarization presumed in his account of Joyce's subjectivity. Lacan did not evoke "defamiliarization" to describe what he sees Joyce to be doing but it is discernible where symbolic appropriation is in effect at work in his notion of pere-version. But we cannot speak of the father without speaking of history again.

The father's history

Lacan understands history not as chronology but as crisis. For this we can begin with how Lacan offered his historical account of the master–slave dialectic as a corrective to Marx. For Lacan does not regard colonialism to be a phase or a geographical condition in the history of capital. It rather situates the agency of the colonized in a different logic to capital qua the master's discourse, insofar as capital itself is the beyond for surplus jouissance. To see this is to consider how Lacan's account of history critiques the Marxist and Hegelian presumption of progress. Psychoanalysis is "progressive," situated in a history that can be told as a sequential development, when viewed as an evental formulation in the longer story of the hysteric's search for knowledge as a discourse of mastery. But psychoanalysis also speaks to a process in crisis insofar as the objet petit a is encountered at a point where the master's extraction of the slave has reached a breaking point in its constant pursuit of the impossible. Where the symbolic margins in *Seminar V*, qua the racialized and marginalized Jewish standpoint, could still be understood for a view into the particular mechanics fueling the impossible beyond motivating symbolic reproduction, the symbolic margins by *Seminar XVII* are construed as inaccessible.[2]

Crisis to be sure does not refer to a decline. From Lacan's perspective any talk of progress and decline, indeed of history, is only salient in light of the pursuit of impossible jouissance. Indeed, what the master would call progress is just time as it "brings an unnatural knowledge out of its primitive localization at the level of the slave into the dominant place, by virtue of having become pure knowledge of the master, ruled by his command" (Lacan, 2007, p. 104). Time is measured in other words by how epistemic clarity is produced out of the "nothing" that is "raw" savoir-faire as it were. Consequently, crisis is the inability to temporalize progress qua extraction, to realize the future for the pursuit of the impossible object. Lacan does not put it in such specific terms but the crisis of the object as the crisis of empire comes together in *Seminar XVII*'s re-theorization of the Oedipus complex. Here Lacan expectedly takes for granted that "the father" is the symbolic and imaginary locus of identification and desire. This indeed informs the seminar's account of the father as a "structural operator" (Lacan, 2007, p. 123).

This refers to how the Other's jouissance in knowledge is regulated by an identification with the father's jouissance. But more particularly, the father is structural in how the object is symbolized by identifying with the castration in the father's desire. This is how the Other's jouissance is in effect a jouissance of being deprived, moved, that is, by the urgency of recuperating an impossible loss. To identify with the father in this case is not simply to identify with someone productive – "the word 'father'" itself suggesting "there is something that is always in fact potentially creating" – but that desire is such is always compensatory (Lacan, 2007, p. 95). This lack is where the master, construed historically, manifests as the father in the imaginary and the symbolic: "the real father carries out the work of the master agency" insofar as the father's desire is so oriented to the impossible satisfaction in a lost jouissance (Lacan, 2007, p. 126). This impossibility is where we find the father's significance as a figure of decline most apparent. It pervades the standard picture of the persevering father in Freud's case studies. He is "the entrepreneur of decisions, in his relationship to the capitalist, whose accumulated resources, the capital of libido, will enable this decision to pass into action" (Lacan, 2007, p. 98). But the father also desires in the remains of some legacy:

> It is implicitly to proffer that the father is not merely what he is, that it is a title like "ex-soldier" – he is an "ex-sire." He is a father, like the ex-soldier, until the end of his life.
>
> (Lacan, 2007, p. 95)

The point is not that the father was once the master and is now no longer. Rather it is that his manner of desiring reflects the crisis of the object. The myth of his decline is the condition for his idealization as he derives jouissance after a certain purification of his ideal. Consequently, if the father is to be refused it is precisely where he lacks in light of the ideal as he is unable to fulfill the promised jouissance. Thus, the hysteric's discourse's "living function with respect to the master's discourse" occurs in relation to "the castration of the idealized father," insofar as the father seeks satisfaction in the impossible object (Lacan, 2007, p. 99).

That the father's castration is intrinsically linked to the crisis of the object speaks to how Lacan understands the impossibility of the hysteric's body. The pursuit of the Other's jouissance attests to how the objet petit a is inscribed with a fantasmatic promise of wholeness, in which knowing becomes as much about the mythical possibility of "completing" the body. For what the concealment of the slave's labor also produces is the anticipation that knowledge can provide the satisfaction for a "body" that is conceived as lacking. This "lost body", however, is nothing more than the real difference that must be excluded where knowledge is formalized to be mastered. The materiality in what formalization must exclude – the materiality in the slave's labor – accounts for the excess energy that moves the master's jouissance in knowledge, thereby granting the desire to know its libidinal intensity. In other words, the suppression of the slave in the production of knowledge also lends the signifier its mysterious aura, as the appeal of knowing is imbued with an excess energy that cannot be accounted for. Knowledge is thus reproduced at the expense of the split between signifier and body, in which the encounter with new knowledge comes with the anticipation of bodily satisfaction:

> there is a use of the signifier that we can define by starting out from the master signifier's split from this body ... the body lost by the slave which becomes nothing other than the body in which all the other signifiers are inscribed.
>
> (Lacan, 2007, p. 89)

From Oedipus to pere-version

The jouissance of the castrated father is evoked in *Seminar XXIII* but only as a counterpoint to see what Joyce's savoir-faire does. That Joyce's sinthome works against any need for a paternal metaphor is widely taken for granted. Indeed, this is a key premise for pere-version. Less acknowledged is how Lacan situates this refusal in the fact that John Joyce, James' father, also did not and could not function as a transmitter of values. John did not live up to the colonial-bourgeois ethos imposed on him: "Not only did he teach him [James] nothing, he neglected pretty much everything" (Lacan, 2016, p. 72).

Contrary to the paternal entrepreneur - the imaginary father Lacan presents as a trope in Seminar XVII - who bases his identity on sustaining the family, John was a debaucherous drunk who disregarded his parental responsibilities. The absence of an ideal father – ideal that is in oedipal terms – was crucial as the opening that enabled Joyce's defiance. Rather than to construct a myth of the ideal father, to thus erect a master in the form of a discourse about what a father should be, James opted for indifference to endure the collapse of a paternal symbolic.

We should be careful, again, to reduce pere-version simply as a sign of individualistic protest. Colette Soler's reading of Joyce's divergence from the Father is here instructive. Soler sees it as a mark of Joyce's heresy and frames it as "the Nego" (Soler, 2018, p. 32). Soler applies the psychiatric notion of "negativism," which refers to the refusal to heed the request of others, to indicate Joyce's "rejection of the commonplace, 'hell of hells,' his search for an epiphanic beyond" (Soler, 2018, p. 32). But this "beyond" while clearly going against tradition, does not see Joyce sliding into a solipsistic subjectivity. On the contrary, we should regard it as the basis for Joyce's de-individualization. Pointing to the final words in the *Portrait of the Artist as a Young Man*, Soler locates Joyce's heresy where the Nego becomes act: "the moment when, refusing reality to all experience predating his departure, he makes himself into a beginning, fashions himself, sublimates himself into a conscience born – not carnally from a father – but from his race," race understood, that is, as a social link (Soler, 2018, p. 72). Soler does not express this in decolonial terms, but the implication is not difficult to see from here. Soler treaded the point but does not pursue its radicality. To situate Joyce in the social link is to also see how Lacan situated Joyce's heretical non-conformity in the anti-colonial politics at the time: "The 'sint'home rule,' the symptom on wheels, this alone commanded him, allowing him both to sustain himself as autonomous and to sustain himself in the world" (Soler, 2018, p. 23). It is an individualism founded in the anti-colonial circumstance.

But beyond this, pere-version is evoked also to show the corporeal implications of savoir-faire. This is important to note for what is perhaps *Seminar XXIII*'s most overt decolonial gesture. The sinthome's heretical relationship, culminating in the radical reworking of psychoanalysis' notion of perversion, amounts to a similarly divergent embodiment. It is when the body is discussed in *Seminar XXIII* that we see Lacan defining empire as "*imperium over the body*" to describe how corporeality is subjected to the master's epistemic drive [italics in original] (Lacan, 2016, p. 10). Against this Lacan presents an instance when Joyce embraced his corporeal dissolution, namely, when he simply moved on "after having received the strikes of the cane from his four or five classmates", treating the violence as nothing more than shedding the skin of a fruit (Lacan, 2016, p. 129). Where the imaginary always amounts to a defensive body lined along a fictional boundedness, the

Joycean body is not objectified. Lacan describes it in fact as "cheapened" for being unamenable to the master's need for knowledge. Consequently, the ego too is not functioning in the same way. If the ego is ultimately about the failed pursuit of a beloved semblant, then in Joyce's case "The rupture of the Ego sets the imaginary relation free" (Lacan, 2016, p. 134).

With this Lacan presents pere-version not as another structure, drawn out of the subject's relation to the Other, but the dissolution of the idea of structure itself. The body consequently manifests this dissolution with the sinthome serving as the fourth term where the Other of the Other is absent: "It is not a break between the symbolic, the imaginary, and the real that defines perversion, it is that they already stand apart in such a way that a fourth term has to be supposed" (Lacan, 2016, p. 11). This informs Lacan's conception of pere-version as a turning to the father where the Father is clearly lacking. The sinthome's perversion consequently allows us to think of entirely novel relations between pain and pleasure. Now sadism and masochism "bear strictly no relation to one another" and this unboundedness is what Joyce can explore (Lacan, 2016, p. 69). This is why the psychoanalytic difference Joyce represents is not to be regarded as an example of a "malfunctioning subject" but a subjectivity that diverges from what is psychoanalytically familiar. He "has an *Ego* of a quite different nature" [italics in original] (Lacan, 2016, p. 131). But this difference, with all the history it evokes, cannot be fully grasped without Joyce's decolonial circumstance. Psychoanalytic rethinking consequently is fully embedded in the antagonisms produced by empire.

Joyce's decolonial circumstance therefore ushers in the possibility for psychoanalysis to be defamilarized. The "coloniality of the analysable," that is to say the coloniality presumed in psychoanalysis itself, is undone to allow for another voice. Joyce's savoir-faire enables this to be explored to its most radical conclusion, as Lacan demonstrates its creative possibilities by evoking topological links and knots of symbolic decline. With this we can chart a point of departure for a politics of psychoanalytic defamiliarization. The difference between the coloniality of the "Joycean subject" shall we say and the coloniality of the slave vis a vis the master's discourse stems from Lacan's pursuit of decentred knowledge, one that he explored through the possibilities afforded by savoir-faire as a conceptual compass. Lacan in *Seminar XVII* describes how the analyst's discourse' is moved by savoir-faire conceived as "analytic know-how" (Lacan, 2007, p. 35). Lacan describes it less in *Seminar XXIII* to emphasize analytic know-how's situation at the margins of mastery. But certain similarities are evident as both are about overcoming knowledge that is centered upon an identification with the Other. Just as Joycean savoir-faire diverges from the need for an epistemic guarantor, analytic know-how emerges where the analyst "eliminates himself completely from his own discourse", from the transferential projection that has him positioned as the Other (Lacan, 2016, p. 63). Analytic know-how, like

Joycean savoir-faire, is "a discourse such that it is not semblance" as it refuses the subject–object duality that is sustained by the objet a (Lacan, 2016, p. 5). Thus, Lacan would also characterize it as "non-knowledge" (Lacan, 2007, p. 186).

The general similarity in their marginal position nonetheless comes together to also highlight a stark difference. Joycean savoir-faire is situated upon the failure to imaginarize. It is a real resistant to becoming an image. Analytic know-how, however, departs from the real in a certain failure met *after* the image. Consequently, this difference allows us to posit two forms of real agency at work in Lacan's psychoanalysis. Analytic know-how is derived out of the hysteric's speech that analysis galvanizes. Joyce's decolonial know-how is characterized as a pere-version as it represents a language whose form cannot be structured. Whichever way you have it the direction is clear. The future of psychoanalysis is about knowledge at the underside of signification which cannot be considered without colonized speech. This is the slave's speech in the real of decolonization. But how do we go beyond the confines of psychoanalytic formalism and begin to imagine what this politics might be? The next chapter on Malcolm X will offer some suggestions.

Notes

1 For other accounts on Lacan and Japan, see Parker (2008) and Shingu (2010).
2 We should not read this as if a sequential account of what Lacan takes to be taking place in historical capital. "Crisis" is mentioned far more often in *Seminar V* than it is in *Seminar XVII*.

Chapter 3

"Turn to Allah, pray to the East"

Malcolm X and symbolic dispossession

Introduction: The periphery is central

The two impossibilities discussed in the previous chapter, even when taken at their most general levels, allow us to consider the latent presence in turn of two valuable presumptions in Lacan. The first is that psychoanalysis could take on radically different forms. We may lament Lacan's superficial treatment of coloniality. But we must at the same time acknowledge Lacan gestured toward the simultaneity of different possibilities for psychoanalysis in a way that allows us to posit a distinction between what we can call, to simplify, "establishment psychoanalysis" and the underside of psychoanalytic possibilities. *Seminar XXIII*'s treatment of colonialism, in this regard, is a Lacanian challenge from decolonization, as it were. The second is that it shows how Lacan was compelled to rethink the future of psychoanalysis through difference. This anticipates the present where conversations between different national psychoanalytic approaches and contexts are already actively taking place. But Lacan goes further with the implicit recognition that psychoanalysis will discover its future provocations and potentials in other symbolic orders. *Seminar XXIII*, if one is not worried about being too optimistic about the promise in the very short and difficult text, thus leaves us with a precedent: The psychoanalytic response to alterity is neither accommodation nor adaptation to another context or culture. It is about radically refinding psychoanalysis, its possibilities and limits, elsewhere.

This brings us to another point. The defamiliarization we just spoke of, lest it remain fossilized as a textual enigma, must proceed with the right view of difference. Here more difficult problems come into view for while Lacan provided insight into how psychoanalysis could be different, he did not offer a decolonial psychoanalytic theory of difference itself. Knowing psychoanalysis' poor history with difference, we will have to eventually turn to sources outside psychoanalysis for answers and interlocution. But even this would not be enough. Psychoanalysis, determined as it is through clinical practice, a service to be sold, must contend with differences in *global* flows, in the linkages of capitalist networks that shape globalization.

DOI: 10.4324/9781003387978-4

Where psychoanalysts in the majority of the Global South are currently debating their need and use for psychoanalysis, Lacan's reading of Joyce's already 'non-conforming' relationship to language – a non-conformity that was already widely accepted by the academic establishment by that point as to no longer be actually non-conformist – is at best a provocation than an actual theoretical resource. A decolonial psychoanalysis should not just be another product in the marketplace (however much this may be circumstantially inevitable at some point). It must also address the coloniality of its theory and practice as a product that travels, and will be redefined, through encounters with non-European historical dynamics. It is with this in mind that we shall re-construct what the underside of signification might mean in the more immediate realm of anti-colonial politics.

We shall begin with how we arrived at this point. The trace that comprises the underside of signification discussed in Chapter 1, and savoir-faire framed colonially in Chapter 2, enable us to see that Lacan thought of the symbolic and real as historical. The reason why our order of representation could be disrupted cannot be accounted for without a sense of how the symbolic-real tension was produced. Both chapters concur on how this difference between symbolization and its real impasses occur where Lacan understood science (as modern scientific capitalism) expands. It was from this historical outlook that Lacan turned to the margins of the symbolic to theorize psychoanalysis. His return to Freud in *Seminar V* was essentially a return to Freud as a marginalized Jew just as his later turn to Joyce was clearly about the possibilities of conceiving a psychoanalysis beyond the master's discourse, a turn which indicates the importance of defamiliarization as I just introduced. Both cases indicate how central the colonized's standpoint is to the constitution of psychoanalysis. The psychoanalytic center is always-already entangled with the non-psychoanalytic periphery. Psychoanalysis is found at the limits of its questions. The implication therefore is not if there can be a different psychoanalysis. It is whether we can think of psychoanalysis out of the tensions in the underside of signification. But to take this seriously is to similarly take its implications to their utmost possibility. The colonized's relation to psychoanalysis' condition of possibilities is to be found in the materiality of symbolization, not their subjectivity, standpoint, or agency conceived a priori. To move a step forward is to account for what this materiality might look like beyond Lacan's limited and incidental gestures.

What follows is an attempt to detail the political possibilities within this materiality by way of "symbolic dispossession". I introduce this term to describe the politics of speech at the underside of signification. It is "symbolic" in that it refers to speech as it is being incorporated into the symbolic order as a colonial mode of ordering. It is "dispossession" as the speech of the colonized is also where the limits of the ordering, as the limits to the symbolic's abstraction process, are revealed. But this limit, when we pursue the possibility to its most logical conclusion, comes with another revelation in the possibility of a different mode of ordering. For if symbolic ordering is about the expulsion of incommensurabilities, the limits where the symbolic is dispossessed should indicate the endurance of different symbolic possibilities.

The model I present for such a politics is pan-African Muslim liberation thinker Malcolm X. This is on theme for one, where Malcolm X was unlanguaged. His failure to identify with the English language – and the culture and racism that came with it – is reiterated across his autobiography as a dissatisfaction that eventually paved the way for his Islamic radicalization and eventual adoption of the X. Much like what we found in Lacan's use of Freud and Joyce, Malcolm reinforces our understanding of lack as the potent condition for the possibility of new beginnings, against the flow of Western colonial symbolic ordering. But as a disenfranchised Black-American Muslim, appealing to the different temporalities represented by African and Islamic history, he offers us a chance to elucidate how the gap is historical. The materiality of language, where the symbolic order is properly grasped to be continuously expanding as to be at once impeded, opens alternative political imaginaries through new temporal frames. This indeed is how we are to psychoanalytically understand Malcolm X's militancy in a decolonial vein. It is not so much that his adoption of the X entailed an affirmation of lack qua the loss of history. It is that it marked the refusal of white history for another.

We cannot understand this without recognizing how Malcolm X extended his unlanguaged state through other symbolic orders. For Malcolm, even until his death, never actually identified with the Arabic language either. Add to this his frequent dependency on a wide array of translators across his international sojourns as a pilgrim, activist and diplomat for the Nation of Islam and later orthodox Islam. Malcolm X retained his subjectivity *within* the gaps across languages in the plural. This is important to note because it is out of these very gaps that he could produce different combinatorial possibilities of signification, where the fusion of his socialist–internationalist–Islamic Pan-African principles could be articulated. Malcolm offers psychoanalysis a far richer field of symbolic inquiry than Freud and Joyce in this regard, for he demonstrates how the alternative temporalities in the state of being unlanguaged materializes in the real of the global. There is the most evident difference in the politics of naming that they were fated to embody. Where Freud (and Heine) were forced to adopt new names to hide their Jewish origins, and Joyce was further unlanguaged because he had no way of even conceiving of an Irish name for himself, Malcolm was continuously resignified even after adopting his orthodox name in el-Hajj Malik el-Shabazz. During his visits to Africa, his comrades from various African countries granted Malcolm local names as gestures of welcome and solidarity.

Malcolm was clear, however, that the renamings were as affirming as they were awkward. He was aware that the names felt novel because he was not

African. Indeed, Malcolm was in many ways too-named, too uncertain. Rather than finding a home in Africa, the renamings signal how he was able to navigate the new set of symbolic possibilities in a real that was actively unfolding, conjuring newer political possibilities out of his state of linguistic alienation. But this was not a triumphant process. We should see the renamings as a testament to his lifelong sensitivity to the affects conveyed in the fragments of new sounds he encountered on his path to freedom, a sensitivity that was further heightened once he (re)turned to Islam. It was not so much that he had to learn an entirely new language in Arabic to perform Islamic rituals. It is that his turn to Islam saw him meeting newer sounding words, concepts, and names of people and cities alongside a growing intrigue toward the immense world of decolonization and the foreignness of the signifiers found therein. The wave of decolonization that swept much of what was called "the Third World" was not only new in its optimism for uncharted political possibilities, it was also evental in the foreign encounters that expanded the possibilities of a new internationalism. Malcolm shows how this has the crucial effect of elongating the formation of signifiers, where the combination of their sounds and the substitution of their meanings were felt because the fragments were all unfamiliar. Key in Malcolm's biography is his detailed description of how he had to embody the new sounds as awkward twists to his corporeality, further defamiliarizing how the world had always felt before. The real was not met in sudden bursts of sublime acts but the seduction of newer symbolic possibilities in the combination of signifying fragments where language was experienced for its constant strangeness, rather than self-evident meaning.

This is all the more telling where he found his political awakening not through *Das Kapital* or "A Child is Being Beaten," but the English dictionary at the prison library, combing through every word in alphabetical order wherein the gap between the sign and the signified, the words that makeup their literal definitions, are squared with the contradictions that Malcolm found in the colonial racism of the real world. In Chapter 1 we looked at how Lacan describes signification in speech travel across the chain of signification to mean that there is in fact a certain grappling with difference in the real of "time" and "space". Malcolm X shows how this symbolic travel occurs through the constant incorporation of differences wherein the gap in the ordering of language is always met and grappled with. Speech, as the persistent encounter with the incommensurabilities of history, was how Malcolm was at home displaced.

"Symbolic dispossession" should also give us the opportunity to reclaim how Malcolm X has long been evoked in psychoanalytic circles. Key to this is Slavoj Žižek's pacification of Malcolm's politics where the global richness of Malcolm's activism is neglected to uphold him as a personification of a politics of negativity. The politics of negativity has it that the "truth" of what is imagined as identity is actually the gap inherent to the failure to resolve difference via sameness. Thus, it is a politics that has been described at times as non-identical or non-identitarian in disposition.[1] All universality by this is "nothing but the inadequacy of the appearance to itself, of the particular to/with itself" (Žižek, 2012, p. 539). The politics of negativity, consequently, criticizes identity claims that presume an essential seamlessness. Malcolm X is often presented in Žižekian discourse as an example of a politics that defy essentialism, with the X taken as the loss and absence of any real grounding for Blackness or African identity as such: "What interests me in Malcolm X is how he never falls into this trap of Black identity where Blacks should assert their culture, and so on ... He never played this game: 'We black people should return to our roots and identify our own culture,' and so on. 'That is why I am opposed to identity politics'" (Žižek, 2012, p. 462).

There is no issue with this claim insofar as the X in Malcolm's X name was an affirmation of a lost past. This was what enabled his many experimentations with different personas and ethical projects across settings and contexts. But the Lacanians following Žižek who insist that Malcolm is only good for "nothing" would lean on a particular aspect of his non-identity, upholding it as evidence that the post-colonial subject does not need history and with that "tradition". This assumption that the gap nullifies everything is superficial because it does not account for why Malcolm X embraced a variety of mythologies and rituals, many indeed of origins, in absolute earnestness. It does not account for why Malcolm as a colonized subject longed for a different historical experience than the one afforded by the temporality of Western colonial modernity. Key to what this chapter uncovers is how this longing was found in the gaps of speech Malcolm encountered as frequent enigmas throughout his global travels. This indeed is how Malcolm will serve as a fruitful contemporary model for symbolic dispossession where speech is registered in the gaps of the symbolic order in ways that account for how "nothingness" could maintain its potency and power to produce new historical subjectivities.

In this we find greater stakes. If we need Malcolm X to theorize symbolic dispossession it is because he is also being read across psychoanalysis through a Eurocentric lens. This owes a great deal to Žižek's more foundational theorization of the power and political potential of negativity which is conceived specifically with European history in mind. In a sense, it is a variation of the same Lacanian theme. Negativity acquires its power where the voiding the symbolic ordering inflates reaches the point of untenability. This is informed by an avowed Eurocentrism where negativity is treated as a privileged discovery unique to the evental contingencies of European history, in the supposedly irreplaceable profundity of its scientific breakthroughs and democratic experiments. In this view there is only an inevitable freedom in symbolic destruction, where freedom is sought as literal nothingness. The next chapter will unpack the deeper issues with this conception of Europe and negativity through Žižek's historicity of the object, namely how the emptiness discovered in time maps onto how the encounter with the absence of any foundation to thought and morality became the basis of the modern European institutionalization of personal freedoms that has been so universalized as to be the taken for granted way "we" think of freedom today.

But why this must come against a past, coded as "tradition," is rarely accounted for. Tradition to be sure is a slippery term to define, especially in progressive circles, where it is rarely upheld for theorization or as an organizing principle for solidarity and action. This should be sufficient grounds against leaning on the term too much to describe non-identity. Nonetheless the Žižekian logic leaves us with quite a lot to work with in the meantime. Negativity is meant to be theoretically appealing because of its radical refusal of sameness, a radicality which is emphasized through the rejection of all tradition as an example. Losing "tradition" is more profound where it comes with a much more loaded set of implications than losing "culture" and the variegated senses the latter more generalized word carries with it. Losing tradition in the way Žižek sees it is about losing all foundation, of any possibilities of origin and or claims to authenticity. But if this is the case then Malcolm X is neither negativity's best nor most proximate ambassador. To lose the past is to imply losing history (which Malcolm sought throughout his orthodox years), religion (which Malcolm embraced wholeheartedly) and a unique way of life from the permissiveness a secular context would be more amenable to (which Malcolm clearly was consistent about critiquing even from his supposedly deviant Nation of Islam days). Such a sweeping dismissal of tradition's significance, for one, is a misreading of the relationship between culture and progressive politics in the sphere of decolonization. There was never a time when decolonization movements were devoid of appeals or uses of traditional mythology. The harking to a purely secular decolonial period in the Islamic world before it was overtaken by fundamentalists is a gross reduction of history. Reclaiming culture was always central to decolonization. The refusal of tradition, waiting for a decolonial movement to arrive at a secular outlook before being worthy of progressive support, is also a losing proposition when it comes to understanding actually existing decolonization's challenges and possibilities.[2]

But the Žižekian politics of negativity fails most where it cannot compute that tradition could be reconstructed, that "the past" is always in need of retrieving because the need for an alternative historical imagination is key to decolonization. Tradition by this is not "origins" construed in a fixed or ossified manner. The need for such an alternative history already precludes the assumption, which appears to be central to Žižekian negativity, that resistance or subjectivity is to be construed primarily as a solitary endeavor. One cannot re-construct a historical narrative without referencing a collective and with that a world of imagined relations that the history is meant to address. This collective spirit furthermore is not something one dictates but joins in recognition of a broader historical momentum. This is not an Isla-mist thing but an evident strand of thinking throughout decolonial figures from Mariategui to Tan Malaka. There's nothing about the word "tradition" that is self-evidently negative or positive. It is ultimately about how tradition is used, by whom and for what political ends. If we are to stigmatize it from the jump, it would be because we have taken for granted the standard liberal Eurocentric view of history that equates tradition with "the past" on account of some view that whatever is present, or oncoming will be redeeming.

This inability to conceive of "tradition" in a more elastic way accounts for what is probably the biggest neglect among Lacanian abusers of Malcolm's actual legacy, and that is the Nation of Islam, however much they may be operating out of a thick account of Blackness, offers a politics premised upon an affirmation of an inherent displacement. They are African and American only through the terms offered by their alienation. Indeed, Malcolm could adopt the X into his name because it was already a long-established practice by the Nation. But this is not all. The X was not adopted through a momentary brush with the real but a grueling struggle to symbolize the possibility of new political projects. Death here is not faced in morbid meta-phors of solitary suicide and murder - a prevalent figuration in Žižekian readings of the Lacanian act - but revolutionary defiance, immemorialized by the famous photo of Malcolm readily holding a gun and looking out of the window for his assassins. This is where we shall have to make sense of Mal-colm's continued search, and in fact need, for mythologies of origins and purpose. The void was not affirmed for a freedom to be personified in the greater intensification of neurotic suffering, or middle fingers to all tradition and authority, but the discovery of new symbolic possibilities that amounted to the wholehearted embrace of the thickest visions of humanity. This mythology as reinvention, or reinvention through mythology, accounts for Malcolm and the Nation of Islam's enduring relevance in popular culture. This will also offer a corrective to the superficial Lacanian take on tradition as something to be dichotomized from modernity or progress. Tradition isn't a thing to be surgically removed from the present. It is the material with which history is thought.

But let's not stop at just correcting the Lacanian misuse of Malcolm. To read this psychoanalytically as we have across the past two chapters, via Lacan's attentiveness to the underside of signification, is to read Malcolm as deprovincializing the symbolic order. If the underside of signification is the real of signification, then so too should Malcolm be approached for a view into the immanent antagonisms of symbolic ordering Lacan had been inves-ted to uncover all along. Malcolm realized lack not through disrupting the symbolic but in unlanguagedness, in the slippages of dispossessed "English", English as it is simultaneously uttered across its jazz, formal, street, African, Islamic, and international torsions and extensions. What follows therefore is a sketch of what the Lacanian use of Malcolm have yet to address, namely

Malcolm X not as a globality of ideal seamlessness but of symbolic dis-possession. An attentiveness to Malcolm's experience as unlanguaged will culminate in a very interesting evocation of "we" during a notable use of the mirror in his autobiography. But we shall appreciate this further by begin-ning with the foil for our deprovincialization of the symbolic, namely Žižek's popular take on Malcolm X.

Part 1: The politics of negativity

The thing about seeing Malcolm X so frequently in Žižekian and Lacanian literature is that Malcolm is rarely ever cited. He is presented as an example, and as we shall see a crucial example, with little reference to what he actually did, said or wrote. This is noteworthy, not only given the wealth of historical debates and secondary literature that are available on Malcolm X's politics, but more so when compared to the greater degree of textual care and detail Lacanians express for icons in the whitened canon such as Antigone. Whe-ther this is enough grounds to determine that Lacanians haven't read this crucial figure they uphold for their project is difficult to say. But we can find a rather obvious reason for the lack of references when we consider what they highlight about Malcolm X instead. Žižek presents Malcolm X as an example of two things. The first is that the adoption of the X affirms the underlying lack that constitutes all identities. The second, heavier claim, is that this is due to the erasure of the past. Both of these come to uphold Malcolm as a political subject whose futurity is to be actively opposed to a nostalgic politics. This assertion is as reductive as it is ubiquitous. It con-stitutes one of the most common and handy examples of the Žižekian poli-tical outlook. But more than that it has seen Malcolm X become not only the poster child for negativity but also the "right" attitude to colonial trauma. Furthermore this "rejection of the past" resonates with Žižek's broader claims about Europe's continued significance for radical politics, as Europe's radicality for Žižek is premised similarly upon the erasure of the past as such. As we shall see, this constitutes the basis of Žižek's rejection of historicism. In Žižek's reading of Malcolm, we find an implicit insertion of Malcolm X's subjectivity into Žižek's European outlook.

Ilan Kapoor and Zahi Zalloua have done considerable work to construct a political theory around Žižek's conception of negativity and will thus be a valuable resource for grasping its implications. In particular they present Žižek's conception of negativity as the basis for what they call negative uni-versality. This is a universality that is discovered through "what is missing, in what is abjected or doesn't belong" (Kapoor & Zalloua, 2021, p. 185). It recognizes that the universal is only possible through its deadlock in the symbolic, or "the real" as the stumbling block to any attempt at "closure, harmony, or stability" thereby making the excluded an indispensable aspect of the universal's conceptual salience (Kapoor & Zalloua, 2021, p. 17). The universal, in other words, is only thinkable through the real antagonism in what it cannot incorporate thus making "difference" an indispensable constitutive element. This is to be contrasted with the liberal view of the universal in which the universal is to be grasped from the imaginary, in which the other could be "understood" from an immediate rational standpoint. Negative universality, instead, sees the universal conceived at the threshold of the imaginary, where the presumed immediacy becomes unsustainable as it is unable to understand the otherness it encounters. This leads to another key aspect of Žižekian negative universality. It is not enough that it is grasped by a single standpoint. The deadlock at the limit-point of negativity is a collective experience. Thus Žižek emphasizes that it should be a "*shared* deadlock," a deadlock that is met through the differences that cannot be resolved [italics added] (Kapoor & Zalloua, 2021, p. 16). This sets Žižek's approach apart from its opposite in identity politics. Where identity politics assumes that sameness is a given and that politics is about the appeal to the same across differences, negative universality insists on the impossibility of sameness. This impossibility is where an essential gap underlying the appeal to sameness is revealed and consequently where a fundamental lack-in-being, the emptiness that governs what we take to be our world in common, is registered. This is the lack that is to be affirmed as universal insofar as it is the deadlock that all measures of sameness will inevitably encounter or grapple with.

Žižek's opposition to identity politics, however, should not be taken to mean that he is opposed to identities per se. It is to show how all identities are constituted over and against the gap. The gap in this sense is ontological as it is confronted as the negative basis of all identities. Identities in other words are crucial for as long as they are understood as contingent, to be constructed and reconstructed owing to the realization that they are not timeless but are subject to a struggle with the lack in being. This informs Žižek's conception of non-identity. It is not an appeal to dissolve identities based on some formal quality of the subject (the liberal appeal to abstract human rights is one example of such a gesture). Rather, identity is key for as long as we see their symbolic ordering and imaginaries as actively grounded on an impossible real. And insofar as this gap is constitutive and foundational it is also the essential antagonism at the core of the social, our necessary co-existence with others qua difference and what Žižek calls "politics proper". This is politics understood not as a compromise across differences, where different identities meet across a stable field. It is the politics that emerges where the gap is faced as differences are actively grappled with upon the recognition that the field is always-already antagonistic. Thus, as real, universality is realized through the conflictual nature of politics as a common predicament: "while each particular responds idiosyncratically to the real-as-antagonism, this same negativity becomes the basis for a shared horizon of meaning and struggle" (Kapoor & Zalloua, 2021, p. 20). Identities consequently are to be expressed not as insulated realities that could be contained (in which politicization is framed as an option). Identities are to be championed and contested owing to their constitutive link to the political as antagonistic gap:

> Politics here is an active response to a deadlock, a retort to the always-already fissured nature of the social. Thus, queer or gender politics happens, not because the political is "naturally" inscribed in social identity, but because the out-of-jointedness of each position necessitates an active intervention.
>
> (Kapoor & Zalloua, 2021, p. 21)

Politics proper therefore happens upon the universal recognition that what we may put forth as identity is in actuality non-identity.

That the lack in being is encountered where the real is grasped as constitutive to identity, leads to what is perhaps the most crucial implication to Žižek's formulation of universality, and that is how it emerges only through difference. The limit to identity in other words is not something logically deduced. It is faced only through difference. Indeed, it is through meeting difference qua difference, where the otherness is not to be deflected or pacified via another rationale, that identity could be questioned to begin with. This in fact is where many critics of Žižek's position on refugees miss the mark. Žižek is not anti-refugee based on their purported" backwardness." Žižek is against the liberal outlook that refuses to engage with the question of difference that the refugee crisis compels. The liberal multiculturalist position in other words does not sufficiently recognize the opportunity to think the real, preferring to represent the refugee within whatever is available to the liberal symbolic. Žižek's Eurocentrism, consequently, is not racial. He is Eurocentric in that the question of difference could only be thoroughly handled through the legacy of radical politics that he takes to Europe to have pioneered and thoroughly exhausted, in which the question of "otherness," in its various philosophical, religious, racial, gender, and sexual manifestations have made entire European intellectual traditions and political movements. This, it goes without saying, is based on Žižek's more foundational assumption that the real's historical location in Europe. For Žižek, the negativity in the political is realized only through the deadlock represented in the encounter with otherness. The gap that constitutes politics therefore is real only upon having encountered difference as an impasse, an encounter that Žižek takes for granted as definitive of European history. If Europe is to be privileged it is as where real political antagonism has been most dealt with.

A proper reading of Malcolm X will give us a lot to critique here. Before that we will do well to charitably consider the extended potential of Žižek's outlook. It also ascribes the grappling with otherness, rather than its mere inclusion, to be the basis of radical politics. It differs from the commonsense take that progressiveness is about the extent to which the otherness could be properly accepted. It is rather that there is no proper "inclusion", other than that which would radically rewrite the symbolic order. The excluded therefore is to be situated outside to the extent possible, by which difference – be it racial, historical or cultural – must be met. This no doubt will come across as crude for the liberal multiculturalist who believes that difference could be understood or that we could move from tolerance to acceptance. But for the Žižekian lens, it only marks the recognition that politics occurs through the real as the constitutive "outside". Negative universality is determined by the real qua those at the threshold of the existing political framework. These are subjects who "belong to the system but has no proper place in it" (Kapoor & Zalloua, 2021, p. 23). To describe this subject, Kapoor and Zalloua turn to Jacques Ranciere's notion of part of no-part: These are the underclass, the subaltern, "the permanently unemployed, migrants, refugees, sweatshop laborers, etc" – indeed whatever capitalism produces but cannot subdue (Kapoor & Zalloua, 2021, p. 1). As symptom, they reveal the system's repressed truth: "The fact that the part of no-part belongs to the system but has no proper place in it reveals the truth – the injustice – of the system. The excluded are precisely those who must be negated for capitalism to function 'normally'" (Kapoor & Zalloua, 2021, p. 23)

Žižek and Malcolm X

Žižek's commitment to universality as the non-identity in the real of politics prepares the ground for his take on Malcolm X. Žižek reads the X to mean first and foremost a "reversal" of paternal identification, where Malcolm undergoes a transformation from identity, in which "the lack of the signifier" is denied, into non-identity where subjectivity is formed around "the signifier of the lack" (Žižek, 1993, p. 78). For this Žižek turns to a *New York Times* review of Spike Lee's film on Malcolm which emphasizes how the "X" that Malcolm adopted affirms the rejection of the identity granted under the slave master's historical gaze. This does not only remove Malcolm from the white-European colonial symbolic order. It also poises Malcolm to affirm a new subjectivity as difference, an unknown that disrupts:

> X stands for the unknown. The unknown language, religion, ancestors and cultures of the African American. X is a replacement for the last name given to the slaves by the slave master ... "X" can denote experimentation, danger, poison, obscenity and the drug ecstasy. It is also the signature of a person who cannot write his or her name ... The irony is that Malcolm X, like many of the Nation of Islam and other Blacks in the 60's, assumed the letter – now held to represent his identity – *as an expression of a lack of identity* [italics added].
>
> (Patton as cited in Žižek, 1993)

Žižek highlights how the review curiously evokes the notion of lack in ways that are resonant with its Lacanian meaning. Žižek from here elaborates how Malcolm's choice of X as the unknown translates to an affirmation of freedom in the new. Rather than to refuse lack, Malcolm instead ensures its affirmation. With this – as the X "stands all possible future meanings" – Malcolm also personifies how negativity is the basis of a new politics: "X qua void exceeds every positive symbolic identity" (Žižek, 1993, p. 78). But Žižek takes it further. Malcolm is not simply an example of lack-affirmation. Žižek presents Malcolm as an example of the sinthome as Malcolm enacts a naming, and fashions a singularity, without any appeal to a paternal metaphor or a symbolic "center":

> this identification with the unknown, far from being an exception, brings to light the feature constitutive of symbolic identification as such: every symbolic identification is ultimately identification with an X, with an "empty" signifier which stands for the unknown content, i.e. it makes us identify with the very symbol of a lack of identity.
>
> (Žižek, 1993, p. 79)

As an example, Žižek points to Malcolm's "singular ethico-political achievement" in the latter's eventual renunciation of the Nation of Islam's ethnocentric theodicy for a "universal" orthodox Islam (Žižek, 2016, p. 77). Malcolm affirmed the emptiness of the signifier through fashioning more identities. Lack, the absence of essence to any identity, is realized through a universal, presumably more abstract, symbolic order as opposed to a strictly more particularist one. In this regard Malcolm is the personification of non-identity, in which strict claims of belonging are refused for a voidal or more "lacking" sense of subjectivity.

Žižek goes further to stress Malcolm's evental value in the historical implication of his experimental singularity. It is through affirming the X against what was internalized as the universal vision of history imposed by the whites that Žižek describes Malcolm as "whiter than white," as he was able "to freely form a new identity much more universal than white people's professed universality" (Žižek, 2014, p. 17). By affirming the X, Malcolm was affirming the gap in "Blackness". Identity is hereby grasped for its contingency which enables the radicalism in the new subjectivity that is consequently formed. We relate to Malcolm through the otherness that is produced between our location in the stable symbolic center and the radicalism that is enabled by the X qua the gap. The gap between us and the X forces a grappling with otherness that instantiates our realization of the universal qua the antagonistic field that shapes our relationship to difference: "the lack of fixed identity. X qua void exceeds every positive symbolic identity" (Žižek, 1993, p. 79). Malcolm's singular reinvention of himself, and the trouble this caused, forces the dominant symbolic reckoning with the gap in the real. Insofar as this universal unseats the historical hegemonic white universal, Malcolm X's negative universal could be said to be "outwhiting" whites, defeating whites in the game that they had long dominated, in a world that has been shaped by their image.

To properly uphold Malcolm as a figure of symbolic defiance, however, requires that we also square Žižek's claims with the politics that Malcolm's adoption of the X produced. This requires that we enlarge our view of Malcolm to consider what exactly is at stake in his experimentation with identities. In this regard, Žižek is less clear. If Malcolm's legacy is just anti-racism, then surely there is nothing about his affirmation of the "X" that is unique. Malcolm was only one figure among countless others who were actively protesting white supremacy at the same time, many of whom did not have to renounce their government name to appeal to the unknown. Malcolm in any case was neither the first nor the last Black activist to take on the X and was inspired to do so only upon being moved by the highly intricate symbolic order offered by the Nation of Islam's idiosyncratic vision of the faith. To take Malcolm's reinvention seriously is to consider how his his embrace of the gap laid the ground for his eventual experimentation with different symbolic orders and this is evident where Malcolm X is regarded as a universal figure on account of his decolonial significance. This, however, requires that we make a significant correction to Žižek's reading. It isn't the white symbolic order that Malcolm disrupted. His disruption spoke to a global political consciousness. Malcolm revealed a non-white universal insofar as his evolution served as a global reference point for a world beyond Europe. Nowhere is this more evident than the international imprint of the antagonisms he provoked. This requires that we see that Malcolm's legacy endures in the questions he left behind not in the symbolic order Žižek has in mind but the symbolic as it was shaped in the global sphere of decolonization. To simplify, the "outside" that renders the universality in non-identity is not embodied in Malcolm X but the more significant "outside" that constituted the decolonial world he traversed and gave voice to.

If this is absent in Žižek's rendition of Malcolm it is because Malcolm's transformation is framed temporally rather than spatially. Malcolm is situated in European time, and thus the European view of man, than he is in the geographical awareness of decolonial internationalism. To see this, we must first describe the reductive vision of history in Žižek's reading of Malcolm, particularly where Žižek attributes Malcolm's subjectivity to the destruction of the Black past. This claim, like everything else in Žižek's reading of Malcolm, isn't textually supported but it is alluded to enough. For Žižek, Malcolm's adoption of the X is intrinsically tied to the total erasure of Black history: "The idea is that this X which deprives the Blacks of their particular tradition offers a unique chance to redefine (reinvent) themselves" (Žižek, 2016, p. 77). The same point was made more polemically in Žižek's television interview with Tavis Smiley (2015) on PBS:

> Because of this Malcolm X ... wasn't playing the Hollywood game, *Roots*. You remember that stupid TV series? The greatest honor for you Blacks' desire is to find some tribe in Africa. Oh, I'm from there. No. Of course, Malcolm X meant by the brutality of white men, being enslaved, we were deprived of our roots and so on. But he wrote about it. He says, but this X paradoxically opens up a new freedom for us ... not primitive tribal, but universal, creating their own space. We, Black people, have a unique chance not to become, not to return to our particular [roots], to be more universal, emancipated than white people themselves. You see, this is the important thing for me.

The irony in this remark wouldn't be lost on anyone who has actually read Malcolm X's autobiography given that it was penned by Alex Haley, the same writer who also wrote *Roots*. If Žižek's reading of Malcolm X comes across as more polemical than theoretical, it is because it does stand out as a thin treatment of what has turned out into a major theme in the Žižekian project. This is obvious when compared to Žižek's other more sustained in-depth readings of European figures such as Kant and Hegel. But if this comparison is worth making it is because Žižek's rendition of Malcolm has become in many ways the instant example of the "point" in all Žižekian theory. It is Malcolm – and not say Keyser Söze as the prime example of the Lacanian act, which Žižek offered in his analysis of NATO's intervention in the Balkans, an area one would like to think he is more familiar with than Africa – that has endured as the shorthand personification of Žižek's theory of subjectivity. It is Malcolm in his ostensive departure from the past that has informed subsequent uses of Žižek for a global era. Kapoor and Zalloua present Malcolm's adoption of X as "inventing a new universal" because slavery had deprived "black people of their roots" (Kapoor & Zalloua 2021, p. 99). Zalloua's standalone use of Žižek for anti-racist critique, where Malcolm is again featured but only ever so briefly, similarly leads us to this renunciation of a lost past: "Adopting X in place of the Patronymic Little represents a universalizing move that does not limit black radicalism to a reified vision of the past as the basis of anti-racist critique" (Zalloua, 2020, p. 116). The same point is in Gautam Basu Thakur's Lacanian-Žižekian critique of post-colonial theory. Thakur (2020) channels Žižek's lesson from Malcolm X to conclude that "the negated cannot be retrieved – there is no going back and the only possibility moving forward lies through embracing the negation claiming it as part of one's identity, hence the 'X' in his name" (Thakur, 2020, p. 192). In many ways this evocation of the X has become the standard example of Žižekian theory, *par excellence*.

By claiming that Malcolm's reinvention of his singularity is tied to the loss of history, Žižek is reiterating the familiar Lacanian premise that the lacking signifier is a modern emergence that trails the historical decline of traditional and religious authority in Europe. Žižek is right to draw from this given how it is essential for Lacan's theorization of the decline of the paternal metaphor, which is accounted for sociologically in Lacan's earlier writings as the effect of European modernization and industrialization. Psychoanalysis identifies the possibility of retrieving one's singularity by way of the truth that the subject encounters within the trauma endured in symbolic decline. The signifier is hereby rendered empty where it is unable to stabilize meaning and this paves way for the subjective destitution so crucial for the Lacanian project. Rather than recourse to a guarantor of meaning in the guise of the Other, the aim is to instead address the unspeakable truth that was excluded to sustain the Other's desire. Žižek applies the narrative of symbolic destruction and its redeeming possibilities to Malcolm, in which the emptying of the signifier qua the emptying of tradition is entailed in the trans-Atlantic slave trade's erasure of the African past. Malcolm could have only realized this emptiness of the signifier through being a subject who was ultimately shaped by the West where all roots were finally lost:

> When Malcolm adopted "X" as his family name, thereby signaling that the slave traders who brought the enslaved Africans from their homeland brutally deprived them of their family and ethnic roots, of their entire cultural lifeworld, the point of this gesture was not to mobilize the Blacks to fight for the return to some primordial African roots, but precisely to seize the opening provided by X, an unknown new (lack of) identity engendered by the very process of slavery which made the African roots forever lost.
>
> (Žižek's, 2016, p. 77)

This should allow us to reflect on Žižek's claim about Malcolm X's whiteness with some curiosity. The historical outlook Žižek presumes has it that Malcolm was not whiter on account of his epistemic position. Malcolm rather was whiter for enduring a more drastic loss of culture that should put an end to all attachments to identity once and for all. Thus the point of embracing the X is to embrace the lack of culture that will ultimately pave the way for "symbolic suicide" (Žižek, 2023, p. 82). This is the gist of Žižek's latest reaffirmation of Malcolm X's legacy: "Malcolm X proposes for Blacks themselves to bring to an end their deracination with a gesture of symbolic suicide, the passage through zero-point, in order to free the space for a new identity" (Žižek, 2023, p. 82). This new identity, beyond the black-and-white framing of the world, is what will finally "render whiteness pointless" (Žižek, 2023, p. 82). Malcolm's negativity too, consequently, is "outside" when viewed from within the white historical temporal frame. It is where symbolic decline is experienced more profoundly than what is otherwise endured under "normal" and "white" circumstances. We have a better sense now of why the overcoming of whiteness cannot happen through a return to Africa. It is because it must be attained through whiteness itself. All that is asserted in the name of non-identity turns out to be loaded with cultural presumptions, that ultimately the symbolic order no matter what culture you belong to, is still the white man's symbolic order. One should not be African but one must be whiter, and not even that. One must be whiter than white. Now we know why.

Malcolm's act

Žižek's Malcolm does at least frame the antagonism in Malcolm's adoption of the X accurately, in that it centered on an irrevocable contradiction. But this not a contradiction between black and white but between the universality of Islam and African nationalism. Malcolm had traversed a temporal tension but it is one beyond European temporality. To see this is to pursue two crucial implications hinted at the introduction. It is to begin by acknowledging that Malcolm was neither the only nor the first Black activist to adopt the X. It was already a common practice for members of the Nation of Islam. Perhaps the most famous other example would be Muhammad Ali and his rejection of his Christian name in Cassius Clay, a rejection premised upon Ali's conversion to the Nation's teachings. Žižek, to be sure, was right to point out how the X marked a break from the past. But this was a break that was formed not before but *through* the affirmation of Islam that the Nation delivered to Black Americans. If the X could be embraced, it was because Islam already appeared as the signifier of a concrete alternative. The X in other words was not empty qua destroyed. It was already loaded with political anticipation. This realization, furthermore, was neither intellectual nor textual but intersubjective. Malcolm first learned about the Nation of Islam by way of his brother Philbert who had converted earlier. Malcolm's journey into orthodox Islam in turn was significantly influenced by her half-sister, and Civil Rights icon in her own right, Ella Little-Collins, who paid for Malcolm's Hajj and funeral. So powerful was the momentum that Black Muslims presented their movement as an alternative to Christian African-American activism, framing the latter as the more inferior emancipatory project due to its roots in the very faith that actively subjugated Blacks into slavery. Malcolm himself attributed his adoption of the X to how the Nation of Islam provided the Black man with a new urgent political agenda:

> "X" replaced the white slavemaster name of "Little" which some blue-eyed devil named Little had imposed upon my paternal forebears. The receipt of my "X" meant that forever after in the Nation of Islam, I would be known as Malcolm X. Mr Muhammad taught that we would keep this "X" until God Himself returned and gave us a Holy Name from His own mouth.
>
> (X, 1999, p. 252)

Nowhere of course was this momentum more manifest than the reason Malcolm wholly embraced the Nation's strict code of conduct. Refraining from alcohol, premarital sex and pork was crucial for the political rebirth of the Black man that Islamic ethics was to usher. This potential for political renewal was also the conviction that informed Malcolm's eventual embrace of orthodox Islam. It wasn't simply theologically sounder than what the Nation of Islam could teach. Orthodox Islamic ethics are also more extensive and rigorous. Malcolm's reinvention was not about the ecstasy of indefinite self-transformation. It was revolutionary discipline. Before Islam, Malcolm said, "I considered myself beyond atheism – I was Satan" (X, 1999, p. 201).

Žižek's reading of Malcolm X is so roughshod that it becomes vulnerable to a more basic Islamic reading that we should entertain for the sake of argument and as contrast with the eventual uniqueness of Malcolm's subjectivity we should actually be exploring. For the basic Islamic reading of Malcom's transformation would recognize Malcolm's subjective experiment but only as a mere prelude to his truer Islamic destiny.[3] After all, Malcolm did eventually renounce the X to adopt a more fitting Islamic name in el-Hajj Malik el-Shabazz. The el-Hajj is not a proper name, but the title earned upon the completion of the Hajj, the pilgrimage to Mecca that makes one of the five pillars of Islam. This could be easily interpreted to mean that Malcolm eventually arrived at the realization of a new universality beyond that of the Judeo-Christian tradition he once belonged to. Malcolm's story as a long-winded journey into Islam is in fact frequently evoked as an example of how Islam stands for the true universal, that where the story of Western progress is exhausted, Islam offers a more invigorated feel of a palpable future. Perhaps more importantly, the mainstream Islamic claim to Malcolm X has the virtue of retaining Malcolm's commitment to a collective politics, which Žižek's highly individualistic interpretation altogether precludes or diminishes.

If the Žižekian reduction and the orthodox Islamic claim to Malcolm X are equally superficial it is because they ignore what is perhaps the most crucial aspect of Malcolm's radicality, and that is his Black nationalism.[4] Žižek wants to sidestep this to emphasize the emptiness that enabled the subjective experimentation that led Malcolm to Islam, while the orthodox Islamic standpoint evokes Islam to show that the experimentation with Black Islam was just a prelude to the eventual meeting with the Truth. Both avoid the crucial fact that Malcolm's most iconic soundbites, lectures, and events – from which we can know and recall his radical politics – were from the 12 years he was a dedicated member of the Nation of Islam. In fact, Malcolm's autobiography, which for all its issues remains the most authoritative document of his life and teachings, would not mention orthodox Islam at all until later in the last two chapters when Mecca is discussed, that is to say until his immersion into the Nation's teachings was already extensively referenced. What we know most of Malcolm in other words was grounded in his conviction, however temporary, in the distinct worldview upheld by the Nation. This should remind us that his conversion to proper Islam was fundamentally sparked by a moral disagreement. It was a departure against the Nation's leadership's hypocrisy, more so than their doctrine, that eventually led Malcolm to Sunni Islam. Malcolm long maintained his affinity with the Nation's teachings despite regular meetings and conversations with orthodox Muslims in the Islamic world. In other words, the Nation of Islam's idiosyncratic teachings were always a given among other non-Black and non-American Muslims. For it wasn't orthodoxy, a true pure Islam, that Malcolm was ultimately after. He wanted a vision of the Black man's place in the world that translated into emancipatory politics. In this, the Nation's ethnocentrism enabled Malcolm to grasp the Black man's intrinsic value, something which he long had difficulties discovering on his own (indeed it was something he had never thought about before he knew of the Nation). Actually, Malcolm never rejected the Nation of Islam. He had to leave because he was forced out.

The challenge of affirming the Nation's primacy in Malcolm's outlook is compounded by what is perhaps the most complicated aspect of Malcolm's nationalism, in that it was a nationalism that was intrinsically internationalist. Internationalism consequently was a defining feature throughout Malcolm's politics, whereby the Black-American struggle was always conceived as one with other decolonization projects across the world. The parochialism presumed in the Žižekian critique of Black nationalism is therefore a gross distortion of what was taking place. For the Nation of Islam's unique political outlook was what actually enabled Malcolm's international appeal. Indeed where the Blackness essential to the Nation's teachings ensured their relevance to American history, Islam afforded Black nationalism a viable international face. This strategy was most evident in the Nation's use of Muslim names. Muhammad Ali's visit to Africa expanded the Nation's international standing because of his name's commonplace familiarity. Here, the Lacanian concern with naming could be oriented to a different set of symbolic possibilities. Muhammad Ali saw the simplicity of his name as the reason for the fanfare he received: "The name is in Ethiopia, Morocco, Syria, Indonesia, Pakistan, Turkey, Algiers, Saudi Arabia. Muhammad Ali [was a common name] when I travelled. Muhammad is the most common name in the world" (Roberts & Smith, 2016). As the report concludes,

> In Africa, Ali discovered that he was more popular abroad than at home. While most Americans refused to recognize his Muslim name, strangers, writers, and dignitaries in Ghana, Nigeria, and Egypt showed him respect by acknowledging it. Everywhere he went people cheered his name like he was *their* champion, a Black hero whose name mattered as much as his accomplishments in the ring.
>
> (Roberts & Smith, 2016)

The international symbolic presumed in these name changes means that we would be wrong to think of it as a fringe Islamic move. It is not uncommon that non-Muslim African-American radicals, nationalists, activists and artists would adopt Muslim names to signal their refusal of Western identity. William Emanuel Huddleston became Yusuf Lateef, Leroi Jones became Amiri Baraka, Dana Elaine Owens became Queen Latifah, Jonathan William Davis became Kamaal Ibn John Fareed aka Q-Tip, Dante Terrell Smith became Yaasin Bei. Islam did not emerge as a refusal of a past that enabled Malcolm's epiphany. It was already by that point an established political alternative, and we can only grasp this if we situate the African-American struggle within the broader wave of decolonial politics and its persistent presence in mainstream political imagination.

This should complicate any attempt to frame Malcolm within a pre and post-Sunni binary to recast his conversion instead as a traversal of a global symbolic, as he was very much a part of the internationalization of African-American nationalism. This should also orient us from a temporal to a spatial plane. Malcolm's turn to Sunnism, unlike how the film depicts it, was not in any case a sudden conversion. It occurred over time through various overtures to Africa and the Middle East. We cannot avoid the fact that Malcolm's Islam for most of his life was steeped in the Nation's teaching. This remained the case even throughout his engagement with the Islamic world. Malcolm X took a total of four trips to Africa and the Middle East. Out of the four, two took place in 1959 as an ambassador for the Nation of Islam. This was when Malcolm visited Egypt (where he met with Gamal Abdel Nasser at the height of Nasser's power), Iran (the first country in the world to feature Malcolm X in a stamp), Syria, Saudi Arabia, Sudan, Nigeria and Ghana. It was upon returning to America, as the Nation's ambassador, that he declared the importance of an international front. But more importantly Malcolm's global awareness did not amount to a total abandonment of Black identity. What Malcolm found in his international travels was the possibility of a middle point between an exclusive Black nationalism and a Black nationalism that could be a portal for an honest conversation with whites, as he himself remarked clearly here:

> One of the major troubles that I was having in building the organisation that I wanted – an all – black organisation whose ultimate objective was to help create a society in which there could exist honest white–black brotherhood – was that my earlier public image, my old so-called "Black Muslim" image, kept blocking me.
>
> (X, 1999, p. 454)

But even then, Malcolm was clear that Islamic monotheism was crucial for Blacks to be successfully a part of this mission:

I said to Harlem street audiences that only when mankind would submit to the One God who created all - only then would mankind even approach the "peace" of which so much talk could be heard ... but toward which so little action was seen.

(X, 1999, p. 455)

Islam and Blackness remained crucial features of Malcolm's political outlook even after his embrace of Sunni orthodoxy where he had grasped a more nuanced view of whiteness and the world. Decolonization was embraced as an opening for an internationalism for Black upliftment, not an internationalism that led to an abstract humanity:

It was there in the Holy Land, and later in Africa, that I formed a conviction which I have had ever since – that a topmost requisite for any Negro leader in America ought to be extensive traveling in the non-white lands on this earth, and the travel should include many conferences with the ranking men of those lands. I guarantee that any honest, open-minded Negro leader would return home with more effective thinking about alternative avenues to solutions of the American black man's problem.

(X, 1999, p. 421)

We cannot dismiss Malcolm's nationalism without at the same time dismissing what remains perhaps the most crucial aspect of Malcolm's legacy, and that is his international appeal as a figure of defiance, discipline, and spiritual awakening. We therefore face the difficulty of affirming Malcolm's radical legacy as formed in the Real of American race relations, while having to recognize the inextricable role Black nationalism played in articulating the politics that produced his subjectivity. To address this, we should pay attention to what Malcolm himself saw in the nationalism that was offered to him in light of the concrete socio-political conditions in which Black nationalism at the time was expressed. Additionally, we should also address the intricacies of American Blackness's engagement and use of "Islam", particularly how it transformed what was a marginal belief system in the American landscape into a universal signifier. We can do so by looking at the spatial imaginary therein as unique to Black-American nationalism as a nationalism of the dispossessed. Like any nationalism it responded to the need for place. In recovering from the historical trauma of slavery this was a redemptive response, one that must account for the loss Black Americans endured in the modernity that was to emerge in the wake of abolition. But where Black nationalism was unique was that it could not simply treat any territory as it wished. As a post-colonial nationalism of former slaves, they expressed a nationalism of the displacement particular to the Blacks across the North Atlantic for they were outsiders to both the West *and* Africa. Consequently, the question of identification was also troubled. It was here in their unique impasse of displacement that Islam served as a globalizing signifier for the Nation of Islam's ambitions, with the X marking a geographical pivot to be a part of an international space among Muslims across Africa and the Middle East. Islam gave the Nation a bridge to communicate the plight of Blacks to other Islamic nations where more expansive alliances of anti-colonial solidarity could be forged. An imaginary of global solidarity allowed for a decolonial spatiality the Nation of Islam could not have in America. But while this afforded the Nation global recognition, it also subjected them to further scrutiny, as their beliefs and practices were revealed to diverge significantly from mainstream Islam. This is the real tension that shows the 'X' to mark a pivot to a different set of historical antagonisms, that is to say from the peripheries of American politics to the center of global Islamic decolonization. This is consequently also where we should situate the formation of Malcolm's self-image, namely, as an imaginary constantly reshaped within the gaps across differing spatio-temporalities. The misidentifications formed within the gap informs what I shall describe as "symbolic dispossession". To explore this further we need to begin by first approaching Black nationalism for the complex phenomenon it was.

The real of the return

Žižek's chronic aversion toward "the Return to Africa" is a good place to start. To begin with, Africa as discourse and political impulse was always a futuristic space crystalized in the anticipation of an emancipated Black situation to come. This resonated across the 19th until the early 20th century when nationalism germinated across the globe, no doubt due to the global extent of European imperialism, to become a universally viable political project. In this regard the back-to-Africa movement grew in tandem with a Western intellectual current. Consequently, the return to Africa was often framed and spoken of openly, even by its Black advocates, as a form of colonization. As a movement that grew from descendants of slaves across the Americas, the back-to-Africa vision was particularly urgent to ensure that the quest for self-determination was met with a corresponding place. But this was not conquest in the name of "discovery" and plunder. It was the pursuit of land upon a history of dispossession. Having land was a material demand for an entire people who were integral to but were then excluded from, the gains of American industry and modernity. It was in this compelling viability of returning to actual land that the back-to-Africa movement acquired its intellectual salience. It is not the yearning for a tribal identity.

But the sheer immensity of what constitutes Africa, not to mention the complexity of origins for descendants of slaves in the new world, meant that the return was articulated in various ways, not all of which were compatible, coherent nor noble. Marcus Garvey wanted to be the President of the entirety of Africa construed as a contiguously united territory and polity. For

Rastafarians in Jamaica, a return to Africa specifically meant Ethiopia under the leadership of the divine Haile Sellasi. Others saw a return to origins not in Africa but in Haiti as the first republic of slave revolt. But these demands, as outlandish as they may appear to the culturally sensitive and more geographically informed ears of the internet era, should be squared with the fact that the return to Africa was a "success" in the very narrow but not insignificant sense that it ultimately birthed actual polities. Liberia was established as a state for freed American slaves. Sierra Leone, first named the Province of Freedom, was established by the British as a refuge for freed slaves. After Independence Kwame Nkrumah, who lived in the United States for a decade, offered Ghana as a destination for members of the African diaspora who wished to return to Africa. We find traces of this outreach in 2019, the year marking 400 years since the first African slaves arrived in Virginia, North America, when Ghana launched the "Year of Return" to encourage the African diaspora to invest in the country.

Consequently, if we are to speak of the actual failures along the way, we should find them from within the tensions in the spatial imaginaries of these purported successes. The literal return to Africa was short-lived because there turned out to be little popular uptake. In the United States, the very thought of uprooting to Africa did not appeal to the latter generation of freed slaves who identified themselves more as Americans than Africans. They insisted that they were less Africans than their white compatriots were British. But that's not all. The return to Africa's success and visibility as a political project owed much to its white-racist benefactors who wanted to rid Africans from America altogether. These reasons, alongside the high financial, logistical and emotional costs of relocation over oceanic distances, ensured that it remained a fringe sentiment and a short-lived movement. There were also tensions that arose in Liberia and Sierra Leone among the settling Americo-Liberians and the Sierra Leone Creole people – in other words of freed slaves and their descendants – and local native Africans. The fact that Liberia was founded by repatriated Americans also tainted its value as a redemptive, fully liberatory, project for the likes of radicals like Marcus Garvey. The political currents in any case changed as the majority of American Blacks felt it more compelling to channel their resources and energy toward the Civil Rights struggle where the opportunities for actual gains were more tangible. This was evident in how the Nation of Islam eventually committed to local repatriation to demand the establishment of a separate Black nation within the United States itself. The point in noting the always-already widely recognized impossibility of the repatriation movement is that it simply proves that "Africa" for Black nationalism was as much a problem as it was a solution. It was never merely idealized space. It was pursued as an enigma more than a crystalized destination.

There was also the fact that for Black nationalists in North America, the appeal for an alternative space in early 20th-century Black nationalism occurred alongside the spatial dispossession in the First Great Migration. This lasted approximately from 1916 to 1940, when millions of Blacks from the American South fleeing Jim Crow, and the increase in systematic segregation more broadly, moved to the North for greater opportunities and a life free of racism. Demographically, this entailed a rapid increase in the Black population of the major Northern cities which also saw an unprecedented flourishing of Black cosmopolitanism unlike any other time before. The Harlem Renaissance, to take what is likely the most familiar event of this period, was notable because of authors such as Langston Hughes and Zora Neale Hurston who were migrants from the South. Jazz also found new heights at this time because of musicians who migrated from the South such as Louis Armstrong, Bessie Smith, and Jelly Roll Morton. But the blossoming was also fueled by the similarly heightened confidence in collective Blackness. The migration did not only reveal the North's racist reality, it also galvanized, as a result, the demand for more radical ideas. It was indeed after arriving where the American promise of freedom was supposed to materialize, upon the cultural and geographical schism of migration, that the more utopian strain of Black nationalism found mass uptake. For the thousands of Blacks incorporated into the Northern industrial labor force, this meant some variant of far-left ideas. Black Communists James Yates and Harry Haywood, for example, were migrants from the South, as was James Boggs, husband of Grace Lee Boggs. The link between the possibility of a new politics and the fragmentation of space and identity in the great migration is an important detail for our discussion because it constitutes a crucial backdrop in Malcolm's autobiography. His father Earl Little, a Baptist preacher and supporter of Marcus Garvey, moved his family from Omaha, Nebraska to Lansing, Michigan in anticipation of the better life the North was supposed to provide. Things took a turn for the worse when Earl was killed for his outspoken activism. Malcolm was just 6 years old but the loss bitterly taught him the deep extent to which racism is entrenched in the American psyche. This was learned in the North's broken promise of a better life, but the more pressing lesson was how this just invented a more dangerous Black man:

> America's most dangerous and threatening black man is the one who has been kept sealed up by the Northerner in the black ghettoes - the Northern white power structure's system to keep talking democracy while keeping the black man out of sight somewhere, around the corner.
> (X, 1999, p. 335)

This detail is important to locate the anti-coloniality of Malcolm's eventual embrace of the X. It is, like the Žižekian position wants to emphasize, about the loss of a past. But this is a past defined, temporalized in fact, out of the trauma of geographical fragmentation encountered for the want of history

It was in the political disappointment found in the spatial fissures of migration that we should similarly understand why the Nation of Islam found its earliest successes in Detroit and Chicago. They were among the major Northern cities that owed their rapid urbanization in the early 20th century to the influx of Southern Blacks. The Nation of Islam in fact found its earliest members among the poorest of this demographic. The Honorable Elijah Muhammad, the self-proclaimed Messenger of Allah who led the Nation of Islam to the heights of their national fame in the 1940s and 1950s, was himself a Southern migrant to Detroit from Georgia. But the fact that this demographic was twice displaced and disappointed, as descendants of slaves fleeing the Christian South for the new but equally racist Northern geographies, could account for the extended spatialities that make up the Nation's cosmology. Africa was expectedly for the Nation a foil with which an alternative space exclusively for Blacks could be conceived and in this regard, the Nation's outlook resonated with the diasporic currents of African nationalism described above. But that the Nation construed Africa Islamically meant that their mythology evoked signifiers beyond Africa. Biblical figures and tales are recounted but now woven with icons of other spaces. The claims – that Mecca is a spiritual state of mind more than a physical location, that Black Americans are actually the lost tribe of Shabazz who originated from the Arabian Peninsula, that the earliest Black men were "Asiatic," and that the human races were invented 6,000 years ago by a mythical Greek scientist named Yakub - saw the notion of Africa and the Black "nation," and with this "the Abrahamic," cosmically outstretched. Islam by this is prominent as a signifier that is replete throughout the Nation's beliefs, teachings, ceremonies and rituals, but as a pivot to new spatial imaginations that mutated the possible meanings of Africa and Blackness. Add to all this, claims to extraterrestrial space: according to the Nation of Islam, prophecy is fulfilled by the Wheel, also known as "the Mother Plane," which by all accounts is not of this earth. The Black-American's impossibility of territorial identification produced a proliferation of territorial imaginaries "beyond".

The widespread and sporadic evocations of foreign lands overlapped, and no doubt had much to do, with the equally enigmatic identity of the man who first relayed this cosmology: the founder of the Nation of Islam, silk-coat seller and Allah incarnate Master Wallace Fard Muhammad.

John Andrew Morrow's (2023) rigorous study concludes that Fard was very likely a Ghulat Shia from present-day Balochistan, Pakistan. But this was only a recent claim after decades of unresolved speculations that Fard could have been white, light-skinned Black, Turkish, Arab, Azeri, Afghan Persian, Bengali, or Punjabi. His constant travels and name changes, which are traced to state documents and news clippings from across the West Coast of the United States, make it difficult to piece together an authoritative, non-contradictory, biography. What could be drawn with certainty was that he dedicated himself to building the very organizational foundations that enabled the Nation of Islam to grow into a nationwide force. He also disappeared suddenly, leaving no indication that he had used the Nation's wealth for self-enrichment. Master Fard was an eloquent and charismatic orator who spoke with a distinct although unidentifiable accent. He could read and write the Arabic script (which was either Ottoman or Urdu). He was also arrested for a contentious murder accusation and was last spotted at the US–Mexican border fleeing arrest. He also claimed to be Allah incarnate on numerous occasions, even when he was interrogated by the police. These historical details and questions do not amount to a merely intellectual problem. The various signifiers of the other spaces and names Fard were associated with continue to pervade speculations around the truth of his identity, and consequently the merits of his teachings. [5] They persist in fact in some of the key debates in the Nation of Islam after Malcolm's death, namely on whether the Nation was to tow the orthodox Sunni line or retain their distinct African-nationalist outlook.

In any case, Malcolm himself took little issue with the myths that structured the Nation's teachings and the vision of the world they offered. For example, "The white man is the devil," uttered matter of factly so many times throughout the autobiography, was not just political sloganeering. It was very much tied to how the Nation saw the world. Malcolm's spiritual awakening was in fact sparked by what he took to be the Nation's most important provocation against his political complacency, namely, that American Blacks were the original people and the whites were originally colored. Malcolm's adoption of this outlook was informed by Master Fard's teaching about the global white hierarchy and how it originated from a mistake in Yakub's experiment. Whites evolved from Yakub's whitening of Black people during which they were discovered to be immoral and had to be expelled as devils. The eventual enslavement of Blacks by whites, and the former's eventual fate in America, was an extension of this story. It offered a theodicy to explain how slavery affords Black Americans unique insight into the true nature of the white man's evil: "It was written that some of the original Black people should be brought as slaves to North America - to learn to better understand, at first hand, the white devil's true nature, in modern times" (X, 1999, p. 215). The ambiguity behind Master Fard's own racial identity was also justified in this light: "he was made this way to enable him to be accepted by the Black people in America, and to lead them, while at the same time he was enabled to move undiscovered among the white people, so that he could understand and judge the enemy of the Blacks" (X, 1999, p. 217).

Malcolm credits this discovery for triggering the vociferous search for Black knowledge that underlined his political maturity. Claims that the Original Man – the hypothetical first human – Moses, Aesop, Homer, Jesus, St Paul, and Spinoza were Black were made without irony. Africa and the Islamic world, and the greater sphere of decolonization that was activating across the Third World – was revealed and discovered through Malcolm's conviction in this mythology. The internationalism other Black radicals may have found from a Marxist-informed dialectical view of world history, Malcolm found in the Nation's cosmology. Nowhere was this more evident than in the hours of readings Malcolm spent in the prison library, where his beliefs in the Nation's teachings were further affirmed as he learned more about decolonial developments around the world at the same time. Interestingly, it was in this trajectory of autodidactic discovery that Malcolm remarkably foresaw how whiteness will be threatened by the coming of what we today call a "multipolar" world and how China, owing to its continental size and massive population, will rise in response to the centuries of colonial subjugation it suffered. Malcolm's negativity was a lack in the excess of historical possibilities beyond the West.

Part 2: From identification to dispossession

The richness with which Africa was discoursed, for all its factual issues, should at least point to the simple point that the "outside" of the Black symbolic was not the white gaze. It was the space of African possibilities in which the gazing as such had not crystallized into a master-slave dyad. But this outside had to be construed in spatial terms. Islam or Pan-Africanism was presented to also articulate the desire for another space for Black Americans. Where the early heights of the back-to-Africa discourse appealed to national affiliation, Islam soon emerged among North American Black Africans as a way of stabilizing their spatial unknown, wherein the gap could be extended for newer political possibilities. Thus Islam did not just offer an identity for the Black man. It provided Black nationalism with a new spatiality. The point here, however, is not simply to recognize how the Nation's Islam provided Malcolm with a tangible world to symbolize his subjectivity. Rather it located Malcolm in a world of dispossession, one that could not be rationalized into a map, from a symbolic order that was equally dispossessed upon centuries of displacement. And we are able to understand the contradictory map that was produced when we consider the real spatial crisis that defined the African-American nationalist predicament as a nationalism of displacement. Black-nationalist spatiality – from the desire for Africa to the harking to Islam – was imagined where the dispossession from centuries of slavery converged with the cultural and geographic dispossession in the First Great Migration. Nowhere was this displacement more obvious than how signifiers of differing spaces pervaded their discourse, where Africa and Islam were brought together geographically and cosmologically to ground Black politics into a spirituality. In a world of rising nationalism of territorial claims, the Nation's Afro-centric Islamic imaginary stood out for a symbolic arrangement that was neither here nor there: The constellations of terms, myths and narratives that formed the Nation of Islam's outlook were neither African nor American, neither Muslim nor non-Muslim, neither nostalgic nor futuristic.

Thus if Malcolm could eventually relinquish his affiliation with the Nation it was because the spatial imaginary the Nation offered was not containable. It linked Malcolm to farther global imaginaries. Indeed, Malcolm's eventual embrace of orthodox Islam was a horizontal rather than a vertical path, by which identification dissolved from a transferential Other to a new transitory space. In this regard "Islam" marked an interstitial space between identificatory events: the failure of identification with the Nation and the identification with Islam. Consequently, Malcolm's sinthome manifested across spatial displacements. Indeed, unique to Malcolm's embrace of Sunnism was the absence of a replacement father figure. Elijah Muhammad may have filled the void in the wake of Earl Little's death, with both being allegories of Malcolm's transition across different ideologies. That Master Fard was the personification of God on earth, who was to be contrasted with the white man as the personification of the devil on earth, was a significant turning point for Malcolm's radical paradigm shift. It enabled Malcolm to look back to the personal encounters with white men he had throughout his life as an encounter with systemic racism. But Malcolm left the Nation without any need for a substitute authority figure. Unlike what is so typical to Islamic-conversion narratives, Malcolm did not lean on a senior religious patriarch in place of the void. Nor did he find an alternative community in the form of a mosque or an Islamic center. His new Islamic subjectivity was rather formed in different figures – from Shorty, Bimbi, his sister Ella, and later the various Muslim pilgrims – met in the real flow of international spaces. To recognize the possibility of this flow, however, is to acknowledge another time imbued in the evocation of "Islam" itself, a compelling antagonism that parallels, indeed rivals, that of Western temporality. In other words, if the spatiality of displacement in African nationalism enabled Malcolm's eventual movement to Islam, then we must also identify the workings of two temporalities therein, the temporality in the African-American condition and its use of Islam on one hand, and the temporality of Islam beyond America, on the other.

The transition from a temporal location within the Western symbolic, to an identification with spaces beyond the West, could be discerned in the crisis of transference that underlines Black-nationalist American Islam by which the "elsewhere" space it requires had to be first instantiated in the form of an actual African-American person. This no doubt had to do with the temporality presumed in the Nation's political project, as it points to a higher stage of liberation beyond the freedom offered by American liberalism. The Nation's Islam, as an outlook from another space, is consequently imbued with the promise of another time "beyond". The ability to see the Honorable Elijah Muhammad as God's Messenger in the flesh certainly added to the palpability of this belief. Malcolm himself drew this conclusion not long after his first meeting with the Honorable Elijah Muhammad: "There is a dimension of time with which we are not familiar here in the West" (X, 1999,

p. 240). And it was difficult not to be persuaded. Malcolm X wasn't the only one who owed his spiritual awakening to the Honorable Messenger. Muhammad Ali also publicly professed the same on many occasions. What was at stake was how Elijah Muhammad ushered a world of new symbolic possibilities for the Black masses:

> This is one reason why Mr. Muhammad's teachings spread so swiftly all over the United States, among all Negroes, whether or not they became followers of Mr. Muhammad. The teachings ring true to every Negro. You can hardly show me a black adult in America a white one, for that matter-who knows from the history books anything like the truth about the black man's role.
>
> (X, 1999, p. 223)

Indeed, for a considerable portion of the *Autobiography*, Islam and the Honorable Elijah Muhammad's teachings about the cosmic tension between the white man and the Black man's fate were interchangeable: "now Islam meant more to me than anything I ever had known in my life. Islam and Mr. Elijah Muhammad had changed my whole world" (X, 1999, p. 237).

But that this necessarily evoked a longer-standing historical Islam with historical antagonisms beyond America, meant that the transference the Nation demanded must always contend with similarly another historical logic. Indeed, we shall be reading Malcolm X closely to chart this temporal divergence and his eventual overcoming of it, a reading that will be aided through a consideration that inevitably leads us to Islam's distinct global-historical temporality. What we must do beforehand, to avoid isolating Malcolm X's journey, is to outline how the crisis of identification he underwent was not unique to his standpoint. It was in fact rooted in the longer-standing challenge of adapting a *global* Islam for the *American* Black-nationalist symbolic order.

The problem of personifying Islam to the American Black-nationalist ideal extended from the earlier Black Islam that came by way of Noble Drew Ali, another migrant from the South to the North, and the Moorish Science Temple of America he founded (of which, according to the FBI at least, Master Fard was once a member). "Islam" here would be introduced by way of *The Holy Koran of the Moorish Science Temple of America*. This bears little relation to the actual Quran of orthodox Islam as the former actually consists of a cosmology accounting for the Black man's origins as an Asiatic Moor. These terms are peculiar to the Temple's view of the world. "Asiatic" appears to be what is today "West Asia" or the Mediterranean, and is regarded as where the scripture was revealed. Moor in turn refers roughly to present-day Morocco and West Africa. These spaces are not arbitrary. They map onto Ali's own prophetic journey. Ali claimed to have acquired his divine wisdom when he met an Egyptian magician in his travels who then declared Ali to be the reincarnation of Jesus, Buddha, and Muhammad. This was to amount to the message that the "Black man" is irreducible to his Blackness and the white man's gaze, but is rather intrinsically human, based on a divine conception of the universal. In fact, the rejection of the slave name as an affirmation of Blackness, a rejection that would be so common among latter-day African-American radicals, began as a gesture among the Moors before the Nation.

Indeed we look further to find that the Black-American crisis of identification was not limited to senior figures in mass movements. Similar claims to Black divinity could be found in a contemporary of Malcolm's and another X: the karateka, schizophrenic and Civil Rights activist Clarence 13X (government name Clarence Edward Smith, another migrant to the North) who left the Nation of Islam to form the New York City-based Five-Percent Nation (sometimes referred to as the Nations of Gods and Earth). Clarence 13X's more radical claim, after officially renaming himself as Allah upon the belief that he was God incarnate, was that every Black individual is divine. This was an egalitarian ethos that he offered as an alternative to the Nation of Islam's highly rigid and hierarchical mode of organization. Its membership dwindled after Smith's death and no leader-figure was elected to replace him since.

To this we can add the indispensable impact of Ahmadiyya Muslim missionaries among Black Americans after the First World War. The Nation's massive growth of membership in Chicago and Detroit was widely recognized as an overlapping effect of the popularization of Islam that the Ahmadiyya Muslims had undertaken in the 1920s. Led by Mufti Muhammad Sadiq from present-day Pakistan and then Muhammad Din from present-day West Bengal, and informed by a clear anti-British, anti-colonial outlook, the Ahmadis concentrated and propagated their outreach in the Midwest in terms of racial equality to attract masses of new converts from the disenfranchised Black population in the region. This ensured a certain cosmopolitanism in Islam's earliest days in America, given the Ahmadiyya's largely South Asian, as opposed to Middle Eastern, base. This, however, did not amount to a separate channel of American-Islamic history. The Ahmadi's outreach marked a significant embedding of Islam into the fabric of American life. The Al-Sadiq mosque in Chicago, the oldest-standing purpose-built mosque in America today, is an Ahmadiyyah mosque. They will, however, inevitably stand out for representing the Promised Messiah and Mahdi in the form of 19th-century Islamic scholar Mirza Ghulam Ahmad, an assertion that continues to stoke the ire and accusations of heresy from Sunnis and Shias alike. In any case, it is widely documented that Master Wallace Fard was among the members of the Ahmadiyya's growing Midwestern flock and remixed much of the Ahmadiyya's theological premises, not least the present-day availability of the Messiah, into the teachings he later conveyed as the Nation of Islam's. The fact that Elijah Muhammad referred to himself as the Mahdi, as Malcolm himself chronicled in his autobiography, does speak to the Ahmadi–Nation affinity. As Fatimah

Fanusie concludes, "The Nation of Islam and the overwhelming Muslim presence among African-Americans prior to the 1965 Asian Immigration Act can be traced directly to Ahmadiyya missionary work" (Fanusie, 2008, p. 36). Indeed the Ahmadiyya's religious and organizational influence on the Nation of Islam, particularly through the former's earliest purchase among Black Americans, continue to be a topic of scholarly interest.

It will be easy to disregard these events and figures as mutations of a distant past, whose legacy is pertinent only during a brief burst of radical activity in the antagonisms of the interwar years. This is unless we expand our notion of politics to also include cultural breakthroughs. Legendary hip-hop duo Eric B. and Rakim (whose full moniker is Rakim Allah) are avowed Five Percenters.[6] The "Kane" in Big Daddy Kane actually stands for King Asiatic Nobody's Equal. The entirety of *Enter the Wu-Tang (36 Chambers)* was inspired by Five-Percenter teaching. The album's producer, RZA, even went so far as to say "About 80 percent of hip-hop comes from the Five Percent ... In a lot of ways, hip-hop *is* the Five Percent" (RZA as cited in Baker, 2022). RZA, like his brother and fellow Wu-Tang Clan member GZA, chose their stage names based on the Supreme Alphabet shaped by Five-Percenter mythology as an esoteric reading of the deeper meanings behind the Latin alphabet. The Z, without going too far into Five-Percenter esoterism, stands for "zig-zag", referring to the enlightenment of the self (a kind of post-colonial short-circuiting if you please). The A stands for Allah. This is far less of a remnant than one might think. SZA is the latest artist to take on this symbolism. As an article reports: "Dropping knowledge (and science), Dropping jewels, Word is bond, Word, Cipher, Peace, Building, Seeds (as in offspring), etc., are all phrases that are heavily tied to 5% lexicon" (Quan, 2022). It is not widely recognized, but Ahmadi Islam was also influential in American jazz history: Ahmad Jamal, Yusuf Lateef, Art Blakey (whose band the Jazz Messengers was named after the Ahmadi message), and McCoy Tyner, to name just a few jazz legends, converted to Ahmadiyya Islam.[7] While he did not become Ahmadi, John Coltrane's *A Love Supreme*, largely regarded as one of the most spiritually and politically significant albums in the history of music anywhere, was informed by Ahmadi Islam. Needless to say, this shows just how much Islam extended the possible meaning of African-American nationalism to inspire subjective experimentation. Put in psychoanalytic terms, the real is met in the unfolding threads of symbolic dispossession rather than to be awaited in the disruption of the transferential dyad in imaginary identification.

Part 3: Malcolm's symbolization of the Muslim body

Malcolm's subjective experimentations occurred along a similar trajectory of dispossession, but his politics took him to more radical conclusions. Noting Malcolm's divergence, however, requires that we first read the autobiography for an account of how the signifiers produced in the above amalgamation of

symbolic re-arrangements were internalized particularly where the production of another body, a cleansed and disciplined body free from crime, vice
and indulgence, was key. Symbolic dispossession consequently is felt where
language was deployed to recognize the new corporeal demands.

Malcolm was sensitive, from the onset, to how being a Muslim meant manifesting an entirely different set of moral codes determined upon equally new
expectations of physical conduct. Ablution, prayer and fasting, in addition to
the temperate body required in more sacred spaces, were described as new and
alien habits to his long life as a renegade and criminal. Note how this new set of
bodily demands took Malcolm to the unspeakable:

> The hardest test I ever faced in my life was praying … But bending my
> knees to pray – that act – well, that took me a week. You know what my
> life had been. Picking a lock to rob someone's house was the only way
> my knees had ever been bent before. I had to force myself to bend my
> knees. And waves of shame and embarrassment would force me back up.
> For evil to bend its knees, admitting its guilt, to implore the forgive-
> ness of God, is the hardest thing in the world … Again, again, I would
> force myself back down into the praying-to-Allah posture. When finally I
> was able to make myself stay down – I didn't know what to say to
> Allah.
>
> (X, 1999, p. 218)

The unspeakable moreover was a new opening. Malcolm did not detail the
theological precepts underlying his embrace of the new codes but one reads on to
find him clearly subscribed to the Nation's unique teaching. The Nation demanded for a liquid-only breakfast and "the Messenger" so frequently mentioned at
this portion of the book clearly meant Elijah Muhammad (although it isn't
always clear if the Allah Malcolm mentioned at these sections of the autobiography refers to Master Fard as the Nation deemed, or Allah as the ultimate
monotheistic God that orthodox Islam upholds). It also appears that the Nation
only demanded two prayers a day as opposed to the standard Islamic five. So
while Malcolm claimed that the rituals were performed "in unity with the rest of
our 725 million brothers and sisters in the entire Muslim world," it is also clear
that this was done under an entirely different set of ideas the Nation propagated
(X, 1999, p. 245). But this newfound spirituality was where Malcolm cultivated
the new corporeality to account for his transformation into an African-American
nationalist with the Nation of Islam:

> I have sat at our Messenger's feet, hearing the truth from his own mouth!
> I have pledged on my knees to Allah to tell the white man about his
> crimes and the Black man the true teachings of our Honorable Elijah
> Muhammad. I don't care if it costs my life …
>
> (X, 1999, p. 264)

The body is also central to the humbling lessons Malcolm faced at the Hajj where his experience of Islam also expanded. But this was not merely the adoption of an entirely new set of rituals, as if Malcolm was simply incorporating new factoids. The embodiment of orthodox Islamic rituals also occurred upon a major political break. Taking place after his fallout with Elijah Muhammad, and a rift with the Nation of Islam's notable activists, Malcolm by this time had effectively parted with the man and organization he credited so much for his moral rebirth and self-esteem as an activist and public intellectual. He knew by this point that he had to avail himself of another transformation. For this, he turned to the global community of Muslims that he had also previously addressed. But where before "Islam" was referenced merely generally and rhetorically, and often only when it suited the Nation's theology or message, the Hajj saw Malcolm counted as one of "them". Malcolm became exposed to the sheer vastness of the Islamic world, of a world that was in many ways only superficially dealt with in the Nation's teaching. Our interest in the psychoanalytic implications of this transformation, however, should pay attention to Malcolm's realization not only of the Hajj's physicality, being a grueling ritual that demands a certain robustness, but how poorly the Nation's teachings prepared his *body* for orthodoxy. But this does not see Malcolm merely recounting the link between physical and spiritual transformation. This sees the transformation situated in a global symbolic, by which his subjectivity as a subjectivity of dispossession becomes more evident. The past awkwardly trailed Malcolm's transformation where his body's failure was exposed as it had to adopt the new demands of Islam as they were found in the fragmented spatialities that shaped the globality of the Islamic symbolic order. If Malcolm's identification with the Nation was situated in Western temporality, Malcolm's identification with Islam's globality saw his identification spatialized.

There is much to draw from what is perhaps the most moving chapter of Malcolm's entire biography, but the following two paragraphs encapsulate the gist of the symbolic dispossession Malcolm underwent at the Hajj:

> Two Egyptian Muslims and a Persian roused and also stared as my guide moved us over into a corner. With gestures, he indicated that he would demonstrate to me the proper prayer ritual postures. Imagine, being a Muslim minister, a leader in Elijah Muhammad's Nation of Islam, and not knowing the prayer ritual. I tried to do what he did. I knew I wasn't doing it right. I could feel the other Muslims' eyes on me. Western ankles won't do what Muslim ankles have done for a lifetime. Asians squat when they sit, Westerners sit upright in chairs. When my guide was down in a posture, I tried everything I could to get down as he was, but there I was, sticking up. After about an hour, my guide left, indicating that he would return later. I never even thought about sleeping. Watched by the Muslims, I kept practising prayer posture. I refused to let myself

think how ridiculous I must have looked to them. After a while, though, I learned a lime trick that would let me get down closer to the floor. But after two or three days, my ankle was going to swell.

As the sleeping Muslims woke up, when dawn had broken, they almost instantly became aware of me, and we watched each other while they went about their business. I began to see what an important role the rug played in the overall cultural life of the Muslims. Each individual had a small prayer rug, and each man and wife, or large group, had a larger communal rug. These Muslims prayed on their rugs there in the compartment. Then they spread a tablecloth over the rug and ate, so the rug became the dining room. Removing the dishes and cloth, they sat on the rug-a living room. Then they curl up and sleep on the rug – a bedroom. In that compartment, before I was to leave it, it dawned on me for the first time why the fence had paid such a high price for Oriental rugs when I had been a burglar in Boston.

(X, 1999, p. 399)

These passages show how the present (Malcolm's encounter with a global mass) is linked with the past (his recollection of rugs) through his struggle to *embody* a new symbolic order. But we shall begin with what is perhaps the most obvious point to this passage, and that is Malcolm's overcoming of the white gaze through "the Muslim gaze." This appeared through the eyes of the other Muslims as they judge Malcom's ability to adapt to Islam's fundamental rituals. But this also signaled a different gaze beyond that of the white (American) gaze which even the Nation of Islam had deeply internalized by then. For Malcolm, to be Muslim was to validate the judgment of Muslims as subjects of an entirely different set of moral codes. Add to this the temporal lag Malcolm manifested as he practiced the ritual movements to force his body into postures that were then totally alien. This reveals the strain of identification unfolding in real time. To become a Muslim was to replicate the moves of another Muslim and to do so, to manifest the orthodox Muslim corporeality, was to drill his body through painful repetitions of unfamiliar physical movements. By this point, it was not enough to merely utter proper Islamic rituals or to grasp certain tenets. Malcolm had to ensure that he materialized Islam as he should have a long time ago. It was during this lag in identification that Malcolm was in effect Muslim and non-Muslim. He realized the deficiencies of the African-nationalist Muslim symbolic, which he already struggled to embody, through realizing the extent to which a different corporeality was needed to become an orthodox, or more properly speaking "global" Muslim. But he understood this only upon the embarrassment of being ignorant as a high-ranking representative of American Islam ("I was angry with myself for not having taken the time to learn more of the orthodox prayer rituals before leaving America. In Elijah Muhammad's Nation of Islam, we hadn't prayed in Arabic") (X, 1999,

p. 400). This gap was reinforced at every point that Malcolm failed to get it right, even when all he had to do was mimic his guide's move. So central was the correct Islamic "comportment" that Malcolm deemed getting the body of identification right as the measure of his proper arrival to Islam. To be a Muslim for him was to be in the same body politic: "Love, humility, and true brotherhood was almost a physical feeling wherever I turned" (X, 1999, p. 396). But this wasn't just about getting the right feeling. Some time after embracing his new orthodox Islamic identity, after extolling the potential for Islam to be a unifying factor across different races, Malcolm declared his arrival to "proper Islam" via how he could finally embody the same object world as his newfound orthodox Muslim brethren:

> My hands now readily plucked up food from a common dish shared with brother Muslims; I was drinking without hesitation from the same glass as others; I was washing from the same little pitcher of water; and sleeping with eight or ten others on a mat in the open. I remember one night at Muzdalifa with nothing but the sky overhead I lay awake amid sleeping Muslim brothers and I learned that pilgrims from every land – every color, and class, and rank; high officials and the beggar alike – all snored in the same language.
>
> (X, 1999, p. 417)

The Real of Malcolm's body had to be symbolized as "Islamic" in a more wide-ranging sense than Malcolm could ever register, in which signifiers of altogether different histories had to be incorporated, that is to say, to be made "body". We can chart indeed a radical transition from a binary view of humanity the Nation provided, which reinforced the symbolic containment the Western colonial order had imposed upon American Blacks, to a vaster, more indeterminate symbolic order across different territories. This was tentatively called "the Islamic world" but it was clear that what Malcolm saw was the immensity of "the global" as a horizontal discovery. When it became overwhelming, and it often did, the masses of pilgrims at the Hajj were listed by nationality and color for Malcolm to make sense of where he was. In this Malcolm gradually chronicled the complexity of whiteness, for he encountered countless fair-skinned and white-complexioned Muslims who showed him a new level of rapport, hospitality and charity he for long did not think was possible for American whites. Indeed he later rebranded his entire post-Nation mission with frequent reference to the kindness he received from the countless whites and fair-skinned Muslims that he encountered in his international travels. Malcolm's anxiety in other words was addressed through the step-by-step traversal of the fragmented spaces that constituted his "global". But to note this is to recognize how Malcolm did not come to this point in a straightforward process of rational deliberation. He arrived to the global, indeed he was invested in it, upon the more fundamental circumstance of symbolic dispossession that underlined his Black subjectivity. There was firstly the dispossession that fueled his embrace of Black-American nationalism, which was worsened by his now public and increasingly violent feud with the Nation. But his discovery of orthodox Islam was by no means a straightforward resolution of these losses. What we find once Malcolm was in Mecca was his disorientation before the sheer immensity of the world before him. The fame that preceded Malcolm's arrival meant that he had the help of eager and kind translators throughout his journey. Indeed, he was welcomed and guided directly by the best minds the Islamic world had to offer. But all this merely stressed the foreignness of his subjectivity and location, a foreignness he forthrightly embraced.

The body of dispossession

If the experience of the Hajj accentuated Malcolm's symbolic dispossession it was not as a new break but an extension of a key feature of Malcolm's journey. Islam was not the first time Malcolm's body had been estranged and if he could avail himself of the dispossession it is because corporeal estrangement had marked his journey the entire time. The reader sensitive to Malcolm's struggle to adapt to Islamic rituals will notice how the body was also evoked in the earlier chapters of his narrative. Recall the lengths and detail with which Malcolm described his experience of "conking", or as he called it "my first really big step toward self-degradation" (X, 1999, p. 89). "Conking" was what many Blacks did to straighten their hair to signify affluence and the greater likelihood of acceptance by whites. But it was particularly of political significance as the first time Malcolm felt the gap between the Black-American real and the desired image he was to uphold for the white Other. He recalled how he was "lost in admiration of my hair now looking white" when he first saw his first-ever fully conked set of hair in the mirror (X, 1999, p. 89). Malcolm's autobiographic retrospection obviously affords a more critical review of this event. As an orthodox Muslim he was able to look back to see: "How ridiculous I was! I vowed that I'd never again be without a conk, and I never was for many years" (X, 1999, p. 89). Key is how this recollection also stressed the extent of full-bodied physical pain a good conk required:

> my head caught fire. I gritted my teeth and tried to pull the sides of the kitchen table together. The comb felt as if it was raking my skin off. My eyes watered, my nose was running. I couldn't stand it any longer; I bolted to the washbasin ... my knees were trembling.
>
> (X, 1999, p. 88)

The state of the body across different levels of political awareness underscored the differences between the old and the new Malcolm. We can distinguish the divergent symbolic cuts by looking into the misrecognition conking demanded. The mirror is a curious piece of detail in this recollection. It had the obvious role of sustaining Malcolm's encounter with the Other's desire: "My first view in the mirror blotted out the hurting. I'd seen some pretty conks, but when it's the first time, on your own head, the transformation, after the lifetime of kinks, is staggering" (X, 1999, p. 89). If this moment was crucial for the misleading "clarity" in the mirror reflection, we should also note the multiple negations - "to never again be without" - with which it would be recalled from Malcolm's "orthodox" standpoint. Malcolm was now reflecting across different versions of himself. But the negations, understood in light of his autobiographical narrative, speaks to the constant clearing enabled by the gaps Malcolm inhabited in his symbolic traversals. We are now able to chart how orthodox Malcolm looked back from having occupied the gaps across different spatial imaginaries. It is noteworthy too that the conking was done less against Blackness itself but Malcolm's indeterminacy. Malcolm was nicknamed Detroit Red because of his naturally red hair (which he later described as "kinky red") which signaled a mixed heritage (X, 1999, pp. 394–395). This and his clearly lighter complexion than other Blacks had always made him stand out to both Blacks and whites. But key is how this was a self-consciousness Malcolm had to register across the country, when he moved from Michigan after his father's death to Boston and then to New York City. The red hair was a detail that no doubt intensified his confusion about who he was, a confusion the conk was thought to have eliminated. But it was a confusion that continued to surface at the encounter with new gazes at different spaces.

The clarity of the mirror image, as the image for the Other, and the spatial imaginaries of Black dispossession underlines Malcolm's evocation of sight in his prison years. There are of course the usual metaphors of truth and understanding that came with the clarity the Nation provided him. There was, for example, the decisive evening, while serving time in prison, when he was visited by what he truly believed was Master Fard's mystical apparition. This meeting, or "pre-vision," as Malcolm described it, decisively confirmed his whole embrace of the Nation's political project:

> It's impossible to dream, or to see, or to have a vision of someone whom you never have seen before – and to see him exactly as he is. To see someone, and to see him exactly as he looks, is to have a pre-vision. I would later come to believe that my pre-vision was of Master W. D. Fard, the Messiah, the one whom Elijah Muhammad said had appointed him – Elijah Muhammad – as His Last Messenger to the Black people of North America.
>
> (X, 1999, p. 241)

Indeed, the fact that Elijah Muhammad himself only went as far as a fourth-grade education was significant for Malcolm's faith in his own ability to transcend his state of Black ignorance. With this, the Nation's world of a Manichean struggle between Blacks and whites as it was relayed through the Honorable Elijah Muhammad was something Malcolm also grasped immediately without question. But this was only one spatial imaginary beside the other one he formulated through his struggle to read. What the Nation also triggered in Malcolm was a ceaseless thirst for knowledge, one that was symbolized gradually in his endeavor to be literate. It is here, where signifiers were ordered through the spatial split the Nation ushered, that the clarity acquired in the mirror image began to crack.

The first book that launched the journey, as is well known, was the prison dictionary, and it was the step-by-step learning through every listed word that Malcolm also learned to write. This was described as both an intellectual and corporeal discovery. The words were met in a dizzying state of overwhelm at all the knowledge he had to digest: "I'd never realized so many words existed! I didn't know which words I needed to learn!" (X, 1999, p. 220). Grasping it all meant writing what he learned down. But this also meant learning to write, which first meant confronting his ignorance: "It was sad. I couldn't even write in a straight line" (X, 1999, p. 220). Therein began Malcolm's process of re-symbolization in which a new world, of other spaces, emerged. Note the physicality – the conjoining of new words for a new body – this required:

> In my slow, painstaking, ragged handwriting, I copied into my tablet everything printed on that first page, down to the punctuation marks. I believe it took me a day. Then, aloud, I read back, to myself, everything I'd written on the tablet. Over and over, aloud, to myself, I read my own handwriting. I woke up the next morning, thinking about those words - immensely proud to realize that not only had I written so much at one time, but I'd written words that I never knew were in the world.
>
> (X, 1999, p. 221)

Malcolm repeated this process for weeks to the point where he knew the entire dictionary: "Between what I wrote in my tablet, and writing letters, during the rest of my time in prison I would guess I wrote a million words" (X, 1999, p. 221). He read so much he acquired the confidence of a bona fide scholar "No university would ask any student to devour literature as I did when this new world opened to me, of being able to read and understand. I read more in my room than in the library itself" (X, 1999, p. 223). This too forced a corporeality that absorbed his thirst for the new symbolic. Malcolm detailed how he read in the dark, even once the prison lights were turned off, granting his eyes a different domain than the misrecognition in the mirror:

Fortunately, right outside my door was a corridor light that cast a glow into my room. The glow was enough to read by, once my eyes adjusted to it. So when "lights out" came, I would sit on the floor where I could continue reading in that glow.

(X, 1999, pp. 223–224)

The symbolic cost to Malcolm's body should also therefore be acknowledged:

I had come to prison with 20/20 vision. But when I got sent back to Charlestown, I had read so much by the lights-out glow in my room at the Norfolk Prison Colony that I had astigmatism and the first pair of the eyeglasses that I have worn ever since.

(X, 1999, p. 242)

It is here indeed, in the new symbolic opening afforded by the Nation, that Malcolm produced an imaginary beyond whiteness. But this to be sure was not an imaginary that sidestepped whiteness. Islam enabled Malcolm to learn the colonizer's language in order to use it against colonialism. Reading in fact was about going against the white man:

Every time I catch a plane, I have with me a book that I want to read – and that's a lot of books these days. If I weren't out here every day battling the white man, I could spend the rest of my life reading, just satisfying my curiosity – because you can hardly mention anything I'm not curious about. I don't think anybody ever got more out of going to prison than I did.

(X, 1999, p. 230)

But this was not merely the instrumental adoption of English. Key throughout Malcolm's readings was the crystallization of an altogether different view of the world. Malcolm's assertion that Greek philosophy originated in Africa was a passing remark, but it iterates the key presumption of what would be explored more elaborately later in the debates sparked by Bernal's (1987) *Black Athena*. Malcolm also reiterated Arnold Toynbee's claim about how Europe prior to imperial modernity was just an extension of the Asian continent. But more relevant for our discussion were the spatial imaginaries Malcolm himself constructed in his own journey. He described how his lectures turned the ghetto into something akin to the heyday of Greek civilisation:

The way we were with each other, it would make me think of Socrates on the steps of the Athens' market place, spreading his wisdom to his students. Or how one of those students, Aristotle, had his students following behind him, walking through the Lyceum.

(X, 1999, p. 258)

Needless to say, the global vision that underpinned his politics reinforced his ability as a persuasive and charismatic speaker. But this was not merely a matter of factual persuasion. The range of his appeal was fueled by his ability to connect with the Black audience in ways only he knew how. The analogy Malcolm draws between the impact of his rhetoric and what a doctor does, highlights the corporeal nature of his symbolic dispossession:

As a doctor, with his finger against a pulse, is able to feel the heart rate, when I am up there speaking, I can feel the reaction to what I am saying. I think I could be speaking blindfolded and after five minutes, I could tell you if sitting out there before me was an all-black or an all-white audience. Black audiences and white audiences feel distinguishably different. Black audiences feel warmer, there is almost a musical rhythm, for me, even in their silent response.

(X, 1999, p. 348)

While the Nation undoubtedly opened Malcolm to the world, it was certainly an insufficient one, as Malcolm encountered the vaster political possibilities offered by the Islamic world. But this as we have seen repeatedly was not a seamless transition. The section on the Hajj in the autobiography is richest where Malcolm most candidly reveals his vulnerability: "I had never been in such a jammed mass of people, but I had never felt more alone, and helpless, since I was a baby" (X, 1999, p. 397). The displacement Malcolm endured does indicate a key point to his subjective transformation. He was, to be sure, eager to adapt to the global Islamic symbolic. But this was not found in a fixed transferential figure, nor an institutional authority. If becoming Muslim means transcending human identification, for Malcolm this took place in the form of being lost among the global span of Muslim masses he encountered. Malcolm felt this furthermost in the linguistic alienation he suffered. Malcolm constantly reiterated how he was lost in a sea of foreign languages ("we passed pilgrims by the thousands, babbling languages, everything but English") (X, 1999, p. 400). The extent of the displacement was worsened when he crossed the paths of two black British converts as they were about to leave. This culminated in the moment when Malcolm was nearly called out as a "non-authentic convert" by the Hajj officials and prohibited from continuing the pilgrimage (X, 1999, p. 396). He risked wasting the entire trip due to lacking paperwork but this was not what bothered Malcolm the most as he found himself limited by the inability to speak: "My friends around me began speaking rapid Arabic, gesturing and pointing, trying to intercede for me" (X, 1999, p. 396). This left Malcolm helpless, which must be crippling for someone who had by now established himself internationally as a masterful orator: "I felt like a stupid fool, unable to say a word, I couldn't even understand what was being said" (X, 1999, p. 396). Indeed, it was a particularly marked impasse given how the reader by that time must have been thoroughly convinced that Malcolm's charisma was realized through how well he deployed the spoken word. He had once described debating "like being on a battlefield – with intellectual and philosophical bullets" (X, 1999, p. 348)

Here at the Hajj, his oratory skills were of no use. He lamented about how exhausted he would be after every rally: "Every time I spoke at our Temple One, my voice would still be hoarse from the last time. My throat took a long time to get into condition" (X, 1999, p. 257). Mecca limited the range of his voice, and left him at a loss for words, where his language had little use.

But this at the same time should not be seen as a helplessness that amounted to subjugation. Malcolm was not excluded from the global symbolic, he was rather retained in the gap where the global continued to unfold. This accounted for the revelatory nature of the perplexities at every moment he was humbled by what he saw at the Hajj. No longer needing the misrecognized mirror image, nor the transferential other, Malcolm extended his displacement by riding the gaps he found in the Hajj, and nowhere was this more important than where he willingly estranged himself through the newfound Islamic rituals: "I may not have been mumbling the right thing, but I was mumbling" (X, 1999, p. 401). It is similarly within these gaps of language that we should now trace Malcolm's subjective temporality. There was a purported linearity throughout the perplexity of difference registered in the linguistic confusions across the Hajj's globality. Indeed Malcolm constantly processed "past and present" through negotiating the global newness. When Malcolm X talked about Muhammad Ali to his newfound pilgrim friends he said "All of the Muslims listening lighted up like a Christmas tree" (X, 1999, p. 399). The above passage about the prayer rug at dawn is similarly noteworthy as it compelled him to suddenly recall his burglar years in Boston. But what makes this stand out is that it was not Malcolm's first remark about the rug for Muslim prayer. He made the same observation earlier when he first saw Wilfred perform the Nation of Islam's version of prayer, in which Malcolm also registered the peculiar way Muslims proselytized according to the movement of the sun. Recalling the prayer rug during the Hajj was then a second registration of the same curiosity about the different embodiment required to accompany another subjectivity. The key difference for Malcolm now, as a Hajji, was that he finally saw the greater value of the rug, beyond the merely reductive exchange value that motivated his thievery.

But past meets present and future in a more radical vein. This happened during his trip across Africa, at a night in Ghana, when Malcolm was asked to make a short speech at a party.[8] He stuck to his activist message and urged everyone's support for the broader struggle for deco-lonization that was taking place: "Now, dance! Sing! But as you do – remember Mandela, remember Sobokwe! Remember Lumumba in his grave! Remember South Africans now in jail!" (X, 1999, pp. 434–435). Malcolm added that he refused to dance out of solidarity with oppressed American Blacks but only to then privately admit the opposite. For a moment he was taken back to the entertainers from his lindy hop days as Detroit Red the petty criminal: "But I sure felt like dancing! The Gha-naians performed the high life as if possessed. One pretty African girl sang 'Blue Moon' like Sarah Vaughan. Sometimes the band sounded like Milt Jackson, sometimes like Charlie Parker" (X, 1999, p. 435).

Notes

1 While often evoked in Žižekian literature, the politics of non-identity is a more fitting and direct description of the politics informed by Adorno's *Negative Dia-lectics*. Adorno is referenced frequently where the parallax is explored in Finkelde, Žižek, and Menke, C. (2023).

2 A "secular" non-religious appraisal of the Nation of Islam's politics, which recog-nises the organization's profound role in reshaping African-American activism during its time, could be found in Baldwin (2017/1963).

3 For an in-depth treatment of the significance of spirituality in Malcolm X's poli-tical outlook, see DeCaro (1996). Particular emphasis is given to the influence of Garveyite politics in Malcolm's youth.

4 In this regard, the Žižekian view of Malcolm as an exemplar of individual experi-mentation with no attachments to a historical vision aligns very well with Mal-colm's more "liberal" interpreters who see him as a champion of non-violent racial reconciliations with whites. Marable (2011) has often been read in this light. The responses to Marable's rendition of Malcolm can be found in Ball and Burroughs (2012).

5 Fard's contribution to black political consciousness is still evident in popular cul-ture even many decades later as exemplified by *Master Fard Muhammad*, Busta Rhymes' 2020 single featuring Rick Ross.

6 For more on the relationship between Hip Hop and the Five Percenters see Miyakawa (2005) and Knight (2013).

7 See Gansinger (2017) for an extensive history of religious radicalism and its impact on the history of North American and Caribbean music.

8 This moment in Malcolm's autobiography resonates with the political history of American black music presented in *Blues People* (1963) by Leroi Jones. Of parti-cular relevance is how African music signifies through the sounds in the drumming and beating required to produce a song's rhythm. The meaning isn't loaded into the signifier but in the "body" required to make the music. The geopolitical history is noteworthy given how Jones engaged with the history of African music to account for Black-American music.

Chapter 4

Where do gaps come from?

Psychoanalysis in non-spaces

We cannot present symbolic dispossession as a viable psychoanalytic concept, without also accounting for a crucial implication. To take Malcolm X seriously as a figure of a differential symbolic order is to address, first, its unique trajectory of negativity, that is to say how the excess in the possibilities of new symbolic orderings emerge as it traverses new geo-temporal terrains. Key is how this indicates a temporality beyond the one long written by Europe, a temporality felt in the combination and formations of signifiers through symbols from different spatiotemporalities that allowed him to continuously refashion his subjectivity. But to take this even further is to also leave Malcolm and account for symbolic dispossession's salience on more conceptual grounds. We shall have to account for the formal basis on which the differential nature of symbolization – understood as a *traveling* trajectory as Lacan clearly thought of it in *Seminar V* – could be better conceptualized. The question then, which this chapter will unpack, is not why or how there could be different symbolic orders than the one Lacan theorized (the existence of different symbolic orders was something Lacan never disputed). Rather it is twofold: why and when does difference become antagonistic to account for the excessive core of symbolic reproduction? Why does this unique experience of difference demand that we think of symbolization as a global movement, that is to say, a movement across the antagonisms of different histories and their spaces? How can we then regard this as a basis for thinking about psychoanalysis' place and potential in the totality we call "the global world"?

Any mention of the global world clearly includes the globalized world of Euro-American economic and political hegemony that has been forced upon us. But I am taking the opportunity here to push for another notion of "the global", drawing from the field of Global History, which refers more specifically to structural entanglements that produce the realization of an integrated world. "Entanglements" implies that no culture or context should be taken to be endogenous and sufficient unto itself and that they owe their cultural dynamics to broader historical patterns of exchange and trade. This requires overcoming the limit of methodological nationalism, in which nation-states or similarly insulated social entities are taken as isolable units of investigation, to think instead in terms of

DOI: 10.4324/9781003387978-5

interlocking and mutually constitutive dynamics that cannot be thought apart from one another. The effect would be to shift our understanding of history and modernity, that rather than a Western first view of modernity, in which modernity was set to have begun in Europe before it was exported to the rest of the world, modernity is understood in terms of interlocking flows between mutually constituting social entities. Thus, a more comprehensive view of the world as global, as opposed to seeing "the rest of the world" as simply derivatives of Europe, could be had.

Situating psychoanalytic thinking in this setting means that it will be necessary to evoke historical facts and situations in the course of my argumentation. The purpose is to establish the basis with which we can begin to outline a formal lens for a psychoanalytic view of difference in a symbolic that moves across a "global" plain. It is for this reason that I shall be introducing what I call "intermundial psychoanalysis". I draw "the intermundial" from Kojin Karatani's formulation of the term to refer to the interstices linking incommensurable paradigms. This resonates generally with the Lacanian premise of a gap in knowledge, but it is not a free-floating gap but one structured by differential other. Through a distinct reading of Kant and Marx, Karatani presents the interstices to show how being and thought are not problems in themselves but are produced upon the need to overcome different paradigms of values. The excess produced in capitalist exchange, and consequently the ethical problem of difference capitalism necessarily produces, is formed out of this interstitial gap. Difference by this is not something to be encountered as a rupture after the fact. Difference is the condition producing the excess that makes the gap a problem in the first place and thus the antagonistic structure of communication in the globalized world. Indeed, it will help our elucidation of the intermundial to see it as a "non-space". Non-space refers to the gap in trade that produces the need for a spatial imaginary. This gap informs Karatani's presentation of the "mode of exchange" – a surplus-producing exchange between differing paradigms – as a basis for the capitalist reproduction of the contemporary world.[1] An intermundial psychoanalysis consequently is a view into the globalization of the psychoanalytic clinic that is attentive to its place in the broader circulation of commodities in the capitalist world, not as another product to export but a product introduced in an exchange process that is structured by incommensurability. Consequently, it will help to check the globalization of the psychoanalytic clinic by similarly casting its flow in the non-spaces of incommensurability underlying purportedly seamless exchange.

But far more than just a formula to apply to psychoanalysis, reading Karatani for this purpose also bears theoretical relevance for psychoanalytic critique, particularly where Karatani characterizes the task of critique as transcritical, in that the critical perspective is situated in the interstices of the intermundial as to implement a parallax inquiry into the gap. As parallaxical, the gap is to be situated across the antagonisms it produces. The standpoint is always indirect, traversing the tensions underlying a given moment, rather than a straightforward view into phenomena.[2]

If the notion of the parallax here is familiar, it is because Karatani is the source of what would become "the parallax view" as formulated by Slavoj Žižek. But where Karatani places the parallax in the exchange regenerated by global capitalist trade, Žižek locates it metaphysically in the gap of being. Thus Žižek takes on the parallax without the need for the intermundial, thereby jettisoning the element of difference that is so crucial to understanding excess. This leads to a key distinction that will be at the heart of this chapter, in which Žižek's use of the parallax strips it of its global historical significance to become a purely conceptual encounter, that is to say, a tension experienced in thought rather than the world of exchange-antagonisms capitalism facilitates. With this, we have a foil with which the more fundamental problem of difference in mainstream Lacanian theory could be addressed. The key difference, indeed, the key problem, with Žižek's use of Karatani is that it Europeanizes the parallax to the effect of retaining psychoanalysis within a European fold. Thus, we shall make the notion of the non-spatiality of the intermundial – and its related concepts in the mode of exchange, the transcritical and the parallax – clearer by way of what it should not be, going by how the parallax has been Europeanized.

Part 1: Eurocentric Lacanians

In many ways the problem of difference is already presumed in psychoanalytic accounts of globality. What is usually called "globalization" is regarded as the imaginarization of the antagonisms inherent to capital's structural expansion to newer territories. Much of this furthermore has been informed, and continuously ensured, by the longer historical convergence of Marxism and psychoanalysis in critical theory. This convergence, to be sure, has varied but it nonetheless sets the precedent for psychoanalysis to be read and applied more critically to extra-clinical questions through a broadly Marxian critique of capitalism. This has been the premise for the Marxist-psychoanalytic lens to be formalized as a lens to understand the contemporary world more broadly, with the rightful assumption that the world as we know it is in essence a capitalist world. Insofar as psychoanalysis' general premises do resonate with Marxist-informed understandings of what happens to the subject and the psyche as they are reproduced under capitalism, and that psychoanalytic concepts consequently could be deployed where capitalism is hegemonic, the link between psychoanalysis and capitalist globalization could be taken for granted as given until otherwise realized.

The psychoanalytic–Marxist marriage, however, comes at a high price for the Global Southern analyst because the globalization that critical psychoanalysis is working with is in effect the globalization of Europe. This is not necessarily a problem in itself. Many theoretical projects build their foundations without an active awareness of the context enabling their ideas. In this sense, the fact that we will more likely come across open appeals to Europe among Freudian-Marxists is a welcomed gesture where the question of context is rarely ever acknowledged otherwise. If you think you're theorizing for everyone it is only fair for you to say how and why exactly you could. The problem is when the European political-philosophical experience is also taken as the basis of formulating a universal outlook. Thus we find an implicit tension where their insistence on lack as the material basis for universality rests on an unquestioned and idealized notion of Europe, particularly a Europe whose horrors are presented with the caveat that they are imbued with a political promise graspable only through dynamics unique to European history. Nowhere is this optimism toward Europe idealized more than through the presumption that its evental breakthroughs are endogenous to its historicity, that the meaning of its temporality is entirely to be registered within the terms and conditions familiar to it. The emptiness of being is universal but Europe gets the idea of this emptiness more than anywhere else.

This assumption is operative at various levels across Freudian-Marxist texts. But the open defense of Europe as a political and moral project has its most avowed defender in Slavoj Žižek. Europe here features in two significant regards. The softer version of this claim takes Europe to be an unavoidable historical detail. Europe is the most definitive political feature of the present given that we are still living through the problems that have historically endured through a basically continuous European-imperial system of oppression. The need for a decolonial politics, however crucial its call for inclusivity is, is symptomatic of Europe's persistent hegemony thereby making Europe, after all is said and done, the more important point of political theorizing. Psychoanalysis could be mobilized to address this circumstance because it is a unique product of Europe's historical contradictions. Ilan Kapoor, who alongside Zahi Zalloua, have done the most to export Žižek's relevance to Global Southern politics, takes this to mean that "Psychoanalysis is globally relevant because of the history of globalization/colonialism, which has ended up imposing a Western(ized), and increasingly capitalistic, symbolic order" (Kapoor, 2018, p. xxviii). This, Kapoor declares, accounts for "the Universalizability of Psychoanalysis" (Kapoor, 2018, p. xxvii).

There are many reasons to question whether Europe's dominance today necessarily means that the symbolic order as Lacan theorised it is also Western. But that is the point that Žižek-inspired Lacanians will lean on for their politics. Key to this view is how the symbolic order Westernizes through engulfing the world into the gap, the excess, that necessarily comes with the expansion of capitalism. This is the affirmation of the universal not as an idea or substance, but as the structuring lack-in-common that produces the antagonism that binds opposing agents – conservative and liberal, colonized and colonizer etc – into a single fate in the emptiness of being now globally construed. Building a progressive politics from within this bind, where all come together as contaminated as opposed to essentialist subjects, is the challenge. Global capitalism is hereby construed very much as a destructive and productive force, with the gap ensuring that all that is sacred submits to the commodity form, and the purported liberation from the past therein allows for a universal future to be pursued beyond parochial provinces.

But why this clearly global phenomenon is to be construed as Western, as opposed to say Asian or African, has much to do with how Europe is regarded as the historical, philosophical and geographical terrain which, owing to the very history of oppression it globalized, has had to grapple consciously and unconsciously with the problem of difference at a universal scale. Europe is where the question of difference has been most forcefully met and refused. This is rooted in how Europe is the historical site for what Žižek (1998) calls "politics proper" in which the antagonisms inherent to the real are known where a given order of things is disrupted upon the insistence of what is called, borrowing from Jacques Ranciere, "the part of no-part". This, however, is not about successful political projects but the encounter with pure antagonism. So politics proper could also be discerned through "metaphoric condensation", concealed in fissures that are expressed in demands that do not appear to be most immediately radical or outrageous (Žižek, 1998, p. 990). The picture one gets as one reads through the literature is unmistakable as Lacanian concepts are deployed to revive the European-imperial legacy as everyone's main order of business and thus everyone's problem and solution: "This is why an anti-Eurocentric viewpoint cannot escape a Eurocentric background" (Žižek, 1998, p. 101). This presumption becomes the premise for the stronger claim that Europe, its historical legacy and its institutions, as a result, is the universal solution. This very parochial politics – in their conviction that the fate of the entire world is determined through what happens in a handful of white countries – has not gone unnoticed by Fredric Jameson (2019) who, in a recent engagement in a Žižekian venue, refers to the participants of this tendency as "Eurocentric Lacanians".

Capitalist modernity is global not European

Eurocentric Lacanians are right to assume that Europe, with its global military and financial dominance, is the primary driver of global politics. One could also grant some leeway and not take it too exclusively when "radical egalitarianism, universal emancipation, and justice" are described as "European legacies" (Kapoor & Zalloua, 2021, p. 171). But they contradict their project most when the appeal to the gap inevitably leads to an affirmation of Europe as an ideal. One reads Eurocentric Lacanians to find them constantly juggling narratives. On one hand, the insistence that there is only the gap as the excessive lack in all identities is repeated ad nauseam. On the other hand, European history has the most unique privilege of insight into what this lack can do and is thus the history worthy of being saved. Indeed, the history of the West is upheld as the only historical experience that shows that the gap, far from simply destructive, could be redeeming. Thus while Žižekians are notable for their attentiveness to global movements, they are to ultimately feed into the longer trajectory of Europe's story of emancipatory politics as the true measure of universality. The fate of a universal progressive politics depends on ensuring the survival of the progressive European tradition. Take, for example, how Kapoor and Zalloua offer what they call "a left-universalist Europe" as the solution: "The idea here is for a Europe, armed with its social democratic-egalitarian legacy and socio-economic power, to counter the neocolonial and post-political directions of global capitalism" (Kapoor & Zalloua, 2021, p. 172). There should, of course, be nothing intrinsically wrong about a progressive European response to globalization. But their most upheld example of left-Europe universalism turns out to be the European Union. This is because the EU is "the most effective and long-standing socio-economic union in the world, bringing unprecedented wealth and trading opportunities to its member states, and setting global precedents for progressive common social, labour, and environmental standards" (Kapoor & Zalloua, 2021, p. 169). This statement should come across as outrageous, if not odd at the very least, to any observer of EU politics in recent years, given that it was published at a time when the overwhelming majority of the European working classes were firmly against the European Union. The call for the European Union to wield its socio-economic power reads even more ominously now considering the clear military and diplomatic support that Germany, the country that is the driving force of the European Union, voiced for Israel during the Gaza Genocide.

This idea that Europe, as the universal, is at the heart of all politics is similarly at work in Kapoor and Zalloua's critique of what they take to be the more purist tendencies in post-colonial theory, wherein the most vociferous post-colonial theorization of difference is merely regarded as a symptom of Europe's enduring epistemic hold over the colonized: "the very conceptual tools they use are part of (what these same critics identify as) the European philosophical tradition, evidence precisely of these tools' subversive universality" (Kapoor & Zalloua, 2021, p. 171). Thus they also endorse a post-colonial return to Europe. Note a key point to this claim: it is not so much that the colonizer is a given circumstantial fact of the colonized's subjectivity. The colonized must also redeem the colonizer's legacy: "It means fully immersing oneself in the matrix so as to exploit its liberatory potential and outsmart Europeans on their own terrain" (Kapoor & Zalloua, 2021, p. 99). Consequently, Kapoor and Zalloua do not only demand that post-colonial theory recognizes itself as a European product but to also affirm that embracing their existential bind to Europe is actually the more radical goal: "negotiating the real internally (self-reflexively) rather externally (locating it only in the European Other) implies not a delinking from, but a more radical incorporation and destabilization of, the colonial matrix" (Kapoor & Zalloua, 2021, pp. 98–99). Never mind the fact that this inner struggle has always been openly admitted by countless decolonial thinkers – confessed so eloquently in so many of their memoirs to account for their steadfast commitment to a lifelong confrontation with the European other in the real – it is noteworthy that Kapoor and Zalloua's call of action prioritizes inner Europe somehow as the real challenge of post-colonial theorizing. So evident in their eyes are Europe's virtues that they are at a loss as to what more needs to be explained. The following statement by Žižek, which Kapoor and Zalloua endorse, is a telling summary of the Eurocentric Lacanian worldview:

> To put it bluntly: do we want to live in a world in which the only choice is between the American civilization and the emerging Chinese authoritarian-capitalist one? If the answer is no, then the true alternative is Europe.
>
> (Kapoor & Zalloua, 2021, p. 172)

That this is why the only choice is Europe is also perplexing, especially as we keep in mind that this sentence was reproduced as the emerging multipolar world was plainly in sight, a topic of everyday commentary on global affairs as newer antagonisms and democratic experiments are taking place among demographics that are more culturally complex and numerous than anything Europe had ever imagined. China saw through the biggest Industrial Revolution in human history while there are single provinces in Indonesia and India respectively that boast electorates equivalent to that of seven Western European countries, to take just three examples from one side of a continent.

The effect of this contradiction, between stressing the fundamental lack of all things on one hand, and the eternal virtues of Europe on the other, is that it amounts to salvaging much of the status quo. Thus, on one hand Kapoor and Zalloua continuously assert that what Žižek wants is not some naive salvation of European tradition but its radical transformation: "What he is after is an effective engagement with Europe's symbolic order (its laws and language) – an intervention that would 'touch, and change the Real' disrupting its societies' seamless representation of reality" (Kapoor & Zalloua, 2021, p. 130). On the other hand, the European Union's existing laws are taken to be the final reference to suggest that the EU has the symbolic figured out:

> Not only does the EU allow for the imposition of standards on such things as women's rights, antiracism, and environmental and labour codes, but more than ever it is proof of the success of multilateral cooperation to establish executive power at a supranational level.
>
> (Kapoor & Zalloua, 2021, p. 172)

In other words, their critique of ideal notions of universality quickly makes way for the support of a highly idealized European Union. Or we could also conclude that there is no contradiction here for there is the high likelihood that Kapoor and Zalloua really believe that the European Union is radical by design. They qualify their arguments with elaborate explanations of how the European Union had been co-opted by neoliberalism as if it was never a neoliberal project to begin with. At no point was the fact that the EU was founded on Judeo-Christian values ever raised. Indeed what their claim all boils down to is that Europe was first to figure out the real of universal modernity, and you can take it or leave it. This "Europe knows best" attitude explains Kapoor and Zalloua's sweeping dismissals of actual socio-political struggles and gains in the Global South. Malaysian Prime Minister Mahathir Mohamed, who boldly defied IMF against conventional free market wisdom during the peak of 1990s neoliberal globalization (of which the European Union was a key global player), is inexplicably lumped together with imperial nostalgists Putin and Erdogan. China, despite the wealth of leftist literature its current antagonisms have produced, is simplified for its human rights violations. China's elevation of over 600 million people from poverty is not at all mentioned, never mind considered of universal value. The anti-imperial quality of Iran's Revolution – which made it one of the most sanctioned countries in the world – was not mentioned. Iran is instead listed alongside the Gulf states and Singapore as totalitarian capitalist. Malaysia, Russia, Turkey, China, and Iran are, to be sure, not unproblematic models of political organization. But it is telling of the Eurocentric Lacanian outlook that they are not discussed for their political complexity or as sources for further universal thinking. They are examples to be brushed aside where European history is upheld as the yardstick for liberation. What we end up getting is the assertion of a global hierarchy. European antagonisms are world-forming. Antagonisms elsewhere are only symptoms of a systemic rot. The neo-colonized Global South is where subalterns are produced, it is not where politics or universal thinking happens.

Global modernity

One could simplify the entire Eurocentric Lacanian outlook to say that it offers a universality from the privileged view of a global minority who "get" the reality of the gap by virtue of their leading place in the longer history of politics proper, while the majority world, trapped as they are in the European prism, can only trail in their understanding of what "the political" is really about. It can be seen as an epistemic bait-and-switch: the gap in being is theorized only to argue that Europe is necessary to understand the supposed radicality of the gap. Europe by this is pitched as the fiction most deserving of our faith and defense. The best that progressive politics in the Global South can pursue meanwhile is a belated process of Europeanization. If it is not obvious yet, the Eurocentric Lacanian position is ultimately most defensible on cultural terms, upon the insistence that European politics bears the privilege of being rooted in a history so distinctive for its radicality. This is in many ways evident in the philosophy they present for their project. But we still have some ways to go to grasp their worldview because we must first take the opportunity to also read their position symptomatically, that is to say, as a response to how Europe is actually faring today. For not only is the Eurocentric Lacanian's faith in Europe's ongoing relevance expressed at a time when Europe has lost its significance as the supposed exemplars of transnational trade and peace. They are also being eclipsed where newer trans-continental alliances by economies with far larger populations and markets than all of Europe combined are taking place with little recourse to anything the European Union has done, or was even capable or interested in doing. More simply than the supposedly "peaceful" trade Europe exemplified, the new alliances are aiming to overcome the power of European finance altogether. De-dollarization, the uncoupling of trade from American hegemony, has never been closer to realization because of concrete efforts by China and Russia, with diplomatic cover and sympathies from swathes of the Third World, to work together to circumvent Washington D.C.'s long hold over the global economy in an endeavor spurred by the need for an alternative to the West's long-term imperial interests. The momentum behind Russia and China's alliance, no doubt strengthened by their alliance with Brazil, India, and South Africa via BRICS, has certainly informed the emboldening anti-French sentiment in the Western Sahel region. This, has a longer history in Francophone West Africa given their decades of reluctant reliance on the CFA Franc as national currencies despite being formally decolonized "independent" nations.

Our point should not be about presenting political developments in the non-West as better alternatives than the EU. There is no doubt that the new transnational alliances formed across the Global South are about intensifying the expansion of capital, especially where state capture by global finance has been achieved in the West. The point rather is to indicate how global antagonisms are taking shape beyond what is graspable in Western-historical terms, and this is the more fundamental point Lacanians seeking to think about globalization should heed. But to take this as a start is to already be a step closer to a more accurate picture of the global, namely how it also marks the implicit recognition of enduring linkages and historical networks that limit or transcend the impact of European imperialism. Modernity did not begin in the West before it was then to happen to the rest of the world. Societies are always constituted through entanglements and networks with other contexts. This has constituted the starting point for the different fields theorizing the "international," such as Combined and Uneven Development and Global History to take just two examples, wherein methodological nationalism, in which the nation-state paradigm is taken as the definitive lens for an understanding of history, is refused for a more complete picture of the interconnectedness that shapes the world. For Combined and Uneven Development "the intersocietal" is the most basic unit of the international as it marks the actuality that no social unit had ever existed in isolation and that they are made possible through a relational dependency with other social units. A key insight in Global History is the notion of "simultaneity," that rather than long-term perspectives concerning civilizations and regions, we will have a better sense of the global through looking at "synchronous constellations and external forces" as "important drivers of social change as long prehistories and traditions," that the history of the global could be thought laterally rather than through "deep time" as it were (Conrad, 2017, p. 66).

While it is not within the scope of our inquiry is to delve into the psychoanalytic implications of these innovations, their shared premises nonetheless leave us with a lot to work with, namely that there are always other histories and times that shape any experience of a given present. And this is more evident today because the world is seeing the historical limits to European hegemony, that while its authorship over the world at one point is indisputable, this did not amount to erasing the dominance of pre-existing historical dynamics elsewhere. Consequently, if there is potency in trade and communication it was formed out of longer-standing traditions of diplomacy and outreach. This indeed is the scholarly consensus behind anticipations of what is perhaps the most outstanding geopolitical feature of our multipolar world, namely the anticipation of the 21st century as an Asian century where pre-European linkages are revived in recognition of the need for newer historical possibilities. Being fair to this phenomenon requires a significant paradigm shift to our understanding of the global. Rather than a Europe-first view of modernity, in which modernity began in the West before it was applied to the rest of the world, we are instead compelled to think of modernity globally through key historical parallels across other civilizations and communities. For this we will do well to consider the complexity of Asia as an example.

This will require us to enlarge our notion of "Asia" or the "East" to include the Levant all the way across the central Asian region, the Indian subcontinent, Southeast Asia, to Siberia, China, Mongolia, and Japan. But beyond merely Asia, what will be evident through this larger view is the global story of modernity. Modernity will no longer be about particular states, nations, or civilizations, but their distinct network relations. The point then is certainly not to say that Asia was first before anyone else. It is that with Asia's rise we are now able to see modernity as a global phenomenon rather than a by-product of European national traditions. Notice the decolonial opening: Instead of an original moment (typically thought to be the French Revolution or the British Industrial Revolution), we have instead long-standing linkages that reveal Asia's centrality in the construction of the present. What exactly this all amounts to, if it can produce an alternative narrative of history, is too early to tell and is in many ways being co-opted by different national discourses, especially as the notion of multipolarity increases in political purchase. What could be considered meanwhile is the extent to which the fragmentation of the West's significance as the founding center of modernity could be a foil with which we reconsider Asia's historical centrality. This would require us to take a longer view into the history of modernity where rather than evental breaks we consider momentums that formed over centuries of intercontinental trade networks that extended across the Asian region. Consequently, rather than a transatlantic world of Euro-American dominance and its imperial effects, we can begin to include an Afro-Eurasian world into our figuration of history.

This constitutes the key argument in Janet Abu-Lughod's (1991) landmark *Before European Hegemony*. Challenging the claim that capitalism as a world system emerged in 16th-century Europe, Abu-Lughod points to prior and parallel trade systems that thrived across the Afro-Eurasian space through networks that stretched from the Far East and Southeast Asia all the way across the Mediterranean. The regions, to be sure, were not held together by a stable common market. Rather, they were linked, and mutually impacted, by historical dynamics sustained across the geopolitical struggles that marked the region, forming a truly global space: "never before," Abu-Lughod wrote, "had so many regions of the Old World come in contact with one another" (Abu-Lughod, 1991, p. 3).

Rather than a standard core and periphery, that is to say, a binary view of the world, Abu-Lughod points to the historical activity of multiple centers and peripheries that overlap and cannot be reduced to a simple dualism. The big picture here reveals interconnections across various cities from Genoa and Venice, to Tashkent, Samarkand, and Malacca. Key is how Abu-Lughod's thesis disrupted the prevailing presumption that capitalist globalization is a fundamentally European-driven phenomenon. Instead, historical trade across Afro-Eurasia produced cosmopolitanisms that predated Western globalization:

> All of these units across Europe, the Middle East, and Asia were not only trading with one another and handling the transit trade of others, but had begun to reorganise parts of their internal economies to meet the exigencies of the world market.
>
> (Abu-Lughod, 1991, p. 355)

This diminishes the evental novelty of Europe's supposed discovery of the Americas. The 14th century launch of the Iberian conquest was not an internally European development, but one which was intrinsically entangled with the vast sweep of intercontinental networks that brought Afro-Eurasia together.

Let's be clear that we posit this history not to reveal Europe's debt to Asia. Instead it should first for our specific psychoanalytic purposes diminish the supposed novelty of European progress. European imperialism did not give birth to globalization. European imperialism was just one model of globalization among already-existing others. What Europe innovated, and this is significant, was the acceleration of its imperial model of capital. It did not invent capital itself. Once recast globally, Europe cannot be regarded as the sole force of world-making. What it produced had to be imposed upon other modes of cosmopolitan relations. The political polysemy associated with the rise of the Global South did not suddenly appear out of nowhere but was rather the globalization that enabled the ascent of Western empires. What we call "polycentrism" or "multipolarity" today was always the rule and not a sudden latter-day exception of post-European international relations. Consequently, the legal, institutional and philosophical legacy inherited from Western imperialism cannot be the sole, nor even the most causally significant, element of the story of interconnectivity that must be told to account for the vast world that is modernity. To enlarge our view of the world to be sure is not to assert an ontological stability to the notion of Afro-Eurasia. Fisher-Onar and Kavalski think of this development as a model for "interlocking regional worlds," which could portend the way international relations will take place in an increasingly multipolar world (Fisher-Onar & Kavalski, 2022, p. 5). While we should also not take this picture as a story of world harmony it is also true regional worlds do not just interlock suddenly out of nowhere. The political momentum attests to the fact that the intercontinental vastness that is Eurasia endured as the site of globalization before the rise of European hegemony.

This more importantly should not be considered purely for historical interest. We should also keep the globality of trade networks in mind to explain the rapid formation and reinforcements of current linkages. China's Belt and Road Initiative, wherein Africa and Asia will be linked through the Indian Ocean, and the rivaling Indo-Japanese Asia–Africa Growth Corridor are just two examples. Taking place at the same time are concurrent trade and infrastructure initiatives across the Eurasian region linking Asia minor, the Caucuses, Eastern Europe, Central Asia, and South Asia in different ways. These include Turkey's Middle Corridor, the Shanghai Cooperation Organisation (SCO) which, spanning across Central Asia, is the largest regional organization in the world, the Organization of Turkic States (OTS) and the South Asian Association for Regional Cooperation (SAARC) between countries of the Indian subcontinent. Key in all this is the repurposing of age-old maritime trade routes across the Indian Ocean where historical evidence of Asian and African cultural entanglements – such as the Indian diaspora in Southeast Africa and the Cape Malays in South Africa, to name just two – are not hard to find. It doesn't take a keen observer to notice that all this amounts to a geography that constitutes the vast majority of the globe's population.

We cannot fully decentre the contemporary world from European history without taking China into account. Not only is China the leading power in the Global South's emergence, but its rise is also producing competing narratives of its progress which appeals to a different history of globalization than the one centered on the transatlantic story of history. The first, which is most familiar to the English-speaking world, charts China's rise to the revisionist counter-revolution in the 1970s in which China was opened to the world economy in tandem with the neo-liberalization of US and Western Europe: The post-war Euro-American welfare state was formed upon mounting pressures from leftists and trade unionists before Western capital, facing rapid losses of profits, sought new sources of cheap labor in the third world, effectively granting China its moment in history. This paved the way for China to become the factory of the world, serving as the productive basis for the contemporary capitalist object world, from which its present global prominence began. Notice the Eurocentric nature of this outlook, in which China's emergence matters only to the extent that it can explain Western capitalist history: Western capital modernized rural China where Maoism failed as China's rise only matters to explain Euro-American deindustrialization. But this narrative does not account for the relative rapidity with which it all took place. For this we need to recognize the fact that China, was long before the Opium Wars, the biggest economy in the world known for its advanced agricultural practices and sophisticated system of governance. Euro-American neoliberalism may have a lot to do with how China was incorporated into late capitalist globalization, but this alone cannot account for the speed with which China has thrived globally.

To properly grasp this, we must recognize how China was not a backward latecomer to globalization but was once its key pioneer. Pre-colonial China accrued its wealth over the twelve centuries of trade that formed the Silk Road, the most significant commercial network in the Afro-Eurasian space. Much of what is associated with modern prosperity today such as urbanization, systemic taxation, cultural cosmopolitanism, and technological diffusion – in an unprecedented use of paper currency and printing – could be seen in the interactions that formed along this vast intercontinental network. Baghdad, Aleppo, Samarkand, and Tashkent, to name a few key cities, found key moments of their history through trade across the Silk Road. Nowhere perhaps is the historical legacy of this intercontinental network more evident than in what has become one of liberal media's most favorite topics, namely China's problems with Muslim-majority Xinjiang, a problem rooted to the latter's strategic location for China's Central Asian historical commercial interest. China's Belt and Road Initiative represents China's attempt to forge its roadmap for globalization in the 21st century but it does not do so out of nothing. It appeals to centuries of exchanges that were forged across Eurasia. The Western Freudo-Marxist will likely reduce all this to a perverse nationalist fantasy. But in doing so it misses the more crucial point that China's civilizational presence is a more familiar protagonist to those situated in the historical flows of Asian modernity than the self-evident truths that we are to believe is inherent to the British Industrial Revolution or whatever it was that Europe supposedly universalized for us. To take one example, the taken-for-granted political reality across Southeast Asia is that capitalism was never just Western. Chinese capital, which in certain cases as Malaysia came prior to British capital, was historically as prominent. But the Eurocentric reduction makes the more fundamental mistake of neglecting the increasingly compelling thesis, championed no less by Marxists Andre Gunder Frank (1998) and Giovanni Arrighi (2009), that Asia from 1400–1800, with China as its most dominant power, represented the global economic center. Europe assumed a peripheral position until it had the wealth of the Americas to exploit for gold and silver, the wealth Frank claims it used to buy into already-established Asian businesses that dominated the Eurasian region. China's esteem in the European imagination, materially enabled by historical trade across the Afro-Eurasian network, was evidenced in the appeal of "Chinoiserie," the genre of Chinese motifs and design elements that featured in 17th- and 18th-century European art.

But we should not mistake the Silk Road as the invention of China. If China could develop trade links across Eurasia, it was upon the prior order established by the Mongol Empire. Spanning across the 13th century it enabled the exchanges of goods, ideas, and cultures that linked Eurasia, and in effect "Asia" as we know it today, in such a way that they could be analyzed as a coherent historical category of analysis. The significance of our reimagining of the globe is crucial. At its height, the Mongol Empire incorporated China, Iran, Poland, and a significant portion of present-day Russia under its authority, making it the largest contiguous cosmopolitan empire in history. Anievas and Nişancıoğlu (2015) chart the Mongolian empire as a key geopolitical factor for the eventual concentration of capital in Western Europe. Ayşe Zarakol (2022) goes further to show how the Mongolian empire for Asia is historically comparable to what the Roman empire was for Europe, as it initiated a novel approach to centralized governance over a multicultural polity, whose influence was evident in early modern Ottoman, Safavid and Russian administration. Indeed recent scholarly rediscoveries of Mongol history have emphasized its multicultural and administrative novelties rather than its sheer brutality. This in any case will appear less academic when we note how the Mongolian legacy remains a live reference in contemporary Eastern Europe. Hungary – the country of Ferenczi, Klein, and the Balints – became an observer in the Organization of Turkic States upon the former's claim of Turkish heritage via the Mongolian empire. The Mongol past also lurks behind Russia's recent overtures to its Eurasian heritage. 80 per cent of Russian territory is Asian anyway.

It bears repeating that this horizontalization of "the international" – where global time is understood as lateral flows marked primarily by spatial encounters rather than breaks in linear time – is not about presenting an alternative to Europe so much as a more expansive and accurate account of how the present world, "the global" as an object and problem, came to be. But there is enough here to trouble establishment psychoanalysis where it must now conceive of modernity in a way that also accounts for the temporality of a universal possibility of progress with "non-Europe" in mind. Europe to be sure is a part of this world but it can no longer be conceived as the sole or most significant aspect of it. The view of the lack in the real must therefore be similarly enlarged. There is an opportunity here where the notion of the parallax, so crucial for the Eurocentric Lacanian view of how the void is encountered, could be extended in consideration of global dynamics. The incessant switching of perspectives that lack compels could now be embedded in global flows. It so happens that the recognition of capitalism as the value form of a differential world informed Kojin Karatani's original conception of the parallax that Lacanians have repurposed, and as we shall see water down, for their own project. But to recognize this is to first identify that the main problem as far as the relationship between Europe and Lacan is concerned, is neither the development of capitalism nor the historical centrality of non-Europe. The new geo-spatial sensibility that comes with an affirmation of a global rather than a European modernity rather forces us to cast a critical light on what I take to be the key theoretical presumption at the heart of the Eurocentric Lacanian outlook, and that is the temporalization of the lacking object. This requires that we turn away from the general European Lacanian tendency to reconstruct Žižekian Eurocentrism more specifically. We shall see how he temporalizes the object to also temporalize the parallax, after which we shall consider what a return to Kojin Karatani's specifically transcritical parallax can offer.

Part 2: The Object in time and history

The temporalization of the object

The temporalization of the object as we know is essential for psychoanalysis' developmental outlook, for how it structures the subject's relationship to other people and the things and feelings that stand in for them, in the course of the subject's passage from child to person. It has since Freud expanded to become the clinical focus for object relations theory and attachment theory while becoming a topic of philosophical scrutiny. The coloniality of the developmental outlook is evident where it takes for granted that time is – or has been – revelatory. There is a "point" to where things are going and that ultimately Europe is where thinking about this temporality takes place. But where the Eurocentric Lacanian outlook outdoes what was colonially given by standard Freudian developmentalism is its stress on the duality of lack and excessiveness in the object, that it is not so much the development in time that Europe knows, but that Europe also knows lack as the reason for it. Indeed conceiving of this lack in time is what gives Eurocentric Lacanians their link across philosophy, psychoanalysis, and politics. Philosophically, the object is excessive because it lacks and thought will pursue the truth of this object until it meets its limits to become aware of its contingencies as an instrument. Psychoanalytically, this excessiveness of the object will be the basis on which consciousness is produced against the unconscious, in which the subject eventually comes to terms with the excessiveness by virtue of time itself. More fundamentally for our purposes, the lacking object also accounts for capitalism as a measure of regulating the excessive nothingness. Žižek has exhaustively detailed lack in theoretical terms with his constant appeal to Hegel and German Idealism, in a body of work that has culminated into a sustained engagement with theoretical physics. But key in the story of the object in time is how it informs Žižek's investment in negativity and the gap:

How can a practice which is fully embedded in a life-world start to function in a representative way, subtracting itself from its life-world entanglement, adopting a distanced position of observation and denotation? Hegel praised this "miracle" as the infinite power of Understanding, the power to separate – or, at least, to treat as separate – what in real life belongs together ... Language never "fits" reality, it is the mark of a radical imbalance which forever prevents the subject from locating itself within reality.

(Žižek, 2017, pp. 30–31)

This as we shall see constitutes the philosophical basis of Žižekian Eurocentrism: the revelation of the object in time also reveals how lack structures the most evental political antagonisms of history and is thus the basis of thinking the universal. All of this is to lead to Europe as the place and point of view which "gets" lack and thus gets universality to be the point of it all. Thus all political ruptures are about informing how the European project could be improved as the fundamental universal gesture. But we are not given a proper account of how and why all of this is to be burdened on the supposed potency of lack. This takes us to how Žižek conceives of the existence of the object and capital in idealistic terms, as a pure tension between appearance and essence. In Žižek's Hegelian view, the founding problem centers around whether things either are there or are not in the dialectic of being and nothingness, and self-consciousness is realized to the extent to which thought encounters its limits in the contradictions met in its pursuit of actuality. Consequently, surplus is experienced in the mismatch between language and reality where an attempt to crystalize the object is pursued to failure.

This particular account of how surplus is produced in time is important to note because it marks the point of Karatani and Žižek's theoretical divergence. Žižek is committed to a reified notion of exchange, where the truth of the gap is where the commodity is traded as an already-formed fiction. This is how the ideology in capitalist exchange – as actually being about money rather than the satisfaction of human needs – could be critiqued. On the other hand, Karatani places capital first to assert that there are no "objects" as such until they are subjected to fungibility. For Karatani the excess is not in the formation of the object of certain failure. Excess only happens qua the thing as capital, as partaking in the object world shaped by the circulation and exchange of money for more capital. The difference here is key to grasp before we detail their differences to think of the unconscious in global terms. To take the conversion of money to capital seriously is to also take seriously the different terrains that are necessarily involved to ensure that the object is rendered exchangeable for money – or anything "more" really – in a way in which the thing partakes in the broader process of regenerating surplus value. Excessiveness happens to objects that appear to us within a broader circuit of exchange and we cannot account for this without a global view of the object's constitution. A capitalist view of lacking objects consequently would have it that things don't just lack because of linguistic displacement. They lack because they are rendered fundamentally fungible.

None of this, to assure the Žižekian, takes us to a vulgar materialism. We are still in the realm of negativity and constructs. But it does take us to a simpler, more persuasive account of the lacking object. This object is a construct traced and moved through the global circuit of capital. Insofar as capital is globally uneven – wherein it is about products made in time as measured monetarily by how fast it moves across differentiated spaces – then the thing's excessive-quality, the fact that it demands value, meaning and our hermeneutic intervention, happens within a broader field of consumption rather than the encounter with the problem of appearance at the end point of pure thought. It is in this field of market relations that we can more accurately account for capital's at once fictional and tenuous universality, which colors our relationship to objects.

Mode of exchange

It is with the need to consider this more all-encompassing conception of capital's excess – a horizontal one as opposed to its Eurocentric temporalization – for a decolonial Lacan that we shall turn to Kojin Karatani's "mode of exchange". Theorized against the dominance of the mode of production approach, by which capitalism is determined by the nature of the technology that produced its distinct world of excessive "objects" (basically technology for equally excessive mass industrialization), the mode of exchange operates with the claim that capitalism is structured within a field of social relations in which money is exchanged for more money to resolve the incommensurability between paradigms: "what we grasp as objects of the political economy are never the 'things-themselves' but only the 'phenomena' that are constituted by the commodity economy" (Karatani, 2005, p. 198). With this general premise, the mode of exchange understands capital essentially as a mode of incessant homogenization in a world where difference is the definitive horizon of all thinking. This for Karatani is the essence of capital by which its other problems – the state, the alienation of the worker from the object of its labor and colonialism – are centered. Capital grows through the homogenization of incommensurabilities with surplus value as the binding formal paradigm: "only where there are heterogeneous systems can money transform into capital that gains surplus value from the exchange between systems" (Karatani, 2005, p. 227).

The cosmopolitan world that birthed capitalism is shaped fundamentally through the repeated encounter with difference, and this experience of difference is for Karatani the consequent structure producing the abstractions outlining surplus value as capitalism's fundamental value form. With this emphasis on difference we can describe the mode of exchange in more particular terms to say that there is, much like the idealist premise, a gap at the heart of things. And like the Žižekian idealistic reworking of Marx, capital is construed as a product of this gap. But there is in this gap that Karatani has in mind the problematic of the other as such. This is not an unknown or unknowable Levinasian other. Nor is this other a fictional projection in response to some prior trauma. This is an other recognized transcendentally as an immanent contradiction that we cannot avoid. Karatani theorizes capital as a product of this gap through a most distinct link between Kant and Marx. With this, incommensurability is not the motive force of transcendental idealism, as if otherness is a regulative ideal beyond the realm of reason. Karatani reads Kant for an idealism that has already internalized incommensurability as its basic structure wherein the gap between phenomenon and noumenon needed to be posited. Idealism is the product of difference and not the other way around. Capitalism is similarly the value form forged by the internalization of an externality conceived through the exchange that occurs across differing value systems.

Capital therefore is instantiated in the moment of exchange that necessitates that an inside is determined from an outside, or sameness from difference. This is where Karatani conceives of transcritique as an oscillation across an active gap, wherein capitalism could only be grasped through a critical perspective that is possible upon the structuring presence of difference. Note that Karatani is not presenting "the global" as an answer to Europe. What he is showing is how capital works through the very cosmopolitanism it produced in a problematic that very much mirrors the global world we speak of today wherein the antagonisms of difference is constitutive.[3] The basis to theorize a different relationship between Lacan and capital is not difficult to miss here: the thing is excessive, as the carrier of surplus, only insofar as it could obscure difference through an Other's desire, in the need to direct the lack elsewhere. This accounts for the anxieties, doubts, and apprehensions that underline our relationship to the capitalist object world. Karatani's mode of exchange has it that the object is excessive, put simply, because of the enigma of difference inherent to exchange value.

But the mode of exchange does not just allow for a properly global capitalist use of a Lacanian premise. To take the expansion of capitalism as the basis of our contemporary world is to also demystify the Lacanian notion of the symbolic order. Karatani does not use Lacan but he does leave us with a very fruitful opening for our discussion: the transcritical view of capital would have it that the otherness of language, the gap between word and thing, is merely the incommensurability occluded in capitalist exchange. There is, against the Lacanian view of language, no primary inaccessible trauma that launches the enigma of time. There is instead just the problem of difference. The gap in language consequently is just the gap qua difference structuring the mode of exchange. This is where the decolonial opening is most fruitful in the transcritique, for Karatani would present his alternative by reframing the gap as an ethical imperative to the other. This takes the merely theoretical to the practical where psychoanalysis, when it is all said and done, is about the point of monetary exchange that grounds the exchange with alterity that gives the transference its unconscious. We shall have more to say about this implication later in this chapter. We need to firstly make the more necessary comparisons.

The parallax of exchange

Our more specific textual consideration of the two will center on the different ways in which the parallax is conceived. For in many ways the decolonial opportunity for us to make this contrast was given by the fact that Žižek drew from Kojin Karatani to coin the parallax view. Žižek's readers know this term as referring to the encounter with the inherently voidal nature of the object at the threshold of cognition, where lack surfaces in the surplus manifesting the oscillation between contradictory standpoints. Žižek's temporal use of the parallax is evident where it is presented as a lens into contemporary political antagonisms in which the threshold at the grasp of the object is conceived as something met through contradictions over time. This is temporal, in fact avowedly Eurocentric, not only on account of how Žižek builds on Hegel's philosophy of history, where freedom and the void are discovered mutually through meeting with the failure of the object in time, but that politics and the place of freedom in other cultures are also to be judged from this standpoint. We have an opportunity to introduce a Karatanian corrective to this temporal use of the parallax not only through Žižek's minimal reading of Karatani but in showing how Karatani's parallax is treated in light of Žižek and the Eurocentric Lacanian's core political concerns. Key is how Žižek evokes Karatani's definition of the parallax while neglecting the transcritique. Žižek sees no value in Karatani's Kantianism, preferring to affirm Hegel immediately from the onset for positivizing the lack, for affirming a grounding gap in all thought and value.

By centring the discovery of the universal through the discovery of the lacking object in time, Žižek neglects the parallax's motive force as it were, for why it is that the oscillation happens between two possibilities rather than say a Deleuzian rhizomatic multiplicity. What Karatani shows with his reading of Kant and Marx is the difference in structuring the exchange of objects: Objects cannot be sold, and are thus excessive in the anticipation of a hypothetical buyer, without also the anticipation of the alterity from which the purchase will happen. The structuring difference is what makes Karatani's parallax transcendental in the Kantian sense of an a priori structure of thought. The Kantian thing-in-itself by this is the thing that is exchanged in a global market, and the suprasensible "surplus" is the value form that is produced as a result. It is here, in the antinomy of sameness and difference that capital is momentarily stabilized, formed around the object as exchangeable qua a "more" reproduced through exchange. It is here too that we are brought to the key term that will lead us to a global psychoanalytic potential in Karatani, namely, his use of the notion of "intermundial" to describe the gap that the globalization of capital encounters and its value form could only temporarily occlude. There is as a result no need to posit a standpoint beyond or behind the object for as long as the tradable commodity produces a parallax across differing epistemic standpoints, a parallax to be grasped in the continued shifting of perspectives produced by the process of exchange. And it is here too that we get a global parallax. It is a perspective from the differences that capitalism contends with in homogenizing the value form. What this means more theoretically is that, against what Žižek wants to insist, there is no perspective as a totality of lack after the fact. There is only the transcritique that perpetually looks into the transcendental basis of production in exchange for an ethics of otherness in the intermundial. There is as a result no "ultimate void" accounting for the torsion in the pursuit of being and nothingness. There are just "moments" that are bracketed from the transcritical oscillation in how the object is now commodified for global trade networks. We can, to be sure, still retain much of Žižek's premise about the voidal impasse inherent to objects and how this produces the parallax shift of perspectives. What we must now consider is how this is an object cast in the capital value form qua the formation of the world as we know it.

The intermundial gap allows us to understand the parallax as a transcritical operation embedded in the expansion of the very cosmopolitan world capital produces and alienates. Consequently, with the transcritique we also have a crucial way of repositioning the Eurocentric Lacanian's view of the universal. For the Žižekian views difference as a problem after the fact, in which the refusal of difference is prior. Thus he can speak of an already excluded otherness, or the identification of those outside with the inside, that the marginalized can disrupt. The universal is consequently conceived as foreclosed, as the outside that disturbs the fictional completeness of the inside. The parallax is to be circulating across these hard and fast borders. This it goes without saying is also how Europe eventually becomes the constant measure of "sameness" with which other civilizations are to be judged. Europe is stable until something else disrupts it to provide us with an expanded universal. The transcritical parallax, on the other hand, sees the universal as already given qua the universal economy where money is proliferating to neutralize difference across the intermundial. What is alienating is the sameness forced through this economy. Difference is not something that must be rediscovered upon disavowal. It is always already there to be regulated in the exchange. Difference is never successfully repressed nor expelled. Karatani thus summarizes the transcritique as follows: "this is not to say that our thought could never be universal because of future others. On the contrary, the question of universality could not be *posed* without taking the others into consideration" [italics added] (Katatani, 2005, p. 44). Where the Eurocentric Lacanian sees the world in terms of a civilizational race to nothingness, the transcritical parallax sees that the interstitial, intermundia, gap is always already given to be re-perpetuated by the production of surplus value on a global scale.

Žižek's historicity proper

We have a suitable entry point into Žižek's notion of historicity – which for our interests, accounts for the object in time, and thus the account of the object in European time – in his politicized view of history. We find a curious and telling moment in *Surplus Jouissance: A Guide for the Perplexed* where Žižek (2022) states his approval – after and despite the decades of sustained criticisms – toward Fukuyama's declaration that "history" as we have known it has ended. Žižek is in general agreement with Fukuyama that we have come to an endpoint with the possible ways that the future could be imagined. But Žižek pushes this to a more radical conclusion to ground it in capitalism. History has ended "in some properly metaphysical sense" because our immersion into late capitalism is now final and total to ultimately confirm "the end of historical experience as we know it" (Žižek, 2022, p. 137). All historical thinking, and thus all experiences of time, cannot avoid capital as the ultimate horizon of all thought. The impending implosion of global capital is universally clear to determine the shape of *all* possible philosophy and politics to come. History in this sense is over because there can only be one overarching story to tell about the present, and there can only be one story because there is at the core of capitalism the crisis that has engulfed everyone to face the same fate.

In a dialectical move, Žižek points to the clearest evidence for the end of history in the proliferating demands for more history. For it is only at the overwhelming face of capital's intensifying totality that the need to make sense of time and origins, of how we got to the here and now, becomes a pressing demand. There are two ways we can understand this. The first is political. We can only have history if we recognize that "history" in some sense is impossible, where an anxious "end" to things is already anticipated and alternatives are needed. But to recognize the present as the condition for historical thinking is to also recognize that we are effectively trapped in capitalist temporality, that is to say, the temporality of a system that forces us to question time. Consequently, history from now on can no longer be a history of pure difference, of a past that is beyond the comprehension of the present. There is no longer a naive neutral historical stance. Whatever difference that is found in the past must be understood as a response to contemporary universal urgencies. Under capitalism "We cannot ever occupy a neutral place exempted from history from which we could compare different epochs" (Žižek, 2022, p. 10). The second, more important way into Žižek's historical outlook, is philosophical in that it pursues the ontological implication of this claim. If history is the central preoccupation of our time it is as a response to a more fundamental lack that underlines the production of history. As the cause of historical thinking this lack is ahistorical. It is outside the "time" it produces as "history". The more loaded claim that follows is how the time is produced out of a traumatic relationship with the lack that lends the need to produce history its urgency.

Žižek calls this philosophical approach to the politics of history "historicity" to present it as a critique of the constructivist approach to history that he calls "historicism". By historicism, Žižek has in mind the tendency to understand socio-political phenomena by way of contextualizing them within their historical conditions. "The historical" in this view provides the frame with which the social and the conceptual could be more expansively thought. Deconstruction, Žižek believes, is emblematic of this approach. Žižek understands its importance and affirms its fundamental premise: "all social reality is ultimately contingent, constructed in historically specific circumstances, there are no trans-historical essentials, the basic form of ideology is the eternalization of some historically specific constant" (Žižek, 2022, p. 136). But Žižek also claims that this outlook does not go far enough because it exempts its own standpoint from being historicized: "Such a historicist approach exempts from the domain of historical relativism its own stance which is silently universalized, i.e., historicism applies the same notion of history to all historical epochs," namely by thinking that all epochs are historical in the same way (Žižek, 2022, p. 137). This is compounded by the assumption that all objects are historical to begin with:

> we should always bear in mind that historicisation can also be ideology, not only because it applies a procedure of historicisation clearly grounded in our time to all epochs, but, more importantly, when it reduces to a historical variable a basic feature of a certain domain.
>
> (Žižek, 2022, p. 158)

Historicists are not aware that they are "naturalizing" and taking as self-evident, and thus universalizing, the historical approach.

To be truly historicist is to historicize history by de-universalizing the desire for "history" itself and show it for the historically situated attitude and impulse it is. To be historical, by this, is not to know history through the particular details of a given narrative but to recognize lack as the structure causing the production of histories. To recognize this traumatic relation to lack is to understand that we cannot encounter it directly as if it were an object. Rather we know it through the distinct tensions and dynamics unique to the given situation. To describe this, Žižek points to how the lack is felt through the failure of history, particularly in the tension between the assumption that everything could be historicized, on one hand, and the recognition that the process of historicizing itself is a construct, on the other, that all narratives fail insofar as they must be reproduced and sustained. This tension indeed is what accounts for the movement of historical thought. Consequently, history's structuring lack cannot be known directly, as if an object to behold for contemplation but through history's productive tension. But describing the basis of historicism this way allows Žižek to make a stronger claim and present this underlying lack as what is truly universal. What is truly universal about history is that everyone is trying to think historically and failing, anchored as they are to their situation. This is why Žižek highlights the ahistorical kernel of history for its inherent antagonism, as

> something that cannot simply be explained, accounted for, in terms of historical circumstances, conditions and reactions, but acts as a structuring principle that displays dynamics of its own … More precisely, we should engage in the dialectic between a universal notion and its reality, in which the very gap between the two sets in motion the simultaneous transformation of reality and of the notion itself.
>
> (Žižek, 2000, p. 106)

To grasp this as being at work in historical thought is what Žižek means when he claims that it is imperative to "Radicalise historicism itself" (Žižek, 2022, p. 10).

With this we can understand the motivations behind Žižek's distinct evocation of history's end. It is a philosophical "end" where we can go beyond preoccupations with particular histories to think of history as a universal experience. Žižek's historicist claim about the end of history therefore should not at all be dismissed as hyperbolic. It is a claim about what we now "finally" know about the need for history. Žižek is pointing to a lack in the real that structures the history that fills the imaginary and the symbolic. Žižek's conception of lack's impossibility as the antagonistic cause of history enables him to explain capital's regenerative capacities, in which the traumatic lack accounts for the reproduction of the commodity and capital's value form. This is how the lack in history is also isomorphic to the lack of capital in which the circuit of commodity exchange is similarly a fiction to anticipate the timelessness of endless trade. But what all this also means is that the historicist is inevitably reliant on a conception of time. For Žižek also presents lack as a standpoint afforded only through a distinct temporal politics unique to the here and now. We may never know the cause of it all directly but we know it is a product of a discernible present where the conditions of knowledge and understanding have been irrevocably transformed. Thus Žižek has no choice but to evoke some kind of temporal marker in "Modernity" however much he leaves it undefined, as the epistemic game changer: "Modernity not only introduces a new horizon of understanding, it changes the entire field" (Žižek, 2022, p. 10). It is only under the circumstances of this modernity that the need to think universally – for which history is indispensable – became a problem to begin with.

The parallax at the end

This requires us to go further and account not just for what underlies history but how lack is accounted for. For this we need to turn to Žižek's most important resource in Hegel's critique of Kant's transcendental commitment to a noumenal realm of things-in-themselves. Hegel works with the immanence of appearance to conclude that instead of a substance lying in wait beyond appearances there is only a negativity around which all objects are abstracted. It is to detail our understanding of the experience with this negativity that Žižek describes the real as "purely parallactic": it is not a "thing" so much as a "gap" between competing perspectives, "perceptible only in the shift from the one to the other" (Žižek, 2022, p. 131). The parallax view to be sure does not just describe *any* meeting of contradictory ideas. It is when the contradiction cannot hold as to cause two primary effects. First, an object could only be graspable if its opposite is excluded, that is to say, bracketed. Conversely, the once-excluded object could be understood only after the initial one was removed from view. Thus the parallax view is often described as a movement, an oscillation between contradictory ideas. This takes us to the second effect. Being is to be placed on neither side of the equation but within the antagonism itself. There is therefore nothing beyond the object. There is only the antagonism where the lack of the object is encountered: "We do not have two perspectives, we have a perspective and what eludes it, and the other perspective fills in the void of what we could not see from the first perspective" (Žižek, 2006, p. 29).

The salience of the object being cognized is retained but it is not some truth beyond phenomena. It is in the antagonism within the lack from which it was produced:

The Real is thus the disavowed X on account of which our vision of reality is anamorphically distorted; it is simultaneously the Thing to which direct access is not possible and the obstacle which prevents this direct access, the Thing which eludes our grasp and the distorting screen which makes us miss the Thing. More precisely, the Real is ultimately the very shift of perspective from the first standpoint to the second.

(Žižek, 2006, p. 26)

Key for our discussion is how the real of the parallax is evoked to highlight a temporal point. It is temporal as the threshold at the endpoint of philosophical exploration, or put in Hegelian terms, when thought has run out of appearances to sublate: "is not 'parallax' yet another name for a fundamental antinomy which can never be dialectically 'mediated/sublated' into a higher synthesis, since there is no common language, no shared ground, between the two levels?" (Žižek, 2006, p. 4). It is also temporal insofar as the parallax occurs where there is nowhere left to go because whatever truth could be gathered from appearance itself has been exhausted. The parallax in many ways could be considered as the perspective from the crisis within appearance itself. Nowhere is this temporal dimension more evident than in the subjectivity revealed, for the parallaxical undulation scrutinizing the nature of the object is ultimately for the thinking subject. The parallax reveals the active presence of a subject shaping the nature of the object, in which "an 'epistemological' shift in the subject's point of view always reflects an 'ontological' shift in the object itself" (Žižek, 2006, p. 17). This, however, does not confirm the subject's authority. Instead, it confirms the subject and object's mutual impossibility. The parallax underlines the negativity in the constitution of things as it speaks to the subject's search for the object. Negativity is the condition for both positivity and consequently the subject's detection of its lacking state. Hegel again looms large here, namely his account of the Night of the World which sees subjectivity as a pure self of empty nothing, a fragile placeholder for a plurality of representations coming and going. The parallaxical undulation between an object and its opposite is a moment when this plurality is captured for contemplation. But it instantiates in effect a subject divided across two opposing realities of the object and thus a knower shaped by the vagaries of what can and cannot be known. The object eventually manifests the gap in "reality" as the subject registers its abyssal condition.

It is also here, on this Hegelian note, that we can see how Žižek incorporates Lacan in a more specific register. Žižek details the nature of the parallax object with reference to the objet petit a as "the very cause of the parallax gap" (Žižek, 2006, p. 35). This refers to the minimal opening around which "reality" is shaped, where the subject is constituted as knowledge appears. The object's main feature, however, is difference. This is what Žižek describes as the "minimal difference that divides one and the same object from itself", that is to say the constitutive difference that renders an entity lacking (Žižek, 2006, p. 35). But the Hegelian void stresses how the objet petit a hosts the "'pure' difference which cannot be grounded in positive substantial properties" by which the objet could be more fundamentally understood as the condition for difference to be a problem at all (Žižek, 2006, p. 35). Needless to say, the object's groundlessness also underlines the lack in the subject–object distinction, namely, as the site of where the subject, in his short-circuiting objectal pursuits, ultimately registers its own lack. The object "is the paradoxical object which directly is the subject" (Žižek, 2006, p. 213). As the structural basis of subjective failure, the objet a is a "pure parallax object" (Žižek, 2006, p. 36) This parallaxical conception of the Real constitutes the core feature of Žižek's dialectical materialism. It is materialist in its commitment to the fundamentality of negativity, and thus the antagonistic gap shaping ideas. It is dialectical in its attention also to how the very antagonism that structures the lack in the object constitutes the subject. The evocation of dialectics also works as a philosophical alternative to the limits of historical materialism. Dialectical materialism does not simply present a more solid epistemic anchor to historical materialism, it also introduces the subject's unconscious role in historical change. Žižek does a great deal with this philosophical use of the object as he emphasizes how the parallax encounter underlines "the fundamental feature of today's society" (Žižek, 2006, p. 162). For at the heart of all this is really the parallax view as an account of social reproduction, namely how the world we know it today happens upon the antagonisms of the void. The parallax, indeed, is not "that which remains the same in all possible (symbolic) universes: the parallax Real is rather that which accounts for the very multiplicity of appearances of the same underlying Real" (Žižek, 2006, p. 131). It is less a thing than it is a "hard bone of contention which pulverises the sameness into the multitude of appearances" (Žižek, 2006, p. 131).

With this we can properly deepen our inquiry into how Žižek accounts for Europe's greatness as "politics proper" by appealing to the impossibility of lack. Politics proper is not to be identified in the particular agents of disruption but rather what they reveal of the gap that enables the continuous disruption of the social order in the first place and here the histories of politics and philosophy are brought together. Žižek traces the actuality of politics proper from the democratic experiments of Ancient Greece to include "all great democratic events" (by which he really means European events):

> from the French Revolution (in which the Third Estate proclaimed itself identical to the nation as such against the aristocracy and clergy) to the demise of European socialism, in which groups such as the Czech Civic Forum proclaimed themselves representative of the entire society against the party nomenklatura
>
> (Žižek, 1998, p. 989)

"Something emerged in Ancient Greece" to set "politics proper" off in historical motion "from the very beginning" (Žižek, 1998, p. 992). This basically forms the basis of his "leftist plea for Eurocentrism" as the reminder that we cannot think of the political without some reference, however generalized, to European democratic events. With this he charts a particular, and one might add classicist and actually conservative, view of European history through taking for granted a cultural and intellectual continuity between Greece and Western Europe to show how Europe has seen the most eventual instances in which the parts of no-part rose to disrupt the given order of things.

Part 3: Karatani's parallax and the intermundial

That the parallax view is presented to us as a Hegelian operation should come across as rather curious, given that Žižek drew it from a Kantian source in Kojin Karatani's conception of the transcritique. Just as how we've seen in Žižek, Karatani describes the parallax as "The reality that is exposed through difference" where contradictions are grappled with (Karatani, 2005, p. 3). As we also saw in Žižek, Karatani describes the encounter as one through a "critical oscillation" (Karatani, 2005, p. 4). But Karatani originally formulated the transcritique upon finding "the parallax view" quoted where Kant himself describes the perspective imbued in the antinomies. The transcritique is consequently presented as the thinking that happens in the movement therein. Žižek's appropriation of Karatani then takes the parallax without the transcritique on the basis that Kant did not go far enough as to affirm the void: "Hegel's move is not to 'overcome' the Kantian division but, rather, to assert it 'as such,' to drop the need for its 'overcoming,' for the additional 'reconciliation' of opposites: to gain insight – through a purely formal parallax shift – into how positing the distinction 'as such' already is the looked-for 'reconciliation'" (Žižek, 2006, p. 27). This is supposed to apply to Karatani by implication. There is no transcritique other than the potency of the void itself: "Kant is not unable to reach the infinite – he is unable to see how he already has what he is looking for" (Žižek, 2006, p. 27). Žižek in other words points to the supposed givenness of the Hegelian void to falsify Karatani's use of Kant, namely for retaining the transcritique without getting the fundamental ontological point that the antinomies were just circling around the more primordial negativity:

> This means that Karatani is wrong in the way he opposes Kant and Hegel: Hegel who can think the parallax in its radicality, as the priority of the inherent antagonism over the multiple/failed reflection of the transcendent/impossible Thing.
>
> (Žižek, 2006, p. 25)

What Žižek neglects to mention is that Karatani's reading of Kant was put in dialogue with an equally distinct reading of Marx. It is in the combination of the two that the transcritical perspective was produced. To see this we need to consider Karatani's project more fully. For while Karatani did draw the transcritique from Kant, he understands the object as not an isolable thing but qua the process of exchange capitalism facilitates. For this we need to begin at the very basics to consider Karatani's distinct claim that Kantian metaphysics is ultimately grounded on the ethical imperative to respond to incompatible paradigm of values. The antinomies are not to be read as purely mental operations but one grounded in Kant's fundamentally cosmopolitan concerns, on how a universal set of values could be forged and maintained in a world defined by differences. This very cosmopolitanism was what informed Kant's Categorical Imperative, which Karatani reads as a universalization that anticipates future objections from a potential encounter with literal strangers dead or alive. A statement does not become antinomic without the anticipation of a radical other who can disobey the rules of a given paradigm. Consequently the parallaxical void is not empty. It is excessive because it anticipates another subject. The transcendental position "began with the pronounced parallax between my stance and the others' stance" (Karatani, 2005, p. 112). This cosmopolitan reading of Kant's metaphysics – cosmopolitan in its recognition of a world that can only be open to others – enables Karatani to recast Kant's thing-in-itself as the would-be participant of an ethical community we have no choice, owing to the way the world is complexifying beyond whatever we like and can do, to be accountable to:

> The others – whose who do not share a common set of rules – are not only those in outside communities, but also include those who do not exist in the here and now – future humans as well as the dead. Rather, with respect to otherness, they should be the model. Generally speaking, ethics takes only living beings in consideration, while Kantian ethics, that sees the others as the thing-in-itself, takes hold of *the others who have been and who will be.* [italics in original]

It is important to stress that Karatani isn't historically contextualizing Kant to show how the latter's philosophy was informed by an emerging cosmopolitanism. Karatani reads Kant to make the radical gesture of showing how the limits of what the mind could grasp were found in how the emerging global world reproduces incommensurability as a problem. Karatani wants to demonstrate how the formal rules governing thought that Kant was trying to outline were structured through the deadlocks where the challenge from other value systems are already given. Karatani, in other words, reads Kant to find the gap in being as produced through realizing the inevitability of living ethically among different others. The gap isn't just there. It is valuable because there an incommensurate something on the other side of it.[4] This already leads us to a crucial implication which Karatani does not proclaim but will be useful for our analysis. The gap in being should only be posited if it is about the recognition of other paradigms qua incommensurable. This consequently should not be making us think in terms of "pure" voids: "the Kantian point is that the universality of phenomena (qua synthetic judgement) is taken into consideration only insofar as we wholeheartedly posit the alterity or otherness of the other" (Karatani, 2005, p. 51).

If Karatani points to an isomorphy between Kantian transcendental philosophy and the problem of difference that makes the cosmopolitan world, Marx materializes the same presupposition by tracing the object as it acquires surplus value through the exchange that happens across radically different value systems. Thus where Kant informs Karatani's notion of the parallax view, Marx's critique of political economy will be where Karatani pursues the implications of transcritique. For Karatani, this gap is where money can multiply to regenerate capital. Indeed he takes it to be Marx's most important insight: "only where there are heterogeneous systems can money transform into capital that gains surplus value from the exchange between systems" (Karatani, 2005, p. 227). Capital consequently is described as a synthetic movement. It is firstly synthetic where it binds – a move which internalizes an "outside" – two different value systems together. Put in an overly simplified way, nothing could be sold for surplus if the need and inability to identify with a different desire – the gap that structures capitalist exchange – was there to begin with.

To detail how Karatani links Kant and Marx to describe this gap we shall turn to where they're brought together to inform Karatani's presentation of this chapter's central term. Karatani describes the unique historical location of his transcritical parallax by appealing to "intermundia" to describe the interstices between communities, the gap revealed in the failure of understanding. Karatani, to be sure, does not use the notion of "the global" in the way we are interested in. He was still working for hermeneutic reasons within the ambit of European thought. But we should nonetheless identify how Karatani clearly theorized in recognition of the need to integrate different spaces and circumstances and that this need saw the greater extension of the parallaxical standpoint. He grounds Marx's thought process in the gap between political developments in France and Germany to show how capital could only be theorized through the parallaxical oscillation across different historical settings. The fact that Marx eventually sought exile in London played no small part in embedding a transcritical spirit into his theorizing. Kant is well known for his introversion but Karatani stresses how this should not be taken to mean that Kant was removed from the world. Konigsberg was a major trading city – closer to London than Berlin – whose maritime commerce saw the coming together of traders from different parts of the globe. Karatani similarly stresses how the cogito was formulated while in exile in Amsterdam, where Descartes was deeply affected by a culture of indifferent individualism. The "Cartesian cogito, the subject of radical scepticism, cannot be grasped if separated from this kind of space" (Karatani, 2005, p. 135).

The lateral way in which Karatani pictures the intermundia demands that we understand it uniquely as a "non-space". On one hand, this obviously evokes some sense of "space" insofar as this is the space formed in the recognition of a gap between radically different agents. Karatani himself emphasizes that we cannot help but to think of it first in reference to concrete spaces. He locates the development of modern European philosophy and radical philosophy - its preoccupation with the voidal nature of the object - in the emergence of cosmopolitanism bound through a growing global money economy. But on the other hand, these are very much provisional constructs for they are only posited in the gap in historical thinking, particularly when different spaces appear incommensurate enough that they must be brought together (through the mode of exchange) in order to understand the present. Put in more critical terms, the intermundial, as interstices, is an a priori feature of thought that is internalized to link a world together from the perspective of capitalism as the global money economy: "And this interstice is a space of sheer difference; finally, it is insubstantial and amorphous. It cannot be spoken of positively; no sooner than it is, its function is lost. It is a transcendental topos – a space for transcritique" (Karatani, 2005 p. 134).

The intermundial therefore could be summarized as a "non-space" as it is not produced by the imaginary to evade difference. It is a negative "space" as the gap that shows how subjects are linked through a common recognition of a lack. Indeed that we have a problem describing the intermundia in spatial terms is precisely why the parallax is required as the view at "the loss of the space of intercourse in the intermundia" (Karatani, 2005, p. 100). It is where difference emerges and the need for sameness can only produce an incessant transposition across different standpoints. Karatani takes this at work in Marx itself. Marx theorized capital through the mode of exchange by tracking the *movement* of commodities as they are exchanged for money to regenerate the capitalist economy. With this, Karatani memorably describes "Marx's transcritical footwork" as accounting for its unique universal theoretical quality:

> Marx persisted in criticizing dominant discourses within systems, from an external footing, constantly transposing and turning. Yet the external position is not something that exists substantively. This footing is the difference or the interstice between discourses which abrogate any standpoint. What is crucial here is Marx's transcritical footwork that opposes historical heterogeneity to idealism, while counterposing the autonomous power of category that constitutes reality to empiricism. This prompt transposition ultimately exceeds any selfsame system of thought that can be attributed to him (and because what he says is often inverted according to contexts, one can induce any thought one likes

from him). This footing is the difference or the interstice between discourses which abrogates any standpoint.

(Karatani, 2005, p. 164)

Indeed, the Marxian dialectic between money and commodities is premised on the transcritical, most importantly non-substantive, footwork Marx demonstrated in his writing.

We will discuss how this gap should allow us to imagine the global for psychoanalysis soon enough. For now it is important to pursue the theoretical implications of Karatani's presentation in more detail. With the footwork demonstrated, we can move a step further and describe capitalism's synthetic operation where commodities become more money to overcome the intermundial gap. It is in this particular way, of how differences are resolved, that Karatani identifies capital's mystifying quality: "What drives us in capitalism is neither the ideal nor the real ... but the metaphysics and theology originated in exchange and commodity form" (Karatani, 2005, p. 221). Money at the same time acquires its sublime quality for its "universal exchangeability" (Karatani, 2005, p. 213). Crisis consequently occurs when there is a halt in this regeneration of surplus, when there is a gap between the standpoint of capital and the standpoint of consumption, and put more simply when money could not be exchanged because things cannot be sold, and money as a result cannot be transformed into more capital. This takes us to the essence of Karatani's transcritique: "Scrutinizing the commodity form thus necessitates a transcendental elucidation of the form that makes objects commodity and/or money" (Karatani, 2005, p. 198). Transcritique requires us to be attentive to the problem of different value systems which the reproduction of capital was generated to overcome. For this it must be situated in the parallaxical movement across the capitalist world not as a smooth process of homogenization but as how the need for exchangeable objects is a response to a fundamentally incommensurate world. By this point a key difference should be evident. Žižek positivizes lack as negativity. In Karatani, the gap is structurally instantiated via a logically incommensurate other.

The implication for psychoanalytic thinking requires a brief stop to its Marxist implications. By now, it should be obvious why Karatani eschews the mode of production as the primary lens of political economy. For Karatani, capitalism is ultimately regenerated by the capitalization of money after the sale of commodities. Thus a mode of production, however industrial, does not necessarily guarantee capitalism unless there is already an existing network of trade through which industrial products could be sold. Similarly, commodification cannot be accounted for without the anticipation of exchange by which the product loses its old value for its market price. This, to be sure, does not mean that mode of production and commodification are insignificant terms. Transcritique is presented as their alternative, rather for two reasons. Taken on their own they cannot account for how the abstractions in the regeneration of capital are produced. Capitalism, understood first as a mode of exchange, means that commodification doesn't just happen. It has to be first subjected to the exchange process in a way in which money is multiplied. What this means is that capital works in a world of already-existing non-commodified objects. It does not produce anything. It can only be a parasite over already-existing things. This leads us to the second key aspect of transcritique, indeed its main epistemic point and presumption, that the parallaxical perspective presupposes that there is nothing before or outside capital. The contradictions – between the capitalist mode of production and pre-capitalist mode of production, the commodified and the non-commodified or the state and capital, historical or dialectical materialisms – are immanent to the generation of capitalism. Differences retain as antinomies produced within the tensions in capital's expansion:

> Marx brackets noncapitalist production as well as state intervention, namely, he treats them as if they were already internalised, because they ultimately have to follow the principles of the capitalist economy; because the capitalist economy has the potency to constantly involve its externality and turn it into its internal given. Such is the autonomous potency of the capitalist economy.
>
> (Karatani, 2005, p. 160)

Where Kant's parallax encountered the antinomies as they orbit around the thing-in-itself conceived as a static impasse, Marx's transcritique addresses difference by trailing how the surplus is reproduced across the exchange of objects that sees differences synthesized. Where Kantian abstraction was produced to overcome difference, Marx traced the driving force of abstraction in the regeneration of capital. The transcritical view in other words tracks how capitalism is produced as a crisis of synthesis.

Žižek appears to recognize how Karatani formulates the transcritical parallax as a cosmopolitan reading of Kant but aside from generalities there is no sustained reasoning as to why the parallax needs to be emphasized at the expense of the transcritical. We have enough however where Žižek points out his biggest problem with Karatani in that the latter supposedly "identifies the transcendental subject with transcendental illusion" (Žižek, 2006, p. 22). Little is explained as to where and why Karatani says this, but we could apply the basic premises of Žižek's Hegelianism to say that Karatani was not able to take the next step of affirming the void as the resolution of the antinomies. Put in plainer Lacanian terms, Karatani's merely Kantian use of the parallax did not affirm the subject "behind" the imaginary. But we turn to Karatani's transcritical reading of Kant to see that this is not the case. There is very much a gap but Karatani's interest is not in the gap itself but how it produced by the otherness in the gap. Difference moves the antinomies:

It is something like one's own face in the sense that it undoubtedly exists but cannot be seen except as an image (read *phenomenon*). What is crucial here is henceforth the antinomy as a pronounced parallax – the sole thing that reveals what is more than an image (phenomenon). In fact Kant poses antinomy not only in the section on the transcendental dialectic but almost everywhere. For instance, as one of the crucial examples, he draws out transcendental subjectivity X from the antinomy between the Cartesian thesis, "There is an identical ego," and the human antithesis, "There is no identical ego." [italics in original]

(Karatani, 2005, p. 50)

Karatani does not "affirm" the transcendental subject as void but this is because of the otherness moving with the introspective framework itself for which the ethical is premised. Let's read how Karatani describes what is "in" the void. The following statement is how he summarizes the link between the ethical transcendental in Kant:

It is not the thing that negates (falsifies) a scientific hypothesis; it is not the thing but the future others who speak. However, while it is the other who can negate our cognition (qua phenomenon), this negation has to be accompanied by the other's sense-datum (qua the thing). What is crucial here is the otherness, be it of the thing or of the other person. But this otherness is nothing mystical. What Kant implied by the thing-in-itself was the alterity of the other that we can never take for granted and internalise just on our whim or at our convenience.

(Karatani, 2005, p. 51)

With this we can also revisit Žižek's primary bone of contention with Karatani. For Karatani, Kant did not posit the void because that would mean eradicating the falsifying other which moves introspection. Remember how Karatani finds in the Kantian framework, an "other" qua an other who can challenge a given paradigm, not an abstract other whose mere existence is to be hypothesized.

Kant attempted to obliterate the complicity inherent in introspection precisely by confining himself to the introspective framework. Here one can observe the attempt to introduce an objectivity (qua otherness) that is totally alien to the conventional space of introspection mirror.

(Karatani, 2005, p. 49)

The transcritique is a void but it is a void that produces the need for critique which does not require a voidal subject to grasp: for Kant, "the 'critique' was inseparable from his 'being as criticising,' that is, externalised existence" (Karatani, 2005, p. 95).

Part 4: Where do voids come from?

The main difference between Žižek's Hegelianism and Karatani's other-oriented futurity will become more apparent when we consider the former's civilizational emphasis. For Žižek's historicity proper, in its appeal to the void that causes the reproduction of histories, is also temporalized to conclude that it could only be realized by a certain type of subject. If there is a subject that is able to think about this lack it is the subject found through the parallax view after being called to first seek what was beyond the object. The emptiness of the subject was never a given, in other words. It was only found "after" the lacking object was met. There is no need to tell the history of philosophy if that is not the case. It is also through this encounter that the subject's freedom is revealed. This, against the liberal notion of freedom, is not freedom as the exercise of the subject's inalienable right. It is freedom in spirit's encounter with the inevitability of division, wherein the subject realizes the limits of thought in the essential contingency of things. But that this subjective freedom is realized retrospectively, in the contradictions encountered through the pursuit of the object, means that freedom becomes an irreversible feature of thinking itself. Freedom, in the intrinsic divide that binds subject and object, would from thereon underline our epistemic and ethical outlook.

There are two implications that are crucial for us to grasp here. First, the Žižekian-historicist outlook is in effect history with a capital H. The historicist reflects on time after time, the point at which the truth of history could be "grasped". Indeed Žižek defines history proper as the antagonistic self-realization of the universal: "the universal principle is caught in an 'infinite' struggle with itself; that is, the struggle is each time a struggle for the fate of the universality itself" (Žižek, 2012, p. 217). The second implication is that by linking the empty object with the discovery of the thinking subject Žižek has in mind a particular history in which thought itself was a burden, a problem that required solving. Or put slightly more expansively, the need to question reason itself could have only "made sense" in conditions when multiplicity became a problem in time. The lacking real cannot be timeless because it is something found from the standpoint at which multiplicity itself appears as a problem. One therefore does not just question history because it is a good idea. The need to question history could have only emerged through a particular experience of being overwhelmed by history or rather the need to think in universal terms.

The transcritical standpoint also makes a specific point about time, given that the parallax so conceived by Karatani, tracks the regeneration of capital as time. It would as a result paint a different picture of "history". Capital differentiates a present from a past and this occurs in the contingencies realized across differing spaces and their contrary value systems. But there is a sense in which the Kant versus Hegel dichotomy in Žižek's use of the parallax distracts us from a more important universal implication to Karatani's project. For the historical view it generates does not concern itself with time in the abstract. It is rather history as the greater attentiveness to the ethical. This takes us to Karatani's understanding of labor-power as a key aspect of the surplus that renders the otherness in exchange. For Karatani, the different paradigms that ensure the incommensurability in the intermundial are met in capital's contradictory relationship to labor-power, namely as that which is exterior to capital: "capitalist production relies on a special commodity (labour-power commodity). It is humans, who cannot be discarded when they are excessive, who cannot be readily reproduced when scarce" (Karatani, 2005, p. 250). Labor-power to be sure does not refer to individual laborers. By labor-power Karatani has in mind the subjectivization that occurs where different aspects of life are commodified in capital's process of surplus generation. This as far as capitalism is concerned is where the different paradigms of values are met and antagonized. Indeed Karatani considers the subjectivization of labor as one of the *topos* for transcritique: "it is first and foremost the process of the reproduction of labour-power as a topos of ordeal for capital's self-realisation, and hence the position in which workers can finally be the subject" (Karatani, 2005, p. 21). It is capital's limit insofar as it is that which can only be exterior to capital. It is that which capital must always consume. It is consequently capital's crisis point as that which can never be wholly neutralized in the exchange process. As the underside of capital, the underside of the generation of surplus, labor-power understood as a fundamentally human, non-commodifiable, aspect of the commodity is the site of the ethical at the heart of the transcritical project.

This sees Kant and Marx linked together in even greater urgency. It underscores the difference constituting the Kantian imperative as an ethics of futurity:

> the condition for a certain cognition to be universal is not necessarily that it be based upon an a priori rule, but that it be exposed to the judgement of others who follow a different set of rules … The veritable others whom we cannot anticipate are the ones who live in the future. Or, more accurately, the future is truly the future only insofar as it is of the other; the future we can anticipate is not the veritable future.
>
> (Karatani, 2005, p. 100)

This ethical futurity enables Karatani to reaffirm the centrality of historical politics for Marxism. For as long as capitalism occurs through the interstices, radical politics must inevitably force a confrontation with the other, the aspects of life, beyond exchange. Consequently, the differences underlying the intermundial situates the motor of history not in the concept, in which a new abstraction is produced to merely reflect the contradictions of a current "new" time, but in the interstices of differences that necessitated the added abstraction to begin with. This obviously wrests historical thinking away from Hegel. There is no logical development of the concept in the temporal passage of self-awareness. There is only the confrontation with more incommensurabilities in the expansion of the global market. Transcritique is positioned at the parallax across the intensification of capitalism's crisis tendencies in which the greater imperative to be ethical, in the realization of constitutive difference, will be felt.

The contrast between the two, especially where thinking the universal is concerned, is substantial. Where Žižek takes historical difference as a privilege, Karatani posits it as a necessary feature of thinking through capitalism. Insofar as history is to be tracked through the intensification of capital, Karatani emphasizes that temporality qua history is always underlined by a certain opacity. This is not an opacity found through abstract thinking but in the proliferation of surplus through the proliferation of money. There is always then an ethical imperative on the horizon: "The transcendental position that began with the pronounced parallax between my stance and the others' stance persistently entails the problematic of alterity. In this sense, the transcendental attitude is thoroughly ethical" (Karatani, 2005, p. 112).

Žižek theorizes the void to as a basis for his non-identitarian politics of negativity but it is also clear that Europe is upheld as the spatial and historical manifestation of the encounter with this tension. Consequently the end of history means the realization of what Europe has to really offer. This leads to the glaring issue in his evocation of the European, in which his appeal to Europe's inherently democratic modernity, reveals an overestimation of what emptiness, recast philosophically as the voidal-causal object, can do. We know of the reality of appearance only upon meeting the failure to grasp the thing-in-itself. There is no beyond at which one arrives. What is known is simply "the inherent power of negativity" (Žižek, 1998, p. 997). Žižek is clear that this power is not an inherent feature of thought. It is negativity that takes the disruptive nature of revolutionary politics to its most logical conclusion in which thought itself is subjected to disruption: "the suprasensible comes to exist only in the guise of an appearance of another dimension that interrupts the standard, normal order of phenomena" (Žižek, 1998, p. 997). By extension, the part of no-part's political emergence does not reveal a deeper truth about a social or economic system. It is the collapse of the political qua appearance. Politics proper does not point to an inherent good to be pursued or a reality beyond. It reveals rather the fundamental antagonism of politics that we can only encounter through the appearance of the part of no-part. In this regard, the part of no-part emerges rather literally as the part of the structuring nothingness:

this domain of appearance (that is, of symbolic fiction) is none other than that of politics, as distinguished from the social body subdivided into parts. There is appearance insofar as we are dealing with a part of no-part, insofar as a part not included in the whole of the social body (or included/excluded in a way it resists) protests against its position.

(Žižek, 1998, p. 996)

One might wonder why this otherwise interesting account of the structuring gap – even where politics is cast in light of the impossible object – needs to be European or that negativity has an "inherent power." Indeed, he appears to accord European negativity a certain, for lack of a better word, "magic," that politics proper is just a unique feature of Europe:

one can read it in the much more subversive sense of a tension in which the appearance of egaliberte, precisely, is not merely an appearance but *evinces an effectivity of its own* that allows it to set in motion the process of rearticulating actual socio-economic relations by way of their progressive politicisation. [italics added]

(Žižek, 1998, p. 995)

There is indeed something magical more literally where Žižek appeals to Levi-Strauss' notion of symbolic efficacy – a term informed through the latter's extensive ethnographic studies on native magic – to describe just how essentially European politics proper is:

One is tempted to use here the old Levi-Straussian term symbolic efficiency: the appearance of liberty is a symbolic fiction that, as such, possesses actual efficiency of its own.

(Žižek, 1998, p. 995)[5]

Žižek even refuses a socio-historical, account of Europe: "One should resist the properly cynical temptation of reducing it to a mere illusion that conceals a different actuality" (Žižek, 1998, p. 995). It is to demonstrate this symbolic efficacy that Žižek turns to the history of European political philosophy for proof: Just as we can look back to the history of Europe for "apparitions of politics proper, so too can we look back to the history of European political thought to see how the political was confronted to be refused and resolved: Political philosophy is thus, in all its different shapes, a kind of defense formation" (Žižek, 1998, p. 992). Žižek presents the key moments in the history of Western political thought – from Plato's Republic to Carl Schmitt's conservatism – as evidence of a history of failing to close the gap as it were, whose variations merely go to speak to the compelling presence and prominence of politics proper.

The evental moments unique to Europe are easier to account for if we consider if they should be treated as endogenous bursts of ingenuity. Take the

American War of Independence's much-overlooked Eastern cause as an example. While intellectually referencing European political thought, a key material basis for the Revolutionary War against the British was trade with China. The American demand for Chinese goods, mainly tea and porcelain, contributed to the flow of silver from America to China, which, in turn, caused a trade imbalance for the British Empire, further intensifying tensions between Great Britain and the Patriots that led to their divorce. For another example, consider Ian Coller's (2010) account of how the Jacobins, at the height of the French Revolutionary Terror, sought approval from France's Muslim subjects – in St Louis du Sénégal, Pondicherry, and Chandernagore in India and especially the Arabs that were already residing in Marseilles – to legitimize their construction of a new religious pluralism as an alternative to the Catholic Church.[6] Muslim support moreover was important to ensure the survival of the Revolution:

> By 1794, Muslim states were almost the only major powers still friendly to France. The rulers of Europe were allied against the Republic, and even the fledgling United States had cooled relations with its former benefactor. Without Muslim support … France might not have held out against the onslaught of European reaction.
>
> (Coller, 2020)

To this we can also add the unique global conjunctions that also produced the possibility of the parallax to be thought so extensively. Indeed, the way that Žižek frames the parallax as a matter of Kant versus Hegel has unfortunately seen Karatani situated on the former side of things. But there is a greater intellectual theater at work when we consider how Karatani theorized from the standpoint of Japan's historical uniqueness. The centrality of exchange in Marx was conceived firstly by Kozo Uno, Japan's foremost Marxist economist and thinker as the formalist response to a crucial impasse in the historical debate on Japanese capitalism, namely how capitalism could have developed so forcefully in Japan despite the endurance of a feudal mode of production. The key outlines of this debate resonate with discussions on the transition from feudalism to capitalism that centered on the disagreements between Maurice Dobb and Paul Sweezy in the 1950s and 1960s. But as Gavin Walker (2016) notes, Japanese Marxism bears the distinction of anticipating the relevance of this question by at least three decades from the beginning of the 1920s, owing to its uneven status as a military-industrial powerhouse in an Asia that was rapidly being overwhelmed by European colonial powers. Indeed, becoming a competitive global empire at the capitalist periphery saw to it that Japanese modernity and thus Japanese Marxism cannot be understood in the same temporal trajectory as that of Western European leftist politics. Gavin Walker (2020) maintains that Japan, in addition to having the longest 1968 - that is to say, the longest period of second wave leftist militancy - is likely the most Marxist country in the world, owing to Marx's far-reaching influence in the Japanese academy and in popular literature, among other venues.

So if a formal approach was needed it was because Japan was neither central nor peripheral and thus had a view into the interstitial gap undercutting the primary antagonisms that animate Marxist thinking. Thus the Western canon too is not approached as a hermetic whole but as a discourse moved through the problem of a gap. The international setting in which this reading occurred, and the politics at stake, meant that the gap cannot be understood as self-constitutive but geopolitical, compelled as it is by other times and flows. This is how we should similarly understand the formalism unique to Japanese Marxism, where abstraction is produced to enact the transcritical transposition where gaps between differences are too compelling. There was a need therefore to further universalize the purported universality that was already presumed in already-existing Marxism. Thus rather than to totalize the contradiction, and place Japanese capitalism at some unique "stage" of development, Uno opted for a meta-theoretical inquiry into the challenge of applying Marx in the first place. The question consequently became less about whether Marx could be applied to Japan but what it means to apply Marx at all. The need to continuously transpose Marx across perspectives is rooted in this spatial, or non-spatial, differential.

In any case, until the true extent of our lack-in-common is grasped in global terms we will only have the standard story to stick to. The European disavowal of politics proper will be upheld as a developmental achievement in comparison to other civilizations that have been less fortunate to miss out on the civilizational return of the repressed. Just as Hegel charted the passage of spirit in evolutionary terms, by comparing different states of self-consciousness across civilizations, so too would Žižek use lack to measure other cultures. Buddhism is critiqued for its passivity, for advocating a possible peace with the void.[7] Žižek approves of Islam where Muslims are most uneased by it, namely in its more fundamentalist and fanatical manifestations because that is presumably where the impossibility of the thing is most symptomatic and unbearable. By this point it is clear in psychoanalytic terms that the purported order produced as a result, however defensively, is as important as the constitutive disorder. One of the reasons why Europe is upheld as a promising political model has to do with its "*ethical standard* of society" [italics in original] (Žižek, 2013, p. 29). China is Žižek's example of a society that does not uphold such a standard. His evidence? He *heard* that people in China spit in public and throw food away. Meanwhile in Germany, clips of white crowds singing foreigners out are proudly viralized as the German government continues to provide logistical and diplomatic cover for Israel's genocide of Gaza. Eurocentric Lacanians will see this as a test of politics proper that should propel us to salvage the best of what the European legacy has to offer. But they cannot do so in good scholarly conscience without recognizing that the very need to save Europe is occasioned by the gaze of the post-colonial majority world. Rather than insisting that this gaze is actually Eurocentric by its very interest, it might make for a more worthwhile theoretical endeavor to recognize that we are in a global parallax, where Europe needs non-Europe not as a test of its moral mettle but as a gauge of its very historical relevance for a global humanity quite comfortably moving ahead without it. It is in the world imagined out of the perplexity of encountering other histories, rather than a repeated leap of faith into what Europe supposedly has to offer, that we can begin to construct the possibility of a global psycho-analysis, the global that is forced in the gap of speech, the non-spaces, that links the intermundia together.

Notes

1 "Mode of exchange" is elaborated in more detail in Karatani's (2014) work. The psychoanalytic interest in the gap in a global light requires that we turn to Transcritique where the lack in knowledge is central. Crucially, the "intermundial" and "non-spaces" do not feature in Karatani (2014).
2 Karatani (2017) develops transcritique in greater detail with reference to Freud and Kant. However, this chapter will remain within Karatain (2005) given this is where the notions intermundia and non-space were developed to describe the globality conceptually formed out of the mode of exchange. To my knowledge, at least based on what is available in English, he did not return to those concepts again.
3 Karatani's cosmopolitan use of Kant suffers from his neglect of Kant's racism. For more on Kant and racism, see Lu-Adler (2023).
4 This constitutes the yet to be pursued comparison between Karatani and Sohn-Rethel's (2020) notion of real abstraction (whom the former does not cite). On one hand, there is a clear affinity between Sohn-Rethel and Karatani where they emphasise the primacy of exchange as the driving force of production. Sohn-Rethel posits spatial difference as the motor of abstraction qua surplus although he does not stress the globality of it as Karatani does through appealing to incommensurability.
5 For more on Lacan's intellectual debt to Levi-Strauss' anthropology and their colonial issues and implications see Zafiropoulos (2018). Claude Lévi-Strauss' (1955) anti-racism and anti-colonial politics, however, was most inconsistent with his well-documented antipathy against Islam in *Tristes Tropiques*. There is a noteworthy detail to this, as his suspicion towards Islam was borne out of what he saw to be its similarity with French culture more than Islam's foreignness *per se*.
6 There is a basis here for a radical re-theorization of Islamic "terror".
7 See Žižek (2001) for his account of Buddhism's easy philosophical complicity with capitalism. For responses to Žižek's take on Buddhism, see Møllgaard (2008) and Koivulahti (2017).

Conclusion

Overview

This book has approached "the underside of signification" as a general lens into Lacanian theory to demonstrate its usefulness for decolonial thinking. It began with reframing scientific capitalism as Lacan understands it as a historical force, with particular attention to how it spreads through the process of symbolic ordering. Key is how this ordering occurs through the production of a geo-spatial awareness that resonates with science's expanding drive. The sense of history evoked in the awareness – in the discovery of new hitherto symbolic possibilities – clearly shows Lacan to be theorizing the symbolic order as the symbolic order of Western colonial history. The symbolic consequently is a process of ordering the object world in a moving trajectory, a movement that cannot be explored without evoking spatio-temporal difference. Accordingly, Lacan's recognition of the underside of the symbolic order as the material underside of speech is loaded with decolonial potential. The materiality of speech, as the slippages and ruptures the symbolic order cannot contain in its expanding path, should be considered for its potential as a resource for decolonial psychoanalytic thinking. This goes beyond merely applying psychoanalysis to colonial issues to finding the basis on which psychoanalysis could be thought anew for a global world seeking to overcome colonial trauma.

Chapters 1 and 2 took a close look at Lacan's reading of Freud and Joyce respectively to provide the theoretical basis for the significance of the symbolic "underside" in Lacan. The picture we get is the interest Lacan progressively maintains in forms of speech and knowledge that had to be excluded to sustain the dominant symbolic order. This does not only reveal the symbolic order's Western-European situation, it also sees Lacan's interest in colonized speech as the symbolic's suppressed materiality. The implication is that the symbolic order cannot be conceived without thinking about what had to be excluded for the history of Western epistemology to "make sense". This exclusion consequently makes the underside a resource into thinking about the materiality of speech as a historical materiality. Psychoanalysis'

DOI: 10.4324/9781003387978-6

conditions of possibility and the critique those conditions afford, consequently, cannot be thought without the colonized and their history. Where
Chapters 1 and 2 sketched the theoretical basis for this material underside,
Chapter 3 demonstrated its political relevance through a contemporary
example in the *Autobiography of Malcolm X*. Here I introduced the notion of
"symbolic dispossession" to describe the materiality of speech in Malcolm's
anti-colonial activism, in which his critique of whiteness was clearly moved
and informed by his ability to think outside the cultural demands and political limitations of "white speech". Key is how this critique unfolded through
the spatiotemporal ruptures across a decolonizing Africa and Asia as Malcolm grappled with Arabic, the adoption of African names, and the difference between "proper" and Black English throughout his travels and
political awakening. It is in the gaps, the misunderstandings across global
historical dynamics, that he could affirm his relation to Islam as a new anti-
colonial horizon. Chapter 4 left the terrain of speech to see how lack could
be conceived in global as opposed to European terms. We turn to Kojin
Karatani's notion of transcritique to think about negativity as structured by
what he theorizes as the mode of exchange. The notion recasts our understanding of the object more particularly as the object of exchange value in
order to situate our relationship to the object's enigma in the more extensive
network of abstractions that form the single global world market. Lack by
this is accounted for by how objects are rendered valuable insofar as they are
tradeable in a world of incompatible paradigms that the market tenuously
brings together. The transcritical standpoint moves across both sides of the
exchange where the gap is identified as the point at which surplus value plays
the denominating role to link two incommensurate value systems. The transcritical transposition across both sides of the process is understood as a
"non-space" insofar as it is the gap that reveals the difference surplus value
occludes. This has much to offer for how psychoanalysts should think critically about its globalizing circumstance. Rather than a seamless export to
new markets for its services, psychoanalysis could do well to consider how it
might operate transcritically, in the non-spaces that condition the inner
antagonisms of exchange.

The actual way with which the underside of signification could be seriously
considered to radically design a decolonial psychoanalysis is a subject for
another matter requiring more clinical insights. The modest hope is that this
book could offer a general guide for how speech as the very stuff that psychoanalysis works with could be a resource for thinking about decolonial
politics. The materiality of speech would decolonize psychoanalysis not as an
appendage to another clinical or political project but through psychoanalysis'
own terms now recast as a set of theories and practices that was conceived
through a global parallax that oscillates across the tension between the real
and the symbolic. The lining Lacan works with is the lining of the antagonisms that shapes the contemporary world, understood as a world

continuously ruptured by the real that the symbolic will fail to contain. To take this big picture seriously, however, is to pursue a logical implication presumed in all my chapters: that the underside speaks to how the symbolic and the real are continuously repositioned, that there is no moment at which the symbolic is not reconfigured to address the real.

The politics of untranslatability

We can, however, conclude by identifying a point of departure. To recognize the coloniality of the analysable and symbolic dispossession as deeply embedded concerns in Lacanian theorizing is to go a step further and consider if common Lacanian evocations of "failure" should also be recast accordingly. At the very least, we have the opening to radically reconsider two terms that Lacanians have been otherwise averse to: relation and community. Rather than to take them as signifiers of wholeness we can begin to think of them non-spatially in the Karatanian sense. The encounter with the gap only fails where relations compensate for the want of a semblance. There is a different relationality latent in the mutual entanglement structured by the incommensurate, one which sees the gap as the condition for community to begin with.

For a sense of this alternative possibility we need to turn to Naoki Sakai's (1997) notion of "heterolingual address" that describes how translation is structured by the incomprehensibility that shapes communication in a globalized world. The resonance is in how Sakai places failure not in the encounter with the unconscious but as the starting point of all communication. But it is most pertinent for our discussion where "failure" is situated in the excess in the coming together of different languages that form our experience of the global world as such:

> Here, we may as well draw attention to the mundane insight that communication fails all the time, not necessarily because of the gap between linguistic communities, but also because of the fact that communication takes place only as "exscription": to try to communicate is to expose oneself to exteriority, to a certain exteriority that cannot be reduced to the externality of a referent to a signification. When we fail to communicate, we cannot attribute the failure to its possible cause whether it is excessive noise in the medium or the addressee's refusal to respond-precisely because we fail to communicate. In our case, failure in communication means that each of us stands exposed to, but distant from, the other without grasping the cause for "our" separation. It is only retrospectively, and, in the final analysis, subsequent to the representation of translation, that we begin to figure out an experience of noncomprehension of an other's utterance according to the international schematism.
>
> (Sakai, 1997, p. 7)

"Community" consequently need not refer to the gathering of imagined others that promise belonging. It could rather be the common realization of the need to translate owing to the gap that separates one community from another. This harks in many ways to the lack-in-common that has become the mainstay of Lacanian presentations of negative universality. But recasting this lack as structuring the need for translation adds a crucial element to our understanding of what happens to language globally, for the lack-in-common can now be regarded as a mainspring of a relational creativity. For Sakai stresses how the ability to know one language now depends on the extent to which it is relatable to those who do not know it. Untranslatability is not the condition for the act, whose value is premised upon the self-evident desirability of non-conformist defiance. It is rather recast as the default internalization of an incommensurability that becomes the very condition for speech. "Understanding" by this is no longer determined entirely by one standpoint as it must be made vulnerable to the incommensurate paradigm found in the encounter with the addressee. The possibility of meanings within one language consequently is not dictated solely by its native representatives but is authored similarly by the extent to which it could reach the other paradigm. Relation consequently is sustained through a structuring incomprehension. Both come together to form what Sakai describes as a non-aggregate community: "In a nonaggregate community, therefore, we are together and can address ourselves as 'we' because we are distant from one another and because our togetherness is not grounded on any common homogeneity" (Sakai, 1997, p. 7). This is a community of people who don't quite understand each other and affirm the gap therein as the basis of a common bond. The productivity of failure so pervasive in Lacanian thinking is clearly resonant here. But what is revealed in the failure instead is a network of incomprehensibilities.

Sakai to be sure is not working within a psychoanalytic framework, which means that he does not see the problem of speech to be rooted in the big Other. But Lacanians who have placed the non-relation at the heart of their negative universality might find equality in alterity in the very history of psychoanalysis itself wherein the possibility of psychoanalysis' globality was enabled through the limits of translation. This would place psychoanalysis' universality in other words in the failure of understanding, rather than successful "transmission" as the history is often told. The second point Sakai made in the above paragraph is telling, namely how the lack-in-common is to be found after the fact of mistranslation, when the gap is met in the trajectory of (mis)understanding. We can similarly look back to the globalization of psychoanalysis with the same sensitivity of hindsight where we could begin to appreciate psychoanalysis' decolonial potential for how it was universalized despite understanding, despite adhering to a proper form. The non-aggregate community as Sakai describes it might enable us to chart the distinctive story of psychoanalysis' history outside the West. Two examples will suffice to conclude by way of provocation. The first is what Ernest Jones once called "the Russian problem" (quoted in Miller, 1998, p. 61). This referred to the rapid uptake of psychoanalysis in pre-Soviet Russia which saw psychoanalysis institutionalized at a rate that far exceeded the number of actually available psychoanalysts. Associations were set up across Russian cities upon consultation with the Viennese and London Psychoanalytic Associations as the "central" authorities at the time. However, the actual and rapid mass appeal of psychoanalysis in Russia saw various unauthorized translations of Freudian texts, leading to doubts on whether psychoanalysis was properly understood. By 1909, organic demand in Russia produced translations of Freud's entire collected works: "In no other country had the collected works of Freud been published in translation" (Miller, 1998, p. 35). So compelling was Freud's theory in Russia that it would eventually occasion the first psychoanalytic encounter with the Islamic world when a Psychoanalytic Society was formed in the historically Turkic and Muslim city of Kazan in 1922. Much remains to be researched about the richness of confusions in the psychoanalytic spread across continents during this period. It should however signal how defamiliarization is not a need new to our globalized era but is rather essential to psychoanalysis' founding years.

Psychoanalysis in India also began in the same defamiliar vein. None of the founding members of the Indian Psychoanalytic Institute in 1922 were officially psychoanalysts. However, analysis was provided before a training regime was finally instituted in 1930. This divergence had its roots in the most unique figure of Girindrasekhar Bose. Delving into psychoanalysis after a sustained interest in magic and hypnotism, he began to write in analytic terms without access to Freud's writings (Freud's works were only available in India after 1914). Bose pieced together the sparse information he could find about Freud from newspapers and lay articles, thereby producing in effect an unorthodox non-Western psychoanalysis. It was only after Bose completed his first work, titled *On Repression*, that he began corresponding with Freud in a set of exchanges that spanned nearly 20 years between 1921 and 1937. They never met and yet psychoanalysis found its footing in India through a desire that was linked through the universal promise latent in psychoanalytic questioning. The correspondences are available at the Freud Museum upon Anna Freud's request to the Bose estate after Bose's death in 1953. This, however, did not mean that Bose was brought any closer to "orthodoxy". In 1938 Bose had established the 80-bed Lumbini Park establishment – a nursing home that was then classified legally as a mental hospital – as the largest treatment facility run by any Psychoanalytic Society in the world. In 1951 Bose established Bodhi Peet as the first home for children with special needs informed by psychoanalytic principles.

There is much-needed work to investigate how psychoanalysis owes its global appeal to miscomprehensions as much as smooth transmissions, that the need for translation was moved more by the prior recognition of incommensurabilities between psychoanalysis and the non-psychoanalysable. Language similarly acquires its materiality in the gap where right and wrong translations were negotiated, or whether something that counts as psychoanalysis was properly exported. But to affirm misunderstandings at the heart of psychoanalysis' universal capacity is to also see it in the global qua a trajectory found in the non-aggregate community's gaps in translation.

References

Abu-Lughod, J. L. (1991). *Before European Hegemony: The World System AD 1250–1350*. Oxford University Press.

Acharya, A. (2017). After Liberal Hegemony: The Advent of a Multiplex World Order. *Ethics & International Affairs*, 31 (3), 271–285.

Adorno, T. (2003). *Negative Dialectics*. Routledge.

Akhtar, S., & Tummala-Narram, P. (2020). "Psychoanalysis in India" in *Freud Along the Ganges*. Salman Akhtar (Ed.). Other Press.

Almond, I. (2012). Anti-Capitalist Objections to the Postcolonial: Some Conciliatory Remarks on Žižek and Context. *Ariel: A Review Of International English Literature*, 43 (1).

Anidjar, G. (2002). *Introduction: "Once More, Once More": Derrida, the Arab, the Jew in Acts of Religion*. Routledge.

Anievas, A., & Nişancıoğlu, K. (2015). *How the West Came To Rule: The Geopolitical Origins of Capitalism*. Pluto Press.

Arrighi, G. (2009). *Adam Smith in Beijing: Lineages of the 21st Century*. Verso books.

Baker, C. (2022, December 12). Enter the Five Percent: How Wu-Tang Clan's Debut Album Maps the Complex Doctrine of the Five Percent Nation. *Humanities – Washington University in St. Louis*. Available at: https://humanities.wustl.edu/news/enter-five-percent-how-wu-tang-clan%E2%80%99s-debut-album-maps-complex-doctrine-five-percent-nation.

Baldwin, J. (2017). *The Fire Next Time*. Taschen. (Original work published in 1963).

Ball, J. A., & Burroughs, T. (Eds). (2012). *A Lie of Reinvention: Correcting Manning Marable's Malcolm X*. Black Classic Press.

Bell, C. (2022). Lacanian Psychoanalysis in Japan. *Awry: Journal of Critical Psychology*, 3 (1), 199–214.

Bernstein, R. (1998). *Freud and the Legacy of Moses*. Cambridge University Press.

Bjelić, D. I. (2011a). Balkan Geography and the De-orientalization of Freud. *Journal of Modern Greek Studies*, 29 (1), 27–49.

Bjelić, D. I. (2011b). Is the Balkans the Unconscious of Europe? *Psychoanalysis, Culture & Society*, 16, 315–323.

Bjelić, D. I. (2017). *Intoxication, Modernity, and Colonialism: Freud's Industrial Unconscious, Benjamin's Hashish Mimesis*. Springer.

Brickman, C. (2017). *Race in Psychoanalysis: Aboriginal Populations in the Mind*. Routledge.

Burnham, C. (2022). *Can We Decolonize Lacan? Indigenous Origins of the Split Subject in Psychoanalysis, Politics, Oppression and Resistance*. C. Vanderwees & K. Hennessy (Eds). Routledge.

Clarke, R. (1980). Sigmund Freud's Sortie to America: The Father of Psychoanalysis Came, Saw, Conquered – and Didn't Like It Much. *American Heritage*. Available at: https://www.americanheritage.com/sigmund-freuds-sortie-america (Accessed July 16, 2024).

Clemens, J. (2013). *Psychoanalysis is an Antiphilosophy*. Edinburgh University Press.

Coller, I. (2010). *Arab France: Islam and the Making of Modern Europe, 1798–1831*. University of California Press.

Coller, I. (2020, January 27). Islam and the Revolutionary Age. *Age of Revolutions*. Available at: https://ageofrevolutions.com/2020/01/27/islam-and-the-revolutionary-age/.

Conrad, S. (2017). *What is Global History?* Princeton University Press.

Dabashi, H. (2015). *Can Non-Europeans Think?* Bloomsbury.

DeCaro, L. A. (1996). *On the Side of My People: A Religious Life of Malcolm X*. NYU Press.

Deleuze, G., & Guattari, F. (2004). *Anti-Oedipus*. Continuum.

Diop, I. S. (2023). *Adornment, Masquerade and African Femininity*. Palgrave McMillan.

Dirlik, A. (1999). Is there History after Eurocentrism?: Globalism, Postcolonialism, and the Disavowal of History. *Cultural Critique*, 42, 1–34.

Endres, F. (2022). The Crux of the Matter: Lacan's Dialectical Materialism of the Signifier. *European Journal of Psychoanalysis*, 9 (1).

Fanusie, F. A. T. (2008). *Fard Muhammad in Historical Context: An Islamic Thread in the American Religious and Cultural Quilt* (Doctoral dissertation, Howard University).

Finkelde, D., Žižek, S., & Menke, C. (Eds.). (2023). *Parallax: The Dialectics of Mind and World*. Bloomsbury Publishing.

Fisher-Onar, N., & Kavalski, E. (2022). From Trans-Atlantic Order to Afro-Eur-Asian Worlds? Reimagining International Relations as Interlocking Regional Worlds. *Global Studies Quarterly*, 2 (4).

Frank, A. G. (1998). *ReOrient: Global Economy in the Asian Age*. University of California Press.

Freud, S. (1938). *Psychopathology of Everyday Life*. Penguin (Original work published in 1901).

Freud, S. (1955). *Moses and Monotheism*. Vintage Press (Original work published in 1930).

Freud, S. (1960). *Jokes and their Relation to the Unconscious*. Penguin (Original work published in 1905).

Frosh, S. (2023). *Antisemitism and Racism: Ethical Challenges for Psychoanalysis*. Bloomsbury.

Gansinger, M. A. (2017). *Radical Religious Thought in Black Popular Music. Five Percenters and Bobo Shanti in Rap and Reggae*. Anchor Academic Publishing.

Gaztambide, D. J. (2023). *Decolonizing Psychoanalytic Technique: Putting Freud on Fanon's Couch*. Springer Nature.

George, S., & Hook, D. (Eds). (2021). *Lacan and race: Racism, Identity, and Psychoanalytic Theory*. Taylor & Francis.

Greedharry, M. (2024). In Other Theories: Colonial Reason, Language, And Literature in Ankhi Mukherjee's Unseen City. *Cambridge Journal of Postcolonial Literary Inquiry*, 11 (1), 59–65.

Harari, R. (2002). *How James Joyce Made His Name: A Reading of the Final Lacan*. Other Press.

Hart, W. D. (2002). Slavoj Zizek and the Imperial/Colonial Model of Religion. *Nepantla: Views from South*, 3 (3), 553–578.

Hart, W. D. (2003). Can a Judgment Be Read? A Response to Zizek. *Nepantla: Views from South*, 4 (1), 191–194.

Heine, H. (1879). *Pictures of Travel*. Schaefer & Koradi.

George, S., & Hook, D. (Eds). (2021). *Lacan And Race: Racism, Identity, and Psychoanalytic Theory*. Taylor & Francis.

Jameson, F. (2019). Afterword: On Eurocentric Lacanians. *International Journal of Žižek Studies*, 13 (1).

Jones, E. (1925). Mother-Right and the Sexual Ignorance of Savages. *International Journal of Psycho-Analysis*, 6 (2),109–130.

Jones, L. (2022). *Blues People: Negro Music in White America*. Canongate (Original work published in 1963).

Kapoor, I., & Zalloua, Z. (2021). *Universal Politics*. Oxford University Press.

Kenny, R. (2015). Freud, Jung and Boas: the Psychoanalytic Engagement With Anthropology Revisited. *Notes and Records: the Royal Society Journal of the History of Science*, 69 (2), 173–190.

Karatani, K. (2005). *Transcritique: On Kant and Marx*. MIT Press.

Karatani, K. (2014). *The Structure of World History: From Modes of Production to Modes of Exchange*. Duke University Press.

Kardiner, A. (1945). *The Psychological Frontiers of Society*. New York: Columbia University Press.

Khader, J. (2017). Why Zizek's Critics are Wrong – and Where They Could Have Gotten it Right, *In These Times*, December 11. Available at: http://inthesetimes.com/article/18683/why-zizeks-critics-are-wrong-and-where-they-could-have-gotten-it-right.

Khader, J. (2020). Reactualizing Hegel: Žižek, the Universality of Islam, and Its Political Potentiality (Revisiting "the Archives of Islam"). *Sophia*, 59 (4), 793–808.

Khan, A. (2018). Lacan and Race. In A. Mukherjee (Ed.), *After Lacan: Literature, Theory and Psychoanalysis in the 21st Century*. Cambridge University Press.

Kolozova, K. (2011). Slavoj Žižek Imagining the Balkans. *Psychoanalysis, Culture & Society*, 16, 299–306.

Knight, M. M. (2013). *The Five Percenters: Islam, Hip-Hop and the Gods of New York*. Simon and Schuster.

Kossoff, P. (1983). *Valiant Heart: A Biography of Heinrich Heine*. Associated University Presses.

Koivulahti, T. J. (2017). Compassionate Apocalypse: Slavoj Žižek and Buddhism. *Critical Research on Religion*, 5 (1), 34–47.

Lacan, J. (1991a). *The Seminar of Jacques Lacan Book I: Freud's Papers on Technique*. W.W. Norton.

Lacan, J. (1991b). *The Seminar of Jacques Lacan Book II: The Ego in Freud's Theory and in the Technique of Psychoanalysis 1954–1955*. W.W. Norton.

Lacan, J. (1998). *The Seminar of Jacques Lacan Book XI: The Four Fundamental Concepts of Psychoanalysis*. W.W. Norton.

Lacan, J. (2006). *Ecrits: The First Complete Edition in English*. W.W. Norton.

Lacan, J. (2007). *The Seminar of Jacques Lacan: The Other Side of Psychoanalysis Book* XVII. W.W. Norton.

Lacan, J. (2011). *The Seminar of Jacques Lacan: Book XVIII: On a Discourse That Might Not Be a Semblance* [Unofficial Translation Not Meant for Public

Circulation]. C. Gallagher (Trans.). Retrieved July 16, 2024, from https://esource. dbs.ie/server/api/core/bitstreams/8183f3b3-eb66-4a57-8b00-2dcd472ddf55/content (Original work published in 1971).

Lacan, J. (2013b). *The Psychoses: The Seminar of Jacques Lacan*. Routledge.

Lacan, J. (2017). *Formations of the Unconscious: The Seminar of Jacques Lacan, Book V*. Polity.

Lacan, J. (2018). *The Sinthome: The Seminar of Jacques Lacan, Book* XXIII. Polity Press.

Lacan, J. (2020). *The Seminar of Jacques Lacan: Book IV. The Object Relation*. J.-A. Miller, (Ed.) & A. R. Price (Trans.). Polity (Original work published 1994).

Lévi-Strauss, C. (2012). *Tristes tropiques*. Penguin UK (Original work published 1955).

Lu-Adler, H. (2023). *Kant, Race, and Racism: Views from Somewhere*. Oxford University Press.

Ludden, D. E. (Ed.). (2003). *Reading Subaltern Studies: Critical History, Contested Meaning, and the Globalisation of South Asia*. Orient Blackswan.

Manasi, K., Dhar, A. & Mishra, A. (2018). *Psychoanalysis from the Indian Terroir: Emerging Themes In Culture, Family, and Childhood*. Foreword by E. Berman. Lexington Books.

Møllgaard, E. (2008). Slavoj Žižek's Critique of Western Buddhism. *Contemporary Buddhism*, 9 (2), 167–180.

Marable, M. (2011). *A Life of Reinvention: Malcolm* X. Viking.

Marriott, D.S. (2021). *Lacan and Afro-Pessimism*. New York: Palgrave Macmillan.

Miller, I. S. (2019). Doublings Between Bewilderment and Enlightenment: Reading Freud with Heine on the Troubled Identity of Hirsch-Hyacinth. *The American Journal of Psychoanalysis*, 79 (1), 17–39.

Miller, J. A. (2016). The Real is Without Law. *Lacanian Ink*, 47 (1), 90–115.

Miller, M. A. (1998). *Freud and the Bolsheviks: Psychoanalysis in imperial Russia and the Soviet Union*. Yale University Press.

Miyakawa, F. M. (2005). *Five Percenter rap: God hop's Music, Message, and Black Muslim Mission*. Indiana University Press.

Moncayo, R. (2018). *Lalangue, Sinthome, Jouissance, and Nomination: A Reading Companion and Commentary on Lacan's Seminar XXIII on the Sinthome*. Routledge.

Morris, M. (1997). *Foreword to Translation & Subjectivity: On "Japan" and Cultural Nationalism*. University of Minnesota Press.

Morrow, J. A. (2023). *Finding WD Fard: Unveiling the Identity of the Founder of the Nation of Islam*. Cambridge Scholars Publishing.

Mukherjee, A. (2021). *Unseen City: The Psychic Lives of the Urban Poor*. Cambridge University Press.

Obiwu, I. (2015). Jacques Lacan in Africa Travel, Moroccan Cemetery, Egyptian Hieroglyphics, and Other Passions of Theory. In M. Nwosu & Obiwu (Eds), *The Critical Imagination in African Literature: Essays in Honour of Michael JC Echeruo*. Syracuse University Press.

O'Donoghue, D. (2018). *On Dangerous Ground: Freud's Visual Cultures of the Unconscious*. Bloomsbury.

Oring, E. (2007). *The Jokes of Sigmund Freud: A Study in Humor and Jewish identity*. Jason Aronson, Incorporated.

Overy, R. (2009). *The Morbid Age: Britain and the Crisis of Civilisation, 1919–1939.* Penguin.

Pandolfo, S. (2018). *Knot of the Soul: Madness, Psychoanalysis, Islam.* University of Chicago Press.

Parker, I. (2008). *Japan in Analysis: Cultures of the Unconscious.* Springer.

Preciado, P. B. (2021). *Can the Monster Speak? Report to an Academy of Psychoanalysts.* MIT Press.

Psicanálise na Rua. (2023, March 7). Sobre o projeto. Retrieved July 16, 2024, from https://psicanalisenarua.wordpress.com/2023/03/07/sobre-o-projeto/.

Quan, J. (2022, July 18). The 5 Percent Nation's Impact on the Golden Era of Hip-Hop. *Rock the Bells.* https://rockthebells.com/articles/the-5-percent-nation-impact-on-the-golden-era-of-hip-hop/.

Ragland, E. (2006). The Hysteric's Truth. In J. A. Miller, P. Verhaeghe, & E. Ragland (Eds), *Jacques Lacan and the Other Side of Psychoanalysis: Reflections on Seminar XVII, Sic Vi (Vol. 6).* Duke University Press.

Rasmussen, E. D. (2004). The Last Hegelian: An Interview with Slavoj Zizek. *Minnesota Review*, 61/62, 79.

Reich, W. (1949). *The Mass Psychology of Fascism.* Orgone Institute Press.

Richards, S. (2023). A Lesson for the World: Solange Faladé's Anti-Colonial Multiracialism. *Modern & Contemporary France*, 31 (4), 435–450.

Roberts, R., & Smith, J. (2016, June 7). When Cassius Clay became Muhammad Ali: An Excerpt from the Book *Blood Brothers. Slate.* https://slate.com/culture/2016/06/when-cassius-clay-became-muhammad-ali-an-excerpt-from-the-book-blood-brothers.html.

Sakai, N. (1997). *Translation and Subjectivity: On "Japan" and Cultural Nationalism (Vol. 3).* University of Minnesota Press.

Sheehi, L., & Sheehi, S. (2021). *Psychoanalysis Under Occupation: Practicing Resistance in Palestine.* Routledge.

Shingu, K. (2010). *Freud, Lacan and Japan. In Perversion and Modern Japan.* N. Cornyetz & J. K. Vincent (Eds). Routledge.

Smiley, T. [Tavis Smiley]. (2015, March 15). Slavoj Žižek and Black America | Žižek visits the Tavis Smiley Show [Video]. *YouTube.* Available at: https://www.youtube.com/watch?v=examplelink.

Sohn-Rethel, A. (2020). *Intellectual and Manual Labour: A Critique of Epistemology.* Brill.

Soler, C. (2018). *Lacan Reading Joyce.* Routledge.

Swales, P.J. (1982). *Freud, Minna Bernays, and the Conquest of Rome. New Light on the Origins of Psychoanalysis. The New American Review*, 1, 1–23.

Swales, P.J. (2003). Freud, Death and Sexual Pleasures: On the Psychical Mechanism of Dr. Sigmund Freud. *Arc de Cercle* 1 (1), 5–74.

Swartz, S. (2022). *Psychoanalysis and Colonialism: A Contemporary Introduction.* Routledge.

Thakur, G. B. (2013). The Menon-Žižek Debate: "The Tale of the (Never-marked) (But secretly coded) Universal and the (Always-marked) Particular ..." *Slavic Review*, 72 (4), 750–770.

Thakur, G. B. (2020). *Postcolonial Lack: Identity, Culture, Surplus.* State University of New York Press.

Thurston, L. (2004). *James Joyce and the Problem of Psychoanalysis.* Cambridge University Press.

Togashi, K. (2020). *The Psychoanalytic Zero: A Decolonizing Study of Therapeutic Dialogues*. Routledge.

Tomšič, S. (2017). *The Labour of Enjoyment: Towards a Critique of Libidinal Economy*. August Verlag.

Visweswaran, K. (1994). *Fictions of Feminist Ethnography*. University of Minnesota Press.

Walker, G. (2016). *The sublime perversion of capital: Marxist theory and the politics of history in modern Japan*. Duke University Press.

Walker, G. (2020). *The Red Years: Theory, Politics, and Aesthetics in the Japanese '68*. Verso.

Weber, N. F. (2017). *Freud's Trip to Orvieto: The Great Doctor's Unresolved Confrontation with Antisemitism, Death, and Homoeroticism; His Passion for Paintings; and the Writer in His Footsteps*. Bellevue Literary Press.

Weil, P. (2023). *The Madman in the White House: Sigmund Freud, Ambassador Bullitt, and the Lost Psychobiography of Woodrow Wilson*. Harvard University Press.

X, M. (1999). *The Autobiography of Malcolm X as told to Alex Haley*. Ballantine Books.

Zafiropoulos, M. (2018). *Lacan and Lévi-Strauss or the Return to Freud (1951–1957)*. Routledge.

Zalloua, Z. (2020). *Žižek on Race: Towards an Anti-racist Future*. Bloomsbury.

Zarakol, A. (2022). *Before the West: The Rise and Fall of Eastern World Orders*. Cambridge University Press.

Žižek, S. (1993). *Tarrying with the Negative*. Duke University Press.

Žižek, S. (1998). A Leftist Plea for Eurocentrism. *Critical Inquiry*, 24 (4), 988–1009.

Žižek, S. (2000). History Against Historicism. *European Journal of English Studies*, 4 (2), 101–110.

Žižek, S. (2001). *On Belief*. Psychology Press.

Žižek, S. (2006). A Glance on the Archives of Islam. *Lacan.com*. Available at: https://www.lacan.com/zizarchives.htm.

Žižek, S. (2012). *Less Than Nothing: Hegel and the Shadow of Dialectical Materialism*. Verso.

Žižek, S. (2013). *Demanding the Impossible*. Polity.

Žižek, S. (2014). The Impasses of Today's Radical Politics. *Crisis and Critique*, 1 (1), 8–44.

Žižek, S. (2016). *Disparities*. Bloomsbury.

Žižek, S. (2017). The Varieties of Surplus. *Problemi International*, 1 (1), 7–32.

Žižek, S. (2022). *Surplus-Enjoyment. A Guide for the Non-Perplexed*. Bloomsbury.

Žižek, S. (2023). *Freedom: A Disease without a Cure*. Bloomsbury.

Index

Note: Locators followed by "n" refer end notes.

.

For Product Safety Concerns and Information please contact our EU
representative GPSR@taylorandfrancis.com
Taylor & Francis Verlag GmbH, Kaufingerstraße 24, 80331 München, Germany

www.ingramcontent.com/pod-product-compliance
Lightning Source LLC
Chambersburg PA
CBHW070339270326
41926CB00017B/3915